This book offers an original approach to Shakespeare's so-called 'problem plays' by contending that they can be viewed as experiments in the Mannerist style. The plays reappraised here are *Julius Caesar, Hamlet, Troilus and Cressida, All's Well That Ends Well* and *Measure for Measure.*

But how can a category which characterizes a trend in sixteenth-century Italian painting be made relevant to theatrical analysis? Drawing upon famous works by Michelangelo, Rosso, Pontormo, Parmigianino, Bronzino, Tintoretto and others (with examples illustrated in the book), Maquerlot shows how these artists cultivated structural ambiguity or dissonance in reaction to the classical canons of the High Renaissance.

Close readings of Shakespeare's plays, from the period 1599 to 1604, reveal intriguing analogies with Mannerist art, while illuminating the dramatist's response to the rhetorical formalism of his Elizabethan predecessors. Maquerlot concludes by looking at *Othello*, which marks the end of Shakespeare's Mannerist experiments, and his less equivocal use of artifice in the late romances.

SHAKESPEARE AND THE MANNERIST TRADITION

SHAKESPEARE AND THE MANNERIST TRADITION

A Reading of Five Problem Plays

JEAN-PIERRE MAQUERLOT

CAMBRIDGE
UNIVERSITY PRESS

Published by the Press Syndicate of the University of Cambridge
The Pitt Building, Trumpington Street, Cambridge CB2 1RP
40 West 20th Street, New York, NY 10011-4211, USA
10 Stamford Road, Oakleigh, Melbourne 3166, Australia

First published 1995

Printed in Great Britain by Woolnough Bookbinding Limited,
Irthlingborough, Northants.

A catalogue record for this book is available from the British Library

Library of Congress cataloguing in publication data
Maquerlot, Jean-Pierre.
Shakespeare and the mannerist tradition: a reading of five
problem plays / Jean-Pierre Maquerlot.
p.   cm
Plays reappraised are: Julius Caesar, Hamlet, Troilus and
Cressida, All's well that ends well, and Measure for measure.
Based on the author's thesis (doctoral, University of Provence,
1989).
Includes bibliographical references and index.
ISBN 0 521 41083 5 (hardback)
1. Shakespeare, William, 1564–1616 – Criticism and interpretation.
2. Experimental drama – England – History and criticism.   3. Mannerism
(Literature)   I. Title.
PR2976.M388   1995
822.3′3 – dc20   95–49726

ISBN 0 521 41083 5 hardback

SE

Contents

Illustrations

Acknowledgements

This book derives from my French doctoral dissertation and has bene-fited from the sound remarks and criticisms made by the members of the jury before whom I defended my work in January 1989 at the University of Provence. The jury was chaired by Professor Jean Fuzier and included Professors André Bourde, Robert Ellrodt, Marie-Thérèse Jones-Davis and, last to be named but first to be thanked, Sybil Truchet, my thesis adviser. Several months later Mr Leo Salingar, Fellow of Trinity College, Cambridge, whom I had known for many years, was kind enough to express a desire to read my typescript and came up with the suggestion that I should translate it into English and submit it for publication with some very necessary alterations and abridgement. This was an idea that I had not been presumptuous enough to entertain but which subsequently met with Robert Ellrodt's approval. Now that the book has at last made its way across the Channel, it is to me the most agreeable of duties to express my gratitude to these eminent scholars. But translating it is an arduous task, one which I would never have been able to carry out by myself without the assistance of two British-born friends whom I wish to thank heartily: Peter Stone, who helped me in the difficult task of preparing the first draft of the chapters on Shakespeare, and Frances McFarlane, my colleague at the University of Rouen, who directed my hesitant steps into the linguistically less famil-iar territory of art criticism and then considerably improved the whole translation. As for the infelicities of style that have subsisted in the text, they are unintentional Gallic *faux pas* for which I alone must be held responsible.

I also wish to acknowledge my debt to the *CETAS* (*Centre d'Etude du Théâtre Anglo-saxon*). As a member of this renowned team headed by Professor Michèle Willems, I have had the privilege of using its excellent library and working in a congenial and intellectually stimulating envi-ronment.

References to Shakespeare's texts are taken from the Arden editions. Quotations from Thomas Kyd's *Spanish Tragedy* and Christopher Marlowe's *Tamburlaine the Great* (part 2) come from the Regents Renaissance Drama Series editions. References to Marlowe's *Doctor Faustus* are taken from the Revels Plays edition. Concerning Ben Jonson, I have used the Oxford complete edition of his works but I have taken the liberty of modernizing the spelling.

Abbreviations

Introduction

The adjective *maniériste* was first coined by Robert Fréart de Chambray in his *Idée de la perfection de la peinture* (1662). Luigi Lanzi used the abstract noun *manierismo* a hundred and thirty years later in *La storia pittorica . . .* (1792). Thereafter, Mannerism finally became an accepted category in the history of art. Today, in spite of differences of interpretation, no one denies the usefulness of the concept to stylistic denotation and the definition of periods. Later and less boldly than in painting and other visual arts, the category entered the discourse of musical criticism. It is not unusual to read or hear it said today that a particular motet by Roland de Lassus, or mass by William Byrd, or madrigal by Claudio Monteverdi, Thomas Weelkes, John Wilbye or more especially Carlo Gesualdo betrays Mannerist characteristics. It is in literature and the theatre that the adoption of the category is encountering the most resistance. To call a piece of prose, a poem or a play Mannerist, or with more caution to say that it is reminiscent of Mannerism, still arouses suspicion – healthy suspicion according to some – in spite of much remarkable groundwork: the pioneering studies of the first generation (Ernst Robert Curtius back in 1948, followed by Gustav-René Hocke, Marcel Raymond, Arnold Hauser and Wylie Sypher in the fifties),[1] then the work of their successors in the sixties and seventies (Daniel B. Rowland, Cyrus Hoy and Claude-Gilbert Dubois),[2] not forgetting the art historian John Shearman, who also has concerned himself, albeit marginally, with Mannerist style in literature.[3]

More recently, the publication of the fifth number of the review *L'art du théâtre* in the autumn of 1986 revived the somewhat flagging interest of theatre lovers in a category that might have been thought to be slightly outmoded. In an examination of the work of the most prominent stage directors in France (particularly Antoine Vitez, Georges Lavaudant and Daniel Mesguich) the contributors to the review discern reactions not unlike those of the Mannerist artists of the Renaissance 'enamoured of detail and quotation, of extravagance and perfection' as if these great entertainers were intent on reviving 'a movement whose domain was culture and whose aim was artifice' (editor's foreword, p. 9).

Can it really be curiosity about the Mannerist period which is encouraging so many contemporary stage directors to become interested in Renaissance dramatists, more especially of the English Renaissance, which is the richest and the most varied, theatrically speaking? Is it not rather the fact that they consort so unremittingly with the playwrights of this period that fuels their curiosity about Mannerism? It is hard to distinguish between cause and effect. The fact remains that among those dramatists who are able to stir up the most creative energy in directors and actors, and arouse the ever-ready enthusiasm of playgoers, it is Shakespeare who holds pride of place. And no wonder. But the present fashion for Shakespeare among French audiences is due not only to the excellence of plays that continue to appeal to modern sensibility with their exotic mixture of sophistication and savagery, attractive to so many French people since Voltaire; it derives also from the immense ability of Shakespearian drama to engender the boldest innovations in stagecraft.

I wonder whether English-speaking audiences, and the theatrical professionals across the Channel and the Atlantic, fully realize to what extent Shakespearian theatre in France has ceased to be a run-of-the-mill theatrical object and has become, for better and for worse, a subject of research and an area of experimentation, things not permissible to nearly the same extent in French classical theatre (national heritage *oblige*) and even less in contemporary theatre, especially when the staging is supervised by the eagle eye of still-living authors. Is one to ascribe to Shakespeare the tendency in some adventurous stage directors ('the new Mannerists') to juggle with signs, to assemble provocative collages or clever montages that are often puzzling and sometimes enchanting or disconcerting? Or is it because today, at the close of the twentieth century, there is a side to our own culture (the Mannerist side?) that discovers in Shakespeare an ideal medium that can channel our own expressive energy? I merely ask these questions, aware that a lack of distance from the culture of the present day makes it premature to attempt a reply. One thing is certain, however: the Mannerist productions that Renaissance plays give rise to are in no way the result of a desire to reconstitute the style of performances of the period or, in more general terms, to restore the spirit of the age. Rather they attest to an uneasy and typically modern awareness of the significance of the word 'heritage' among those whose job it is to hand it down and keep it alive. To avoid the danger of seeing our heritage disappear from our cultural horizon, it is always necessary to stage again and again what has been staged many times before, but to stage it in another way in order to avoid the risk of its becoming fossilized in an official representation whose canon protects it from the cut and thrust of our own time. At a period when the signature on a painting, a text or a theatrical production guarantees its prestige and notice, another of the implications is that the show must flaunt its status as a work of art, demonstrate its visibility as a creation in its own right, at the risk of sometimes compromising the readability of the text.

To turn to the subject of the present study, I aim to show that Shakespeare as a dramatist (leaving aside Shakespeare as an actor) had his Mannerist moment. Within this period, five plays, written between 1599 and 1604, are relevant to my argument: *Julius Caesar, Hamlet, Troilus and Cressida, All's Well That Ends Well* and *Measure for Measure*. Although these plays are very different in form and content, I hope to show that they have in common something which can be called Mannerism, an aspect that does not stand out so evidently in other works of the same period such as *As You Like it, Henry V, Twelfth Night, The Merry Wives of Windsor* or *Othello*; this indicates, incidentally, that I do not consider this span of five years in the playwright's career to be uniformly Mannerist. Where the dating of movements or styles is concerned, I belong to that school of thought which prefers to think of dates as drift-anchors rather than as watertight compartments, and it was no surprise to me to detect precursory signs of Mannerism in *The Merchant of Venice* (1596?). As it is probably not the only play in this situation, I leave it to more acute observers of the Shakespearian scene prior to 1599 to make their pronouncements. *The Merchant of Venice* is, however, a striking example of the direction Shakespeare was to work in throughout the Problem Plays. With some disregard for the chronological latitudinarianism that I have just professed, I tend to think, not without some feeling of unease, for it is not good to appear rigid in this area, that *Othello* represents a decisive end to Shakespeare's Mannerist period and opens the way to a new development. For, in my view, the mood of the tragedies (including the so-called 'late' tragedies) and the mood of the 'romances' are fundamentally incompatible with the continuance of the Mannerist experiment. This argument is worked out in detail in the closing chapter of my book.

But why, it will inevitably be asked, resort to the debatable concept of Mannerism to discuss plays which are generally referred to elsewhere as 'Problem Plays', a name that has gained a general consensus? Suggesting another label is always a risky business that one seldom comes out of unscathed. My belief is that the Mannerist hypothesis will allow us to take a fresh look at works that have been subjected to the same line of enquiry for too long, even if F.S. Boas' initial proposition of 1896,[4] refined and explored in depth by W.W. Lawrence, E.M.W. Tillyard and E. Schanzer in particular,[5] has yielded remarkable results. In simple terms, the Mannerist hypothesis throws an alternative light on these intriguing plays, allowing various unsuspected or hidden aspects to emerge.

Like the well-established concept of Problem Plays, the Mannerist hypothesis makes no claim to offer an exhaustive vision of its field of application. Indeed, the two terms are in no way mutually exclusive. As I make clear in the subtitle to my book, *A Reading of Five Problem Plays*, I even owe to the existence of this category and the perceptive commentaries stemming from it the origin of the idea that if there was Mannerism to be found in Shakespeare, it was probably to these plays that one should turn. But it is one thing to note, sometimes with surprise, that these works lay bare matters of conscience or moral, philosophic and political dilemmas with a previously unparalleled understanding of intellectual enquiry, or that, as plays to be performed, they represent a theatrical problem in themselves: it is quite another thing to maintain that Shakespeare deliberately adopted new techniques at this stage in his development as did certain Italian painters before him in anticlassical Mannerism around 1520, when the historic and cultural circumstances were extremely different to his. Clearly, there is no question of attributing this parallel development (I do not say identical) to any kind of direct influence or socio-cultural similarity. It would be absurd to suggest that by rubbing away the differences, Florence, Rome, Mantua or Parma of this date could represent in synthesis a preview of London around 1600. On the other hand, in spite of the apparent whimsicality of these matching scenes, it is not absurd to imagine Giulio Romano (to take the only painter mentioned in Shakespeare), who was invited by Pope Leo X in the year 1520 to decorate the Sala di Costantino in the Vatican, telling himself, brush in hand, that it was time for him to free himself from the style of his master, Raphael; or to imagine Shakespeare, pen in hand, at the start of *Hamlet* around 1599 or 1600, also telling himself that it was now necessary for him to show his difference from his predecessor, Thomas Kyd, the undisputed master of revenge tragedy.

The idea of the High Renaissance is an invention of art historians, designating and dating the short-lived period in Italy at the end of the Quattrocento and during the first two decades of the Cinquecento during which there flourished a form of artistic expression that was classical, balanced and harmonious (although in fact less harmonious than is often believed). This label is unsuitable for the English Renaissance. On the other hand, the phenomenon that I call 'rhetorical formalism', as it appears in Spenser, Lyly, Kyd, Marlowe and the young Shakespeare (although here too the formalism is less formal than might appear), seems to me to have played a comparable role, *mutatis mutandis*, in forming the Mannerist reaction. It is the style and mood of Montaigne's *Essays*, the anti-Ciceronianism of certain writers of prose such as Lipsius in Holland, Thomas Nashe and Francis Bacon in England; it is the appearance in the 1590s of so-called 'metaphysical' poetry, the fashion for satire and the attraction of melancholy, the taste for philosophic speculation against a background of insecurity ('And new Philosophy calls all in doubt'); all these give glimpses of certain orientations followed in the Mannerist experiment. But an inventory of the causes or concomitances of literary and theatrical Mannerism in England at the end of the sixteenth century would take up a book in itself, and the same is true of the cataloguing of evidence of Mannerism in the later Elizabethan, Jacobean and Caroline theatre.

The present work is more modestly ambitious. Leaving aside all comprehensive socio-cultural generalizations in the manner of Hauser and all breathtaking stylistic panoramas in the manner of Sypher, this book offers a reading of five of Shakespeare's plays, subjected to Mannerist scrutiny, or rather to my understanding of Mannerism. One thing at least brooks no argument: any definition of Mannerism must first be founded on the visual arts before any attempt is made to apply it to works of language. It is not, after all, the first time that the vocabulary of the fine arts has been used in the description of written texts. In its own way, the Mannerist hypothesis links up with the belief of the ancients in the Concord of the Muses ('ut pictura poesis'), a topic revived during the Renaissance. But nowadays it is no longer good enough to produce facile analogies based on strings of metaphors or superficial inferences about examples of different art forms simply because they originate in the same *Zeitgeist* or share a common *Weltanschauung*. As a belated disciple of Etienne Souriau, who is today recognized as a seminal mind in the semiotics of the theatre, but who is still underestimated as an active proponent of the 'correspondance des arts',[6] I believe that the only satisfactory comparative language, respecting as far as possible the specificity of the arts forms studied, is one which is based on structural analogies (Souriau used the term *figures*). This subject is dealt with in the second chapter, which contains a number of reflections on methodology that I have tried to keep to a minimum.

Concerning the actual analysis of each play, my aim has been to make it readable as an entity, although each obviously fits into what I have to say about Mannerism. There is not perhaps all that much harm done, after all, if eager readers go straight to Shakespeare and avoid the more circuitous paths that I invite them into. Nevertheless, I do hope they will want to turn to my commentaries on the paintings once they have read the essays on the plays, in order to discover other parallels perhaps, or else reasons for scepticism.

In conclusion, I should like to make a few remarks upon the reproductions illustrating my argument: I have chosen, as will be seen, some of the major works of Italian Mannerism. I was motivated in my choice by the desire to show readers who still associate Mannerism with decline or a degenerative process that among the practitioners of this style are artists of the first magnitude and that the term is in no way pejorative when applied to Shakespeare. It is obvious that black-and-white reproduction can only give a very limited idea of painting; this is why my commentary often tends to overlook colour in favour of composition. It is necessary to view the originals, as I myself have done (all are quite easy of access), or at least to consult a good anthology that in all probability will include the works because of their celebrity. The explanatory notes adjoining the reproductions make no claim to be exhaustive. Generally speaking, little attention has been paid to the circumstances in which the works were produced, nor has any attempt been made to situate them in the overall output of a given artist. With so little documentation, the notes would be unworthy of a history of art with any pretension to seriousness. They are not the work of an expert, but stand as the individual testimony of an enlightened amateur – at least I hope so – or of a visitor to museums watchfully detecting certain analogies of a stylistic nature between two different modes of representation, an approach that involves the taking of risks.

CHAPTER I

The problem of Mannerism

Since Mannerism in painting is not the main subject of my book, I have taken the liberty of excusing myself from two pieces of normal procedure: my argument is not prefaced by any preliminary remarks on the etymology and semantic evolution of the word *maniera* from which the concept derives. Although important, it is a point that has been amply discussed by Georg Weise, Eugenio Battisti, Craig Hugh Smyth and John Shearman among others, so that it is unnecessary to return to the topic.[1] It would be a superfluous ritual to repeat what has already been written on the subject without the certainty of adding something new. The second procedure adopted by a good number of art historians, especially when writing for the general public, consists in overlooking the fact that Mannerism is largely problematic and there is as yet no unanimity over the interpretation to be given of this particular style. I myself feel that in this case it is imperative to mention this fact and to take a stand in the debate because my views affect the whole development of my study of Mannerism as applied to the theatre.

To state a complicated problem in rather simple terms, without, I hope, misrepresenting the issues: it can be said that the problem is still to be addressed today roughly in the same terms as thirty years ago at the Twentieth International Congress of the History of Art (whose *Acts* were published in Princeton in 1963), when two brilliant papers, one by C.H. Smyth and the other by J. Shearman, cast doubt on Walter Friedlaender's theories, without, however, undermining them completely.

Chronologically speaking, while Friedlaender was not the first to react against the discredit attached to Mannerism as a pejorative term used by the nineteenth century to stigmatize the decline of Italian and European art from the 1530s to the 1590s,[2] it was, however, Friedlaender who was the first to conduct a thorough examination of the subject and to secure a rehabilitation of the style. This bold step was taken in his 1914 inaugural lecture at the University of Freiburg upon 'the anticlassical style'. However, it was no creation *ex nihilo*; the time was ripe, previous critical directions had already been explored, but Friedlaender then set them in a radically new focus. This great German scholar, who was influenced by the aesthetic and intellectual climate of the early twentieth century, with its desire to emancipate itself from academic and naturalistic tenets, saw more cause for hope than despair in the attack launched by Giovanni Bellori in his well-known *Le vite de' pittori, scultori ed architetti moderni* (1672) against the artists of the generation after Raphael, accusing them of having 'abandoned the study of nature, corrupted art with *la maniera* or if you prefer fantastic idea (*o vogliamo dire fantastica idea*) based on *pratica* and not on imitation [of nature]'; to Friedlaender this showed *phantasia* taking its revenge over *mimesis*. Similarly, positive signs of a desire for independence and originality were discerned in the criticisms voiced by Carlo Cesare Malvasia, a few years after the publication of Bellori's book, in the equally famous *Felsina pittrice* (1678), in which the author placed blame on certain artists who, 'seeking another mode and a different way of doing things', had been so remiss as to turn their backs on the example of their masters.

Friedlaender and other art historians clearly were encouraged by the emergence of the expressionist, stylized and abstract art of the early twentieth century to take a favourable view of the dissident art of the early Mannerists. It can also be surmised that Vasari's condemnation of Pontormo, in which he accuses Pontormo of having ruined his own style by indiscriminately imitating the German manner of Dürer, may well have encouraged Friedlaender to give careful thought to the work of the then relatively unknown Florentine painter and to become convinced that Pontormo was one of the boldest pioneers of the new style.

While Friedlaender's reinterpretation of Mannerism is partly accountable to the spirit of his age, it is obvious that his assessment is based upon an extremely careful reading of the works he examined. When consulting the transcription of the Freiburg lecture, subsequently published in 1925, and the essay that completes it on 'The Anti-Mannerist Style' published a few years later in 1930,[3] one has to admire the niceness and thoroughness of the analysis. It is the exceptional quality of Friedlaender's descriptions of paintings which mainly explains why his theories are so convincing and why they are still popular today. It is no accident that André Chastel, a great connoisseur of the Italian Renaissance, should have adopted this outlook in his important book *L'art italien*, published in 1956.

In Friedlaender's view, *creative* Mannerism, the Mannerism that over-turned the canons of the High Renaissance, was the anticlassical art that appeared in Florence roughly between 1515 and 1520 and then spread to central Italy until the middle of the Cinquecento: the work of Pontormo and Rosso, of Beccafumi, Parmigianino and Bronzino, not forgetting the towering and marginal figure of Michelangelo, 'hovering above them and reaching beyond them'; Michelangelo, whose anticlassical inspiration achieved its fullest expression from the 1530s onwards with the Sistine and Pauline frescos in the Vatican, was to influence mature Mannerism much more considerably than did the Florentine painters.

But if Mannerism is to be understood as the bold, innovating style (Friedlaender calls it 'revolutionary') of those disciples who had achieved at least partial liberation from the tutelage of their High Renaissance masters (Raphael, Correggio, Andrea del Sarto etc.), how then is the style of the following generations of mid and late sixteenth-century artists to be referred to, for whom anticlassicism had long ceased to be a living issue? The question has to be asked, especially as it is precisely these painters that Malvasia accuses of giving themselves up to the vice of *la maniera*, and he lists their names: 'Salviati, the Zuccari, Vasari, Andrea Vicentino, Tomaso Laureti' as well as his fellow citizens from Bologna, 'Samacchino, Sabbatino, Calvaert, the Procaccini and the like'. Friedlaender reacts to the problem by remaining faithful to tradi-tional criticism: these second-rate painters, who were powerless to coun-teract the waning of the anticlassical trend, were the conformists of this new style, the sometimes ingenious, often skilful, but always repetitive practitioners of a watered-down Mannerism that had become academic through over-use of the same figurative conventions. Friedlaender writes that Mannerism 'became *di maniera* by repetition, cleverness and playful exaggeration on the one hand, by weak concessions on the other'.[4] Lacking in true inspiration, these artists overemphasized available models, over-refined existing forms and cultivated virtuosity of execu-tion. Anticlassical Mannerism had become 'mannered', not in the sense of affectation or preciosity, but in the sense of the domination of a manner of doing things which had become mechanical. It was the attempt to find a way out of this impasse, seen by the theorists of the 1580s, especially Lomazzo and Armenini, as the sign of a decline,[5] that explains the emergence of a movement of reform led principally by the Carracci brothers in Bologna and by Caravaggio, who came from Lombardy but who worked in Rome. Their aim was to return to a simpler, more natural, more intelligible way of painting and in particular to revitalize the human figure – the local habitation *par excellence* of *la maniera* – which had turned into something impersonal and almost unsubstantial through excessive idealization. The formation of this trend and the description of the new tendencies appearing at the end of the Cinquecento are dealt with in Friedlaender's second essay, entitled 'The Anti-Mannerist Style'.

On the other side of contemporary thinking on Mannerism stand C.H. Smyth and J. Shearman, who query Friedlaender's leading idea that the anticlassical trend can legitimately be described as Mannerist. Both critics point out that it has only been possible to link anticlassicism to Mannerism (a combination which has no precedent in the criticism of previous centuries) by including among the characteristics of *la maniera* the idea of the primacy of the imagination (*la fantastica idea* as mentioned by Malvasia) over the imitation of nature and the masters. They object, and rightly so, that this is a theme which belongs to seventeenth-century criticism; there are no hints of it anywhere in sixteenth-century treatises contemporary with what we now call Mannerism; it is drawing belated and unwarranted conclusions from the opinions delivered by Cinquecento theorists upon *la maniera*. The value of C.H. Smyth's and J. Shearman's contribution has been to return the original concept of *maniera*, with the diverse meanings that it had during the Cinquecento, to the heart of present-day reasoning. Contrary to Friedlaender's some-what schematizing beliefs, *la maniera* does not merely imply a routine method producing an automatic and stereotyped performance; although it is true that Dolce does give it only this meaning in his *Aretino* (1557), as a term used by painters, probably from Venice and therefore outside the sphere of Mannerism, to refer to a deplorable practice tending to give the human figure and face always the same air. But Dolce is an isolated instance. Vasari, quoted by Friedlaender, gives this meaning along with others in both the 1550 and the 1568 editions of the *Lives*, and the same applies to the *trattatisti* writing at the close of the century in the wake of the Vasari tradition.[6] Although Vasari and his successors did not fail to see the risk of uniformity and artificiality that Armenini's *sola maniera* could create, or the dangers of working purely *per forza d'arte* (as Lomazzo put it), yet more often than not they thought of *la maniera* as a desirable quality when acquired by selecting and imitating the finest specimens of nature and art, including the art of antiquity, and cultivating personal talent. Generally speaking, sixteenth-century aes-thetic thinking saw *la maniera*, used in the absolute sense, as a prerequisite to the creation of ideal beauty, unhampered by the accidental or the contingent, of the type that can be observed in the work of Raphael and Michelangelo. The idea that the art of Vasari and his disciples could be seen as a degeneration of the anticlassical tendency is far removed from the thinking of C.H. Smyth and J. Shearman, who view it as Mannerism of the mature period attempting to make use of the precepts inherent in *maniera* so as to emulate High Renaissance art.

While some of the pictorial conventions of Mannerism are visible sporadically from the 1520s onwards, including in certain works that are reputed to be anticlassical (C.H. Smyth calls this 'the gathering of mid-Cinquecento *maniera*'), it was not really until 1530 that the style took shape definitively. As the conventions gradually became embedded in pictorial practice and increased their hold in the middle of the century, C.H. Smyth notes a move towards 'more elegance, more refinement, more brawn, more directions, more dislocation, more flatness-plus-fore-shortening – that is, more grace, difficulty, novelty, and curiousness in the framework of the conventions',[7] as if the artists were striving to make the most of Vasari's precept of licence in discipline (*nella regola una licenzia*).

At this stage, a word must be said about the differences separating C.H. Smyth and J. Shearman in their approach to Mannerism. Referring to certain stylistic similarities between anticlassical art and the *maniera* idiom, C.H. Smyth concedes that there may be elements or early signs of Mannerism in some of the emotionally charged or highly dramatic works by Pontormo and Rosso (in the latter's early Florentine manner) and, much later, in El Greco. In spite of C.H. Smyth's insistence that 'we should consider as proper early Mannerism only those productions of the earlier painting that clearly anticipate the fundamentals of *maniera*',[8] J. Shearman's view is much more intransigent, in that he would like to deny any trace of Mannerism in the works analysed by Friedlaender. In fact Shearman is not so interested in making a detailed survey of all the conventions or pertinent aspects of the *maniera* style as in highlighting its qualities or attributes. In his view, *maniera*, with its positive side 'a certain poise, cultured elegance, refinement and perfection of performance' and its negative side 'unnaturalness, affectation, self-consciousness and ostentation',[9] corresponds to what we would call 'a sense of style' as when we say of someone that he or she does things 'with style'.

Like G. Weise before him, J. Shearman makes much of the semantic link between the aesthetic concept and the social concept of 'manners', meaning a way of behaving. 'Whether you are walking, standing, or sitting, do it always with *maniera*' is the advice of Lorenzo di Medici.[10]

Following the same line of thought, J. Shearman sees similarities between Vasari's idea of *facilità* ('the effortless resolution of all difficulties') and Castiglione's famous *sprezzatura*, meaning the well-bred nonchalance and artless, easy-going gracefulness of the perfect courtier. It is understandable therefore that J. Shearman should exclude tension, drama, violence, passion and exaggerated overflows of emotion from the aesthetic ideal prescribed by *la maniera*. The above criteria constitute the dividing line between Mannerism, meaning only the art of *maniera*, and anticlassicism, thought to be wholly foreign to this ideal. It was therefore not in Florence but in Rome from 1520 until 1527, the date of the Sack of Rome, that the first choice blooms of Mannerism came into flower as a sort of 'art nouveau' in the budding Cinquecento, thanks to the works of Perino del Vaga, Polidoro di Caravaggio, Parmigianino and Rosso himself once he had turned his back on his Florentine manner. These artists were instrumental in establishing the main features of the new style which was soon to radiate its influence over most of Italy and beyond. J. Shearman agrees with C.H. Smyth in thinking that the most prominent representatives of mature Mannerism in the 1540s were Bronzino, Salviati, Vasari and Tibaldi in painting, Cellini and Bologna in statuary and gold and silver work, and Ammanati in architecture.

But J. Shearman's argument raises a question: of what use are the qualities of *la maniera* as he describes them in telling us about the *forms* these artists turned to in order to embody the aesthetic ideal they were pursuing in their works? Properly speaking, neither the recommendations made by Vasari nor the qualities of grace, sophistication, variety and ostentation that J. Shearman sees in Mannerist painting can be called stylistic features: there is just as much elegance to be found in a cubist figure by Braque as in a portrait painted by Renoir. Unlike C.H. Smyth, who focuses on figurative conventions, J. Shearman is mainly bent on defining what could be called in vague terms the overall 'tone' of a work; but not its style, if this word is taken to mean a combination of figurative schemes. In his book entitled *Mannerism*, published in 1967, J. Shearman rehandles and adds to the conclusions he came to in his paper of 1963. But when he comes to broach questions of form in chapter 3, entitled 'Characteristic Forms', the use of the word 'form' undergoes some shift of meaning: alongside a very pertinent examination of the *figura serpentinata*, which is justly considered as one of the stylistic components of the Mannerist style in painting and sculpture, there are other aspects of the discussion that are put under the heading of forms, whereas in reality they concern aesthetic objects or genres such as pastoral, polyphony and madrigals, intermezzi, the decorative elements of urban or domestic settings like fountains, chimney-pieces, staircases, grottoes etc. Immensely interesting as it is, Shearman's study is perhaps too exclusively dedicated to subjective and qualitative judgements, to assessing the amount of grace, refinement and stylization of a given work of art – in short its degree of conformity with the *maniera* ideal – at the expense of any methodical observation of objective data like colour, composition, the treatment of space and volume, lighting etc. It may well be that J. Shearman implies agreement with C.H. Smyth's remarks on painting, but in this case it is difficult to understand why certain anti-classical works have been excluded from Mannerism on the pretext that their idiom is too seldom 'a silver-tongued language of beauty and caprice' and too often 'one of violence, incoherence and despair'.[11] In spite of these works failing to conform to the *maniera* ideal, close examination does reveal a sufficient number of structural or figurative similarities with those paintings considered by Shearman to warrant their inclusion among those representing Mannerist style.

This is why I have thought it relevant to include among the illustrations a number of reproductions of anticlassical works dating from early Mannerism. By referring to the synoptic table (see table 1.1) of the *maniera* conventions, which is a modest attempt to summarize C.H. Smyth's conclusions that represent the most complete and detailed inventory to date, it will be seen that there are a number of convergences.

Who will deny, for example, that there are elements of Mannerism in Rosso's Volterra *Deposition*, painted in 1521 and praised for its beauty by as experienced a connoisseur of *maniera* as Vasari himself? Or in Pontormo's *Deposition* (1526–8) in Santa Felicità, in spite of his very different treatment of the same subject? I have chosen to include a reproduction of Raphael's *Betrothal of the Virgin* (1504) not to annoy, but rather to hint at the presence of some disharmony within a work which is nevertheless extremely representative of the High Renaissance. *The Expulsion of Heliodorus* (1511–12), for which Raphael secured the collaboration of Giulio Romano and Giovanni da Udine, heralds, in my view, the emergence of a new style. The prophet *Daniel*, dating from the same period (1509–12), and *The Last Judgement*, posterior to it by about twenty-five years (1536–41), serve to exemplify two Michelangelesque representations of space with equal claim to be called both Mannerist and anticlassical. The final reproduction, of Tintoretto's *Last Supper* in San Giorgio Maggiore (1592–4), gives an idea of the way Tintoretto interpreted the Mannerist heritage at the close of the century.

Table 1.1. Synoptic table of the *maniera* conventions

Light	• Often uniform, 'flat', as if beaming from a single source and hitting the surface of the painting head on (plates v, vi and viii)
Space	• Deep (plate ii and the internal organization of its deep, unified space which prefigures Mannerism, and plate ix with its perverted use of perspective)
	• Shallow (plate viii)
	• Almost non-existent (plates v and vi)
	• Plural (plates iv and vii)
Volume	• Foreground flattening, as if parallel to the surface of the picture (plates v, vi and viii)
	• Highly exaggerated, in aid of heightened expressiveness
Composition	• Abnormal highlighting of detail to the detriment of essentials, creating an effect of peculiarity and confusion (plates vi and ix)
	• A taste for piling-up and juxtaposing figures and other objects represented within a reduced space (plates iv, vi, vii and ix)
Figures	• Vertical elongation (plates v and vii)
	• Angularity (plates v and viii)
	• Twisted contortion creating a need for foreshortening
	• Unexpected poses and attitudes, unmotivated by any reference to verisimilitude (plates v and vi)
	• Monumental forms, sometimes increased by means of a foreground platform resulting in a view from below to above (plate vii)
	• The minute treatment of limbs and their extremities, of garments, accoutrements (plate viii)
Drawing	• Hard, sharp, accentuating the statuesqueness of the figures (plates iii and viii)
	• The line is broken into segments (plate v)
	• Refined, idealized, keeping to essentials, inattentive to the contingent and the picturesque (plates v, vi, vii and viii)
Colour	• Uniform, to the detriment of values; flesh looks as if it were made of some inert, immutable substance (plates vi and viii)
	• Often inconsistent with 'naturalness' and verisimilitude (plates v and vi)

In conclusion, it can therefore be said that Mannerism as it appeared in Italy during the sixteenth century was a complex stylistic phenomenon that came to dominate artistic production from 1530 onwards. It was not only of considerable importance in Italy, owing to the quantity of works produced, but also in other countries in that it led to the widespread domination of Italian art. The figurative conventions of Italian Mannerism found their way into European painting either through Italian court painters such as Rosso, Primaticcio, Luca Penni, Niccolò dell'Abbate and Salviati at Fontainebleau, Tibaldi, Cambiaso and Federico Zuccaro in Madrid and Zuccaro again in London, or through native artists who more or less adopted the Italian manner, Maerten van Heemskerck and Cornelis Cornelisz in Haarlem, Joachim Wtewael and Abraham Bloemaert in Utrecht, Bartholomeus Spranger and Hans van Aachen in Prague, Alonso Berruguete in Castile, Nicholas Hilliard and Hans Eworth in England, Jacques Bellangé in Lorraine and Toussaint Dubreuil who gave Fontainebleau the final splendours of its heyday. It is no slight to national and regional peculiarities or to individual idiosyncrasies to accept that Mannerism is easily recognizable even by untutored eyes. The most typical forms of mature Mannerism are coherent and sufficiently recurrent to be considered as belonging to a special style, even if the particularity of this style is its encouragement of individual manner within the frame of a new orthodoxy.

Beginning in Italy, Mannerism took over from a type of experimental art which was anticlassical in tendency and expressed a change of relationship between the artist and his work, as well as between the artist and society. In the sixteenth century, artists were less concerned with exploring new ways of relating to nature – this had been the main preoccupation of the Quattrocento – they were more intent on stating their right to go their own way in the face of the relative dogmatism of the High Renaissance. The idea was emerging that a work of art did more than fulfil a social function; it was also made in the image of its creator. Hence the ever-increasing importance of self-expression; hence the ever-increasing need to posssess a style. The anticlassical movement's achievement was not left a dead letter by the Mannerists. It is significant that all the theorists of this period looked upon the study of the masters and nature merely as a means of strengthening individual giftedness and allowing artists to demonstrate their personal talents.

On the other hand, it is clear that Mannerism was overrun very rapidly by an academic tendency towards uniformity resulting from a belief not only in ideal beauty but also in an ideal way of attaining it. The dread of aesthetic decadence lurked quite early on in Vasari and even more so in his successors. It was their attempts to ward it off that led to the foundation of academies and the drawing up of a set of rules that would ensure quality and continuity in artistic production. Vasari sincerely believed that he and his contemporaries had a manner superior to their predecessors' as a result of the 'progress' made in painting since Giotto. Nevertheless, Vasari did not fail to see that *maniera* might encourage facileness, routine dexterity and over-extravagance in artists seeking to singularize their work at all costs. As a result, at the end of the century, the main task facing the best of them was to steer their way to more realism and simplicity.

Finally, it is important to insist that the fundamental principles of the figurative system built up during the Quattrocento never came to be dismantled either by the anticlassical trend within which the first Mannerist experiments developed or by subsequent mature Mannerism, which by no means adopted all of the earlier innovations. At most, the Mannerists were rebelling against the way the High Renaissance limited its interpretation of this system. It is Pierre Francastel who shows how the High Renaissance developed by means of 'a twofold process of narrowing down and going deeper into certain hypotheses put forward during the previous century, by only retaining some of them'.[12] This is no doubt one of the reasons why Mannerist art seems to hark back to trends cast aside by the High Renaissance. Whatever the playfulness, cleverness or dreams that delighted the Mannerists (either anticlassical or *maniera* adepts), they well and truly belonged to the Renaissance and embodied both its spirit of adventure and its conservatism. However much they juggled with space and distorted orthodox proportions, however bold they were in using light and colour, yet the images of the world that they offered reflected both the stability *and* the flexibility of the principles underpinning the system. It was to take four centuries of painting and profound upheavals in the political, social, scientific and ideological domains, marking the end of an era in the civilization of Western Europe, for the image of a universe conceived as a framework for mankind, 'efficient actor on the stage of the world',[13] to appear to be literally a thing of the past. From then on, the plastic arts were once again on the move, groping their way to some major milestones: impressionism, cubism, surrealism and much that escapes classification; from then on, a new era of research was to open up, as it did during the Quattrocento, in an attempt to objectify the confused feelings of a new perception of the self and its place in the universe of people and things.

CHAPTER 2

From art to theatre:[1] towards a definition of Mannerism

How does one arrive at a working definition of Mannerism? I mean one that is relevant to the description of theatrical texts, while also resting upon minute observation of the painting typifying this style? Either the question has remained too often unasked or its importance, methodologically speaking, has been underestimated by the advocates of Mannerism in literature – and the same remarks apply to the advocates of the Baroque – with the result that critics have not always been able to make the most of these categories.

It is tempting to make facile use of metaphorical language when trying to establish correspondences between different art forms, and I myself would be careful not to disclaim all use, past and future, of such a quick way out. Although Wylie Sypher recognizes that 'form' in literature is of a different nature to 'the visible, tangible structure erected there in the art object before our eye, our hand',[2] pointing out that it is hopeless to try and give a rigorous definition of the structure of a poem in spatial or visual terms, yet he too, occasionally, indulges in metaphor, albeit with talent. Thus, referring to Tennyson, he notes that 'he gains "distance" by presenting minute details in his descriptive foreground and leaving his background dim, vast, glimmering'.[3] This is an interesting impression but one that would need to be transcribed and illustrated in the language proper to literary analysis. When W. Sypher describes Mannerist space 'either as flimsy and shallow, concealing volumes behind a papery façade, or narrow, curving and *coulisse*-like', noting that 'by means of such techniques Mannerist art holds everything in a state of dissonance, dissociation and doubt', he does list a number of readily identifiable features of Mannerist architecture and painting. But the conclusion to the chapter is peremptory and unsubstantiated: 'This is the art of *Hamlet*, where ambiguities and complexities are exploited.'[4] The author of these lines presumes a little too much upon the confidence the reader has placed in him.

Assuming that Shakespeare indeed cultivates dissonant effects comparable to those arising from a Mannerist treatment of visual space, we still have to understand which dramatic (by which I mean textual) devices he uses to achieve his aim. If one believes that Mannerism can indeed designate or denote a particular style or *écriture* and represent something more than simply a useful shorthand to refer to certain effects, then speaking of the theatre requires a discourse that is *different* to the one applied to painting and the other visual arts. The encounter between the visual and the textual (since stage performance does not enter into my argument) needs to be organized along lines that protect each of the two parties from having to disown their identities as specific art forms. The drawback of analogy based on metaphor is that the theatre has to be spoken of in borrowed language using imagery to gloss over the inadequacy of vocabulary. Clearly, it is allowable to speak of 'space' in *Hamlet* only if the semantic content of the image is made explicit in terms adequate to the object described. Inversely, it would be just as dangerous to fall into the trap of draining Mannerism of its visual content (and therefore its origins) so as to allow it to be of immediate use to textual analysis. This in fact would amount to withdrawing everything that grounds Mannerism in the visual arts in order to facilitate its transference. So in place of references to materials (colour, line, marble, bronze etc.) and the treatment they receive at the hands of the painter or sculptor, interest would focus on the idea or aesthetic ideal behind the artist's inspiration. Analogy by withdrawal would strip the stylistic category of its material determinants and serve to define only an aesthetic choice which could be basically the same whatever the art form considered. Instead of the Mannerist style of a given painting being discussed with reference to objective criteria, the Mannerism of the work would be attributed to an intention or an aesthetic impression, such as the cultivation of elegance, a liking for weirdness, a desire to create a feeling of perplexity, with the obvious result that the artist's actual handiwork would remain unnoticed or undervalued.

J. Shearman maintains that Guarini's *Pastor Fido* conforms in many respects to the *maniera* ideal with its sense of artifice, complication and decoration and its rejection of emotional excess, but the main issue remains unaddressed and one is left wondering through what specifically dramatic means Guarini arouses impressions analogous to those created by Mannerist painting. It is indeed reasonable and stimulating to postulate the existence of an aesthetic trend permeating European art in the sixteenth century, but there are still questions to be asked about the special features displayed by Mannerism according to the particular art form that it enters; there is still the question of what the actual process is through which *maniera* leaves its mark on a specific material. The truth is that behind analogy by withdrawal there lies concealed the old separation between content and form, essence and existence, between a part that is lofty, abstract and meaningful and a part that is inferior, material and contingent, seen as the mere embodiment, in various modes, of the Idea behind the artist's work. In opposition to this idealistic position (in the philosophic sense), I believe it is imperative to maintain the inseparableness of the signified and the signifier, expressing the idea of the profound unity of the creative act.

If Mannerism refers to a style – a combinatory order of recurrent schemes – it follows that any analogy between different art forms will need to take the structural organization of the material into account. Etienne Souriau quotes an example of 'legitimate' analogy between drawing and music: referring to 'the delightful effect of a Renaissance arabesque produced by a line swerving off its course, momentarily shunning the expected axis on which it might come to rest, disrupting the movement of the stroke as if indulging a sort of fancy and only reaching its termination after what could be called a trial run, almost a false note, on a parallel axis', Souriau calls it a 'plastic appoggiatura', pointing out that 'in music, appoggiatura is a melodic and harmonic device whereby the singing voice is first pitched dissonantly on an adjacent tone, instead of immediately striking the note that would be expected as a logical outcome of the form and as demanded by the harmony, only then coming to rest on the right tone after making us long for it, as if putting an end to a brief, slightly flirtatious, slightly painful moment of hesitation'.[5] It is clear that the foregoing definition, though couched in metaphorical language, is in itself no metaphor, but the rigorous transposition of one identical scheme or figure achieved by the draughtsman and the musician, each using the technique of their craft: it would occur to no one to confuse a line in drawing and a line in music, unless bogged down by metaphorical comparison.

Jean Rousset, in an essay entitled 'Saint-Yves et les poètes', makes a similar type of analogy, one that I find equally convincing. He examines four works of Baroque art: on the one hand Bernini's *Fountain of the Rivers* along with Borromini's *Chapel of Saint-Yves*, and on the other hand a poem by Drelincourt (a minor French poet of the seventeenth century) along with an extract from Bossuet's funeral oration for Anne de Gonzague. Rousset notes that they share a common structure: 'a journey through which one contemplates a transformation from instable to stable, achieving a personal transition from agitation to serenity, from the multiplicity of sense impressions to the unity of the sacred'. Rousset further says that: 'The One can be grasped through the many in a dynamic process, by means of a movement breaking itself up and swelling out, leading into a spectacular volte-face that reveals a fixity.'[6] As with Souriau, the analogy discloses a structuring principle, a dynamics of form embodied in stone and in words. This type of comparison invokes a sense of space inherently present in the arts of language and, more generally, in the arts of duration. G. Wilson Knight remarked quite early on that: 'A Shakespearian tragedy is set spatially as well as temporally in the mind. By this I mean that there are throughout the play a set of correspondences which relate to each other independently of the time-sequence which is the story. Now if we are prepared to see the whole play laid out, so to speak, as an area, being simultaneously aware of these thickly scattered correspondences in a single view of the whole, we possess the unique quality of the play in a new sense.'[7] Anne Ubersfeld, commenting on performance (and her remarks also apply to texts), defines it as a moment in time when 'the text is heard as *parole*, . . . as poem or poetic object, but also as the visual, plastic and dynamic projection of the textual networks'.[8]

It is now time to return once again to Mannerist painting in order to attempt to define the schemes it uses in the organization of its particular 'area' or, one could also say, its own figurative networks. It is not, however, possible to do the job properly unless concrete reference is made to what might be called the elementary components of a painting, things such as colour, touch, line or value. The colours are often uncommon, sometimes precious, sometimes thought to be ugly, at all events disconcerting because too remote from reality. The Mannerist painter's palette has been so thoroughly examined already that any protracted discussion of it is unnecessary. There is, however, one important point: in a Mannerist painting, the colour often appears rather unsuited to the object as referent – for example, the aggressively immaculate whiteness of the flesh in Bronzino's *Allegory* in the National Gallery; the overdominance of the yellows and ochres in Rosso's *Moses*; the obsessive stridency of blues and greens in work by El Greco. Colours as a rule are 'misplaced', provocative, metaphorical. In Rosso's *Deposition* (plate v) the blue of the sky refers to the sky (which is blue) but the signified is a dense, opaque substance which is richly and diversely suggestive: it could be lapis lazuli, slate or enamel, something anyway that is unlike the impalpable airiness of a real atmosphere. The touch is smooth, lacquered and vertical, as if to accentuate the impression of an impenetrable screen. The value of the tones is barely sufficient to attenuate the sense of unreality conveyed by the touch: the shading off from darker to brighter tones stands for the dusk (in accordance with Scripture which situates the death of Christ slightly earlier in the afternoon), but the result is technically too faultless; there is something abstract about its very perfection: in the refusal of a credible sky there is a deliberate statement of artifice. It is a truly Mannerist sky, half-way between the 'realistic' sky of the landscape artist and those unfigurative, conventional backgrounds that enhance and symbolically code the figures – the gold of icons and Gothic paintings, the black against which Cranach's figures stand out and the fiery décor of Hilliard's *Man and Flames*. If one attempted to describe the sky in this particular *Deposition*, one would have to speak of a sky that is glazed, polished or varnished, using a metaphor in the form of an oxymoron, which would become all the more necessary if words had to be used to translate the effect created by the personages: the stiffness of the drapery, the blocks of hewn flesh, the volumes of the bodies broken into facets . . . It could, however, be objected that this violently anticlassical painting is too apt an example.

Turning to Bronzino's *Allegory*, which is entirely consistent with the *maniera* ideal in its refusal of cubist experiments and in its adhesion to the High Renaissance technique of using value to suggest volume, here too the glazing of the touch expresses timelessness and perfection, the chilly world of the Idea extracted from the warmth and precariousness of throbbing life. The only humanizing element in the painting is the figure of Father Time, who brings in a warmer, amber tint and a more vibrant touch, like the intrusion of a fact of nature, though heavily allegorized, into the abstract world of culture: time passing within everlasting eternity. But, then, what about the almost obscene whiteness starting out to challenge the eye of even the most inattentive visitor to the National Gallery: it conveys beauty, but it is cold beauty that spurns desire; does it spell purity as convention often expects? But what kind of purity can be enshrined in such a courtly Venus yielding to the fondling fingers of an ambiguous Cupid? This flesh that might be thought to be intended for pleasure is oddly spiritualized; paradoxically it suggests the idea of chaste lasciviousness or, to put it another way, lewd frigidity.

In French it is *pointe*; in Italian it is called *concetto* and in English 'conceit'. It is the choice figure of Mannerist rhetoric, for conceits glorify dissonance and are themselves the most obvious tokens of artistic ingenuity. Classical writers who hold that art should conceal artistry prefer metonymy to conceit. Metonymy is unobtrusive and reassuring; it reckons on the coherence of the world by acknowledging the interchangeability of its parts. When metonymy decomposes an object, it does so in order to show immediately the ways in which it can be recomposed into a viable whole. Metaphor, on the other hand, even when it stops short of oxymoronic extremes, postulates a disparity at the heart of the object or, what amounts to the same, an overwhelming affinity between disparate objects. Metaphor endows signs pertaining to the visual arts or language with a strange power as if by some master-stroke the most dissimilar things were enjoined to display unsuspected relationships. It will be argued that all artistic creation results from this process (Aragon's *mentir-vrai*), but it is perhaps the peculiarity of Mannerism that it quite shamelessly lays bare the manufacturing secrets of the art object.

In Bronzino's *Allegory* (plate VIII), the space in the painting is not dependent on the representation of any kind of referential space, but results from the expert conjugation of three formal and iconographic schemes: the rhythmic counterpointing of the bodies of Venus and Cupid opposite each other, their being inserted into the complicated network of emblematic figures and objects filling the empty spaces, and the patterning of colours. The positioning of Venus' legs is contradictory to the positioning of the rest of the body; the direction imparted to the arms is contradictory to that of the forearms and they themselves are in conflict with the hands. It is as if Venus' body was carefully avoiding subordinating all its gestures to the accomplishment of one clear gestural intention, but tentatively and simultaneously exploring several possibilities of action. The personage's energy is not summoned up from a desire to carry out a particular act (this is more often a characteristic of classical and Baroque art), but from a desire to perform a gesture that will be graceful, puzzling, unmotivated and superlatively pointless. Reasons for acting are changed into pretexts for posing. Such examples of *contrapposto* abound in Mannerist painting and sculpture. It was thought to be the height of elegance, as well as the unquestionable evidence that art can free itself from the laws of anatomical and psychological verisimilitude. In Mannerist eyes, the Beautiful often lies in what does not exist.

The posture of Christ in Rosso's *Dead Christ with Angels* in the Boston Museum is in subdued *contrapposto*. But the daring mainly lies elsewhere. The work is a variation on Michelangelo's motif of the masculine nude in sitting posture as it appears in the *Ignudi* in the Sistine Chapel. Rosso has made every effort to outdo his model in manly grace in spite of a subject which, in principle, might be thought hardly suitable for this type of one-upmanship. Christ has been given the features of a slightly over-ripe Adonis, snatched away by death or rather ravished as in amorous ecstasy. The pose of voluptuous abandon, as well as the expression on the face, deprive the image of much of its spiritual content. Unless one is ready to admit that a Christian's love for his Saviour feeds on the mingled drives of Eros and Thanatos, this representation of Christ seems incongruous, not so much because it celebrates the profaneness of a beautiful male body as because it betrays a secretly sacrilegious purpose. The body of the Godhead is clearly being used for other ends than religious devotion: it is a fine example of the deflection or perversion of a sign whose referential value wavers dangerously (and delightfully) under the weight of metaphor.

However, there are cases – in fact they are the most numerous – in which the spatial organization of the painting depends in great part on the treatment given represented space. Anticlassical Mannerism revived and heightened a tendency prior to the High Renaissance, which consisted in juxtaposing heterogeneous spaces. *The Madonna of the Long Neck* (plate VII) contains several spaces construed according to different scales but linked together, although without the presence of any rationalizing element, by the use of false perspective, perhaps an ironic concession to the standard of unified space. On the left hand are a set of exaggeratedly tall figures crowded into a confined space; on the right is a more extended space reaching towards the horizon and marked out by a column rising to giddy heights, the first of a row that is almost entirely concealed; and near it is the tiny but over-elongated figure of Saint Jerome holding out his parchment. There is no discernibly intelligible link between these two elements. It is rather as if each object or group of objects were in a self-contained space, estranged from the space contiguous to it. Without this assemblage of heterogeneous spaces, the spatial organization of the painting would naturally have been extremely different. Without it, Parmigianino could not have done what he did, basing the structure of his work on a play of oppositions between gigantic and miniature scales, empty and crammed spaces, a foreground view from below and a middle ground view from above etc.

Even a single, unified space, when handled by *maniera* artists, can result in a thoroughly Mannerist mode of structuring a painting, provided regard for perspective is joined to a desire to subvert the rules of classical representation in some other way. Michelangelo, in the *Prophets* and the

Sybils in the Sistine Chapel, Salviati, in *Saint Andrew* in San Giovanni Decollato (Rome), and Bronzino, in *Saint John the Baptist* in the Galleria Borghese (Rome), are past masters at obtaining striking effects of contrast between oversized personages and cramped surroundings. The human figure is incapable of 'living' comfortably in its allotted space and seems to be trying to depart from it by flinging itself so far forward towards the observer that it almost 'invades' our personal space and upsets our normal relationship with painting. Classicism assumes that the active engagement of the observer is obvious and natural; Mannerism is apprehensive of indifference in an audience known to be blasé. *Castiglione* painted by Raphael (the Louvre) can be gazed at serenely, but the *Lady* portrayed by Pontormo (Frankfurt Museum) is an act of solicitation: the portrait is intended to catch the eye and hold it fast. Critics always refer to the uncommon refinement of Mannerist art, but it can also be outspoken and obtrusive, as if secretly preyed upon by the anxiety of not being noticed enough, should the powerful presence of the model blot out technical performance or originality of manner.

In the work of Tintoretto, an irrational use of perspective gives the viewer a feeling of strangeness verging on anguish, as can be seen in *The Finding of the Body of Saint Mark* (Pinacoteca di Brera, Milan) and its companion piece *The Removal of the Body of Saint Mark* (Galleria dell' Accademia, Venice). In these paintings, an uncanny use of foreshortening implying a considerable distance between the foreground and the background is instrumental in heightening the drama of the two scenes. In no way does perspective suggest real space; rather it becomes frenzied, abuses its power and ends up denying any appearance of reality to the space and objects represented. Images appear as hallucinations and the observer feels drawn into a sort of *terra incognita* which flouts the actual experience of concrete space and the cultural or iconographic experience of painted space. Tintoretto's pictorial statement is that perspective is not necessarily something 'natural', to be taken so much for granted that it can be overlooked. Perspective can thus become insolent, tyrannical and troublesome. In Tintoretto's work it sometimes goes wild, steals the show and, while its derangement lowers its credibility, it also focuses attention upon itself as an *écriture*, as a mark of style and rhetorical grandiloquence. Space itself becomes anomaly, enigma, an element of drama.

It emerges from the foregoing remarks that the principle underlying these Mannerist innovations is that of disparity or dissonance or the systematic exploitation of incompatibilities. This is corroborated at every level in the organization of these paintings. It is the common denominator of the Mannerist idiom and the articulation of its discourse, with conceit as its favourite figure.

But a word must be said about the corollary principle of off-centredness. In Tintoretto's *Last Supper* (strictly speaking, the institution of the Eucharist), which was designed as one of the two lateral pieces for the chancel of San Giorgio Maggiore in Venice (plate IX), the perspective is once again overemphatic, unlike its companion piece on the wall opposite, *The Gathering of the Manna*. It is therefore not, or not alone, the intended location of the piece that can account for the intense foreshortening of the composition, since equally overdramatized perspective spaces are to be found in works meant to be viewed frontally. The main consequence of this treatment of space is that it is largely responsible for decentring the composition; it causes the eyes to stray beyond and away from what should be seen first by giving value to secondary elements placed along the vanishing-lines: for example, the space allotted the servants, which is disproportionate to the space given Christ and his disciples; the proliferation of unknown personages; the gloom pierced by intense light coming from the lamp, as well as from Christ's halo, and conferring an oblique glow on the kitchen utensils; the cloud of angels caught on the ceiling; the asides of the disciples – all so many microevents that disperse the attention. Is, then, the Last Supper still the 'true' subject of the painting? The consecration of the bread and the wine occupies the centre of the painting at the intersection of the two diagonals, but is the geometric centre identical with the major centre of interest, the point of convergence of the signs? Deliberately insignificant, mundane items (the shine on the carafes, the cat clinging to the basket) compete dangerously with the spiritual event. Tintoretto hovers between two requirements: the desire to root the event in the solidity of material life and the wish to dramatize it with maximum pathos. The haloes of Christ and the disciples and the cloud of angels testify to the presence of the divine, but a closer look reveals that nothing could be less appropriate for the exaltation of religious feeling, and more openly theatrical, than that blinding light around Christ's head searching the surrounding darkness like a projector, or those diaphanous angels made of the same evanescent substance as the smoke from the lamps. The same subject treated by Leonardo on the back wall of the refectory of Santa Maria delle Grazie in Milan celebrates the solemnity of the moment stripped of all contingency and vain theatricality; Leonardo situates it in the eternity of sacred things. In Tintoretto's work, the material struggles with the spiritual, the spectacular vies with the ritual. Caravaggio and Baroque painters are also fond of expressing the material nature of the world (the Council of Trent enjoined artists to appeal to the senses), but the enhancement of matter invariably leads back to the sacred; incarnation guarantees transcendence. In Tintoretto's work, and in Mannerist art in general, the religious and the profane face each other like the players in a drawn game with no winner or loser.

Rosso's *Deposition* (plate v) produces an even more noticeable feeling of discomfort: the attitudes, gestures and facial expressions of the personages induce the viewer to transfer his or her gaze to details of little or doubtful relevance and the eyes have to exert themselves to avoid succumbing to the artist's vagaries and impertinences.

The other *Deposition* included here, the work of Pontormo in Santa Felicità, Florence (plate vi), is supremely orderly in construction: the lines, colours and volumes are balanced harmoniously without confusion or overloading. However, not a single figurative element manages to hold the observer's gaze in any lasting way, not even the body of Christ. As D.B. Rowland notes: 'The eye can never come to rest on anything, but is kept constantly travelling around and around the composition, following the curving lines of drapery until a sense of nausea is produced.'[9] All of the personages achieve the Mannerist feat of directing their gaze to something other than the body of Christ. Not that their eyes are turned, like those of Rembrandt's *Cloth-merchants*, towards the viewer of the painting, who has become an object of curiosity to the notabilities whose confabulation has just been interrupted and also the invented vanishing-point of the perspective. No, in Pontormo's *Deposition* each figure is looking away to a private somewhere impossible to localize, perhaps the somewhere of the conscience in personages who are divided within themselves, withdrawn from themselves, as if absolved – by whom or by what is not clear – from taking any real part in the scene which has brought them together. The personages that perform in Mannerist art are often made into an absent presence, as seen in Bronzino's portraits of Florentine aristocrats.

In the first glance cast at a Mannerist production in whatever art form, there is always some degree of nostalgia for a lost unity, a longing to overcome the impression of disparity, to compensate for the absence of logic, to recentre the composition around the main subject and restore the correlation of the sign and the referent: but it quickly becomes apparent that from these tensions there emerge works that are unsurpassed in their ability to give *in-sight* into the processes of the art to

which they pertain and into the artistry to which they owe their existence.

Off-centredness, dissonance, disparity, ostentation . . . one could go on
and on reeling off all the items in the Mannerist paradigm. But enumer-
ation betrays an inability to produce a true definition. At the risk of disappointing those who were hoping for a definition as neat as Rousset's
formula for the Baroque, it has to be admitted, however reluctantly, that
the Mannerist style is even more protean than the Baroque and cannot
be encompassed – still less encapsulated – so easily. Although without an
'Open Sesame', we are at least equipped with a few keys wrought into
shape through an encounter with some of the major works of
Mannerism. It is to be hoped that these keys will open a few doors when
applied to Shakespeare's drama.

Illustrations

The size of the *tempietto* is incompatible with the distance between it and the foreground. Raphael at least partially contravenes the laws of perspective, which in this instance run counter to his figurative intention. He no doubt deemed it important to treat the monument as a separate structure and not as an ordinary part of the décor subjected to the effects of distance in the same way as the paving and the figures in the background. It is as if Raphael's aim was to impose the ideal and therefore unreal character of the temple by withdrawing it from the ordinary laws of perspective. What matters is not the verisimilitude of the building's size but its function as a signifier. One could go as far as to advance that this vast monument grandiosely witnessing the espousal of Mary and Joseph itself testifies to the presence of God through its circular form, evoking divine perfection. It is also possible to see the roundness of the temple as the architectonic expression of the created world, as may be suggested by the groups of figures whose presence humanizes the building without affecting its perfection.

Whatever the interpretation of this deliberate remissness in orthodox representation, there is no doubt that Raphael brings an element of disunion into his painting, a sense of disparity which none the less results in no discordance, since the monumental serenity of the temple is such an important factor in the sense of harmony felt by the viewer.

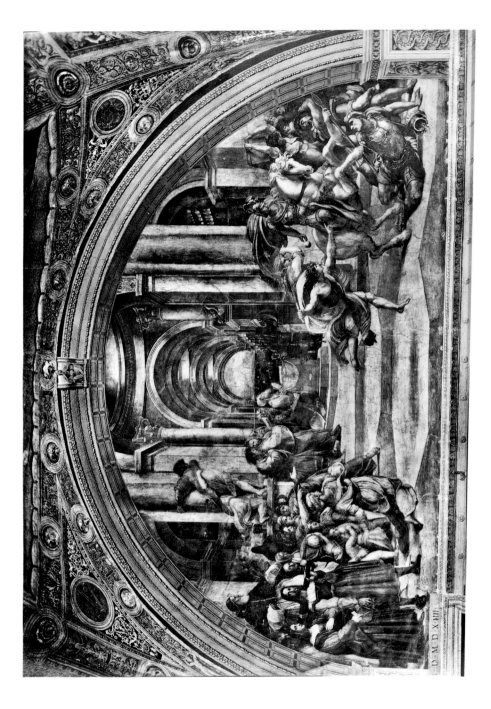

PLATE II Raphael with Giulio Romano and Giovanni da Udine: *The Expulsion of Heliodorus from the Temple*, 1511–12, Stanza dell' Eliodoro, The Vatican, Rome.

The space is organized in a coherent manner around the central vanishing-point of the background *veduta*, the semicircular window open to the sky and below which the high priest is kneeling. Yet the subject of the fresco is not the high priest at prayer, although the viewer's eyes are drawn irresistibly to him, but the expulsion for which the high priest is rendering thanks to God. The expulsion, which is due to the intervention of three avenging angels, takes up the right-hand side, while the left is devoted to the witnesses of the scene. The symmetrical arrangement of the groups in relation to the central axis further stresses the contrast between the two atmospheres: the turbulent violence of the expulsion, giving rise to dramatic gestures, and the relative calm reigning on the left, even if a few women have been seized with terror. There is no doubt that this arrangement using symmetry and contrast reveals the artist's classical ideal of clarity and intelligibility. On the other hand, the big empty space in the centre of the composition is problematic; it is emphasized to an exaggerated extent as if the figures, as actors or witnesses, were destined to occupy only the aisles, not the nave; nor do the outflung limbs of the angel flying in pursuit of Heliodorus in any way cut into the central area, which remains obstinately deserted.

In addition, there is a remarkable insistence or even repetitiveness in the use made of the geometric figures of semicircles: the *trompe-l'oeil* of the archway defining the almost theatrical space in which the scene is played out; the double arches that make up the vault of the chancel half drawn in along the aisles; and, finally, the *veduta* upon which the perspective lines converge. The omnipresence of this architectural motif suggests that its function is not merely to mark out the receding space, and this is where the structural relationship between the pattern of semicircularity and the central emptiness referred to above begins to emerge: from the coexistence of these two modes of structuring space comes the impression of a whirling movement, powerful enough to have swept the figures away from the centre of the periphery. The attitude of the two youths clinging to a pillar whose pedestal they have climbed in order to obtain a better view of the scene, the movement of the drapery wrapping itself around them, the position of their encircling arms and the very precariousness of their posture convey a sense of an invisible, centrifugal force, something like a vortex flinging the figures onto the lateral walls.

With the spectator's eyes thus drawn towards the *veduta*, one may well overlook the recognized subject of the fresco (the expulsion of Heliodorus); nor is one more tempted to pause over the reactions of the witnesses to the expulsion. The eyes can only survey the scene in its entirety through a renewed effort and a deliberate toing and froing between the two opposed areas, so that an impression of some visual discomfort is added to that of a turning world, due to an inability to achieve any immediate, global vision.

Finally, a word must be said about the three or four figures foregrounded at the extreme left. In view of the tornado raging on the other side, these figures (that include Julius II on his gestatorial chair) are astonishingly unmoved. As Raphael's own contemporaries, they are exterior to the subject of the representation. The presence of the pontiff has a symbolic meaning that goes beyond the homage paid by the artists to their patron and commissioner. As the distant successor of the praying high priest, the Pope incarnates the continuity of the Church of God. As for the bearers with their eyes turned away from the scene of action so that they strike up a sharing relationship with the viewer of the fresco, the indifference that they and the serenely impassible lady betray is a visual expression of the distance separating the biblical episode from modern times: they are the vehicles of the commentary.

One realizes here how iconographic inconsistency and compositional oddity contribute to the meaning of the work. It seems that this fresco exemplifies the 'discord of parts' noted by P. Francastel as a fairly recurrent feature of Quattrocento painting, a practice still perceptible in some High Renaissance works but to which anticlassical Mannerism was soon to give fresh impetus.

(I am indebted to R.E. Wolf and R. Millen, joint authors of *Renaissance and Mannerist Art*, New York, 1968, for the remark concerning the centrifugal animation of the composition.)

DANIEL

There is an obvious lack of proportion between the massiveness of the figure and the narrowness of the space allotted to it. The reduction of the surrounding space is meant to accentuate the figure's monumental effect. However, the artist's intention goes beyond producing that sort of illusion. The *trompe-l'oeil* cornices and pilasters are used as surrounds to a constrictive spatial framework from which the figure seemingly strives to escape by throwing itself forward towards the viewer. The overriding impression, as often in the work of Michelangelo and Mannerist painters, is one of pent-up energy powerless to flow free because of deliberately restricted spatial partitioning. Thus Michelangelo suggests both the need for dynamic expansion and the impossibility of its attainment, in contradiction to the style of the High Renaissance which prescribes a rational distribution of space around the figures, so that they may fit into surroundings adapted to their needs. In the present instance, the overt primacy accorded to the figure entails space constriction. This type of imbalance or unequal relationship is a distinct foreshadowing of mature Mannerism, as shown, for example, by Salviati's *Saint Andrew* (1551) in the Oratorio di San Giovanni Decollato in Rome, an illustration of which is included in J. Shearman's *Mannerism*, p. 85.

Michelangelo's critical questioning of 'classical' space is far-reaching. It is not quite correct to claim that there is no depth at all: at the bottom of the fresco, the gaping rock of hell – the sole fixed point of reference within a dynamic scene where clusters of bodies seem to be suspended in mid-air – then Charon's boat a little further to the right and finally the oval nimbus surrounding Christ all mark out a space that suggests a semblance of depth. On the other hand, it is undeniable that this plural space radically differs from Alberti's monocular perspective.

The layout of the groups is symmetrical: three transverse, and more or less parallel, lines created by the blue of the sky divide the fresco into four levels arranged according to a vertical, non-perspective plan. The size of the figures is not calculated with reference to the viewer contemplating the fresco from below: the personages nearest the viewer are smaller than those situated in the upper half. Therefore, the size of the figures is not dependent on optical logic, but on a theocratic logic founded on the spiritual hierarchy of the actors.

It is to be noted that certain groupings, especially the personages around Christ, are articulated according to the laws of perspective: the figures are not at all on the same plane and some of them stand out in relation to others of smaller size, so that the group forms a coherent whole generating, as it were, its own independent, homogeneous space. However, taken together, these groups cannot be considered from a single viewpoint. The juxtaposition of several spaces prevents any immediate and global perception of the fresco. It can be compared to the telling of a story made up of a succession of episodes that situate the reader/viewer in a scheme of duration. Unsure, at first, of where to cast one's glance, one soon feels attracted into a circular journey drawing one from the resurrection of the dead (at the bottom left) towards the ascension to heaven, where the risen dead seem to be caught up by an irresistible force and ushered into the presence of the Supreme Judge with the blessed pressing around him. Looking then to the right, which is also the left hand of God, one catches sight of the descent to hell, leading the damned to the infernal shores swarming with devils and serpents.

Everything here combines to arouse a sense of amazement. Michelangelo's rather unclassical purpose is to wrench the viewer from visual habits largely conditioned by the use of a single perspective; he baffles commonsense expectations of a reassuring space in which each object looks the way it should with regard to the laws of mathematics and he overwhelms us with the awe that overcomes the spirit when in the presence of such immense mysteries as the resurrection, the last judgement, salvation and damnation. There is no doubt that the viewer's immediate impression is, once again, one of bewilderment, or rather a sort of holy terror when contemplating the imposing sight of this metaphysical *epic* in which eternity is at stake. Michelangelo's artistic choices condition the viewer psychologically and spiritually so that, once bereft of the certainties of reason and experience, there before the altar, if only for an instant, we are allowed to know the meaning of the sublime.

GIAN BATTISTA DI JACOPO

The space is almost unreal. The sky is slate-blue in colour and hopelessly uniform even in the shading-off. It drops down vertically like the painted backcloth of a stage: an abstract sky in a landscape devoid of an atmosphere. What spatial relationship can there be between the depthless foreground with its grouping of paper-thin figures and the far distance both close at hand and very remote, which is indicated by the jagged skyline and the tiny personages visible on the road?

The classical moulding of figures and drapery has gone, replaced by an angular stiffness recalling the 'cubist' experiment of Rosso's *Moses*, painted the same year. The geometricality of the cross and the ladders has, as it were, spread to the actors in the scene. The figure of Christ is hardly treated any less harshly. Replacing the rounded forms of musculature and the pliant sway of drapery is an assemblage of almost plane surfaces, often triangular in shape, whose sharp edges catch the garish lighting that seems to be coming from a hypothetical projector facing the painting.

The details are all meant to be disconcerting. Rosso provokes, puzzles and sidetracks the viewer, jolting us out of our usual system of visual, psychological and religious reference. Only one personage is looking at Christ, or rather at one specific detail, the wound in his side, which this personage emphasizes with arm and eye. The eyes of the other figures are cast in all sorts of directions as if to turn the viewer's attention away from the real subject of the painting, the taking down of the body of Christ from the cross. The result is that the viewer feels that he or she no longer fully controls his or her gaze; as if, inadvertently, the eye comes to hover over certain details that unduly engross the attention: the shocking discrepancy between the size of the holy women and the massive stature of Saint John, whose abnormal height only becomes 'acceptable' because Rosso has made him bend his head; the stiff, forceful arm that the kneeling Mary Magdalene thrusts out horizontally towards Mary and upon which the broken lines of the folds of her dress converge with unswerving regularity; the strange curve of the mantle worn by the old man perched at the summit of the cross; the physical semitransparency of Christ's left leg and foot. And in such an abstract universe, what could cause this uncanny rush of wind affecting some robes and not others? The posture of the figure in the top right, holding up the body of Christ, suggests that it is he who is carrying almost all the weight on his own. But, then, what causes the strange relaxation of his hand dangling limply down the body instead of grasping it, the fingers brushing the wound of Christ? And why does the wound arouse such horrified stupefaction in the man who sees it? Is it plausible to think of him discovering it only *now*, and being the only one to react so dramatically to this sudden revelation?

Turning to the figure of Christ, one is struck with some perplexity. While the general posture is reminiscent of Michelangelo's *Pietàs*, the facial expression, in my opinion, is unprecedented; it shows the artist's taste for provocation, as it is so much closer to voluptuous surrender than to the throes of death or the serenity of the deceased. Another example of this equivocal tendency verging on sacrilege is provided by the *Dead Christ with Angels* at the Museum of Fine Arts in Boston, reproduced in J. Shearman's *Mannerism*, p. 66.

Mantegna's celebrated *Dead Christ* (1480) in the Pinacoteca di Brera in Milan presents a foreshortened view of Christ which strikingly brings home the concrete reality of physical death, with the stiffness of the corpse and the livid hue of the flesh. Conversely, Filippino Lippi and Perugino, who together produced *The Deposition from the Cross* (1503-4) in the Uffizi in Florence, insist on Christ's divinity by conferring an ideal beauty upon the body and face of Jesus. There is nothing like that here. Rosso's great originality lies in thwarting expectations and upsetting aesthetic and religious sensibilities by offering a deliberately 'unacceptable' vision of the deposition. The colours are sharp and precious, polished and enamelled, conjuring up a metallic or mineral world in keeping with the many-faceted forms noted above. The personages are not meant to look lifelike; their function is not to make us become emotionally involved in their suffering, in spite of the side-glance cast at us by one of their number. Taking a scene familiar to the Christian conscience, Rosso introduces incongruities incompatible with traditional schemes of thought and sensibility, and thereby aims at creating a feeling of unease, a disturbance to the eyes and the soul. Considering that the deposition (along with the entombment) is the most harrowing episode in the Christian story, I suggest that such an experience of bewilderment or even stupor imposed on the viewer is the analogue of the spiritual disarray that overcomes the Christian when confronted with the death of Christ.

PLATE VI.   Pontormo: *Deposition*, 1526–8, Santa Felicità, Florence.

When Pontormo came to paint his own *Deposition*, he was in full control of his mature style. The work belongs to the same period as the famous frescos in the Certosa del Galluzzo (1522–5) representing scenes from the life of Jesus, about which Vasari expressed regret that they had undergone the Gothic influence of Dürer.

Pontormo's liking for light, delicate though dissonant colours, together with his avoidance of chiaroscuro and, more generally, any light and shade effects, are bound up with what P. Barucco calls 'the wasting away of the bodies of the personages that are possessed by a haunting anguish and inhabit a space made unreal by the lack of perspective and the painter's choice of a purely imaginary colour-scheme' (*Le maniérisme italien*, Paris, 1981, pp. 30–1). But the point is that this anguish does no more than merely 'haunt' them: there is something ghostly and private about it, falling short of frank expressiveness. As L. Venturi puts it: 'the figures are swaying not in order to express the drama of the event but to create the sinuous rhythm of a complicated and rather mysterious arabesque' (*Le XVIe siècle. De Léonard au Gréco*, Geneva, 1956, p. 233). To the impression of elegance produced by these effete though graceful figures whose oversophisticated grouping and gesturing evoke some sort of vertical choregraphy is added an effect of giddiness (see my analysis of the painting in chapter 2). One is reminded of Alfred Einstein's lines on Gesualdo's *Book VI* of madrigals, quoted in D.B. Rowland's *Mannerism – Style and Mood*, p. 15: 'It is impossible to sing three such pieces one after another without being seized by a sort of nausea or musical sea-sickness, for the dose is too strong and the unsteadiness too prolonged' (Einstein, *The Italian Madrigal*, Princeton, 1949, vol III, p. 715).

This unfinished altarpiece is one of the works most frequently reproduced in anthologies of Mannerist painting. It has become commonplace to point out what makes up the aristocratic elegance and somewhat haughty grace of the figures represented; the elongated bodies, vertical attitudes and flexible poses are stylistic traits also found at Fontainebleau, where this ideal of beauty was much cultivated. It is to be noted, however, that modifying the canon of proportion was not confined to *grazia* Mannerism; it appears likewise in Pontormo's frescos in the Certosa del Galluzzo (see the willowy, slender Christ of his *Christ before Pilate* reproduced by W. Friedlaender), in his *Deposition* in Santa Felicità (see plate VI) and in his *Visitation* in San Michele at Carmignano. Whether the aim is to create a sense of worldly elegance or to spiritualize the human figure, the elongation of forms drains the body of much of its corporeal reality. El Greco was to push this figurative technique to an extreme.

Globally speaking, Parmigianino's composition is ruled by the laws of perspective: it is organized along a diagonal materialized by the oblique edge of the platform in the foreground and that of the stylobate supporting the row of columns on the right hand. This, however, implies that space is treated as a homogeneous continuum. Four autonomous, mutually incompatible spaces are disposed along this perspective: there is the foreground with the figures presssing around the Virgin and Child, then a second space with a figure that is both tiny and exaggeratedly elongated representing Saint Jerome unrolling a parchment; the middle ground is occupied by the very high column hiding the ones behind it and allowing only their bases and projecting shadows to be seen; finally, the background, in the far distance, prolonging the perspective towards a barely undulating horizon. If perspective can be regarded as an attempt to convey an illusion of depth by giving each element represented a size inversely proportional to its distance from the foreground, it becomes obvious that the perspective used here is a pretence. No law of optics can justify the amazing disproportion between, on the one hand, the gigantic figures in the foreground, filling over three-quarters of the total height, and the dwarfed figure of Saint Jerome in the second space, and, on the other hand, between the saint and the column rising to such a giddy height. Similarly, the lack of spacing (owing to excessive foreshortening) between this column and the next ones of the row cannot be justified in terms of verisimilitude. In the absence of any point of reference, there is no means of evaluating the 'real' size of all these elements and the distance between them. The viewer is confronted with the arbitrary whimsicality of a dream-like vision, an effect increased by the unfinished state of the painting.

As in *The Last Judgement* (see plate IV), one can refer to a plurality of spaces, but the originality of the present painting lies in the fact that the treatment of space depends upon a paradox: while the use of perspective prompts the viewer to wonder about the spatial and dimensional relationship between the various parts of the painting, the juxtaposition of contradictory spaces marking out this perspective precludes any possible answer.

The viewer's puzzlement is greatly increased by the esoteric symbolism of the column whose monumental proportions spell out its functional uselessness (had the altarpiece been completed, the row of columns would probably have been part of a whole temple, but still a very odd one) and the inexplicable attitude of the saint averting his eyes from the parchment he is holding as if he were about to address some absent assembly. It is as if one were confronted with an iconographic enigma or an aesthetic caprice.

PLATE VIII. Bronzino: *Allegory* or *Venus, Cupid, Folly and Time*, c. 1546, National Gallery, London.

The title of the piece is conjectural, hardly more than a convenient label to distinguish it from other allegories by the same artist: the *Allegory of Felicity* (the Uffizi, Florence), *Innocence* and *Flora*, the last two being tapestries made by Giovanni Rost after Bronzino's cartoons (Galleria degli Arazzi, Florence).

The work has teased the brains of iconologists in their effort to decipher its subject. The painting appears in Kenneth Clark's *The Nude* (London, 1956) under the title of *Allegory of Passion*. In Jacques Bousquet's *La peinture maniériste* (Neuchâtel, 1964), it is referred to as *Cupid, Venus, Folly, the Sphynx and Time*, in an attempt (though still an unsuccessful one) to name all the protagonists. E. Panofsky sees it as a representation of *The Exposure of Luxury* (*Studies in Iconology*, Oxford, 1939). Reading Panofsky's remarkable interpretation, one is impressed by the extreme subtlety of the allegoric message and the esotericism of the code. It is easy to identify some of the figures such as Venus, Cupid and Father Time, mainly through their respective attributes: the two billing doves and the golden apple, the quiver and arrows, and the sand-glass. However, other personages are more difficult to recognize in spite of Vasari's indications: the old brown-skinned hag tearing her hair in despair may symbolize Jealousy; the 'putto' pelting roses and wearing an anklet of bells like a jester of antiquity possibly stands for Wantonness; behind him, half-hidden in the shade, is Deceit with the body of a reptile and the head of a prim and proper young girl. Finally, Truth, outraged by the behaviour of Venus and Cupid, comes to the aid of Time, as it behoves her, and unveils the lewdness of the disport. But in the 1962 edition of his book (reprinted in 1972), Panofsky adopted W. Friedlaender's suggestion that the angry, dark-clad face in the top left-hand corner of the painting might rather be a personification of Night, not helping Time of course, but trying to hinder the 'unveiling' process. Everything, down to the tiniest detail, contributes to the overall significance: the pink cushion is no mere triviality; as a sign of civilization, it connotes idleness and lechery; Deceit, with an air of mincing demureness, holds out a honeycomb but also harbours a venomous creature. Bronzino's sophistication reaches its acme in the way he embroiders upon this symbol: 'the hand attached to her right arm, that is, the hand with the honeycomb, is in reality a left hand, while the hand attached to her left arm is in reality a right one, so that the figure offers sweetness with what seems to be her "good" hand but is really her "evil" one, and hides poison in what seems to be her "evil" hand but is really her "good" one' (1972 edn, p. 90).

Panofsky's analysis confirms the intellectual, even cerebral, nature of Mannerism, its liking for enigma and the play of ideas.

Bronzino's contemporaries thought the work magnificent ('di singolare bellezza', according to Vasari who recounts that Grand Duke Cosimo presented it to François I). The colours reflect the taste of the Florentine Mannerists. The milky whiteness of the flesh gives it an unreal look and, combined with the sharp-edged drawing, enhances the statuesqueness of the figures. This whiteness is in sharp contrast with the strident blue of the hanging at the back, the acid green of Deceit's dress, of the quiver and of Cupid's quill feathers; the old rose of the cushion matches the flowers that the 'putto' is holding; the brown of Deceit's scaly body recalls the bistred complexion of Jealousy; the ochre-coloured masks, the properties of Deceit, correspond to the amber-coloured flesh of Father Time, the only flesh to look reasonably alive. This chromatic counterpointing shows that ornamentalism is pre-eminent in structuring the picture.

A scheme of vertical and horizontal lines also rules the composition which falls into the general pattern of a square, although the geometric severity and predictability are attenuated by a network of obliques that cut across the painting more or less diagonally. Within this structure, one notes the recurrent motif of right angles giving the limbs that zigzagging which is the hallmark of Mannerism also found in Michelangelo's last *Pietàs*.

There is no sensual eroticism in these smooth, glazed bodies deprived of all power of suggestiveness by a uniform use of light. The *Allegory* achieves the paradox – a true pictorial conceit – of spreading before the sophisticated viewer a learned and decorative display of nudity, which is both lewd and abstract, inside an emblematic picture that almost baffles decipherment.

This is the last version of an iconographic theme that inspired no less than nine different works painted between 1547 and 1594, the year of Tintoretto's death. It is also the most grandiose, the most dramatic and the most Mannerist of all the versions.

The Last Supper of 1547 (San Marcuola, Venice) is classical in style, with the table positioned horizontally – parallel, that is, to the surface of the painting – and Christ occupies the centre with the apostles symmetrically around him. Tintoretto has even accentuated the symmetry by placing two allegoric figures as well as two casual objects on either side of the table: Faith on the left with a carafe on the floor, and Charity on the right with a cat at her feet.

The next two versions mark the transition to Mannerism. In *The Last Supper* of 1559 (Saint François-Xavier, Paris) the composition is still frontal, but the table is perpendicular to the picture plane. The perspective is strongly emphasized with the figures of the apostles overlapping and piling up against each other in a restricted space constructed in depth. The 1561 version (San Simeone Grande, Venice) innovates in that the table, positioned at an oblique angle on the left, puts the composition out of centre. In addition, the main motif seems undermined by the presence of personages uninvolved in the action and, especially, by the overemphasis given to a recumbent dog that attracts the viewer's gaze.

But Tintoretto's Mannerism is even more obvious in the fourth version (San Trovaso, Venice) with its upturned chairs, the twisted, unstable posture of the apostles, the *contrapposto* of their gestures, the way their eyes are turned in diverging directions and, above all, the rows of strongly illuminated columns where two diaphanous, almost disembodied personages (seemingly chalk drawings) move in the midst of an unreal, mystical space extending beyond the unmistakably tangible area of the Supper. It is no accident that, at the same period, Tintoretto should have painted his *Removal of the Body of Saint Mark* (1562–6), which contains similar wraith-like figures.

In *The Last Supper* included here, this technique is applied to the images of the angels. Clearly, the idea is to suggest the supernatural by *other* figurative means than those used to represent concrete reality. This is the final example of Tintoretto's shorthand expression of disembodiment, a boldly unclassical method with which he had experimented in previous works. This type of figurative dichotomy would have been unthinkable during the High Renaissance and the Baroque period, when one and the same code prevailed for temporal and spiritual representation.

Original as it is, stylistically and technically, Tintoretto's approach is none the less comparable to Parmigianino's *Madonna of the Long Neck* or Rosso's *Deposition*: these paintings show the coexistence within the same work of two or more figurative codes resulting in notable effects of disparity. The reader is referred to the more detailed analysis of this painting to be found in chapter 1.

CHAPTER 3

Mannerism in reaction to formalism

In Claude-Gilbert Dubois' stimulating book *Le maniérisme* (1979), the author remarks that 'there can be no Mannerism without the existence of some kind of classicism, or at least a given style of reference', the reason being, he adds, that 'the aim of Mannerism is not to reject the established order or to set up a different order; it is always a follower but also deviant, choosing the mainstream of a previous culture only to act as a maverick towards it'.[1] An examination of Italian art confirms this view. Even in its anticlassical phase, Mannerism did not overturn the figurative order built up during the Quattrocento in any fundamental way, but it did contest the validity of a number of High Renaissance standards whose growing dogmatism had generated the very classicism from which first generation Mannerists wished to escape.

In the views of W. Sypher, P. Cruttwell and, somewhat earlier, F.P. Wilson, something occurred in England at the end of the sixteenth century that can be thought of as a mutation. It is not irrelevant to note that F.P. Wilson attempts to explain this development by drawing an analogy with the visual arts, while insisting on the dangers inherent to this type of parallel:

> but if, as some hold, the essential difference between baroque art and the art of the High Renaissance lies in the attempt to express and enhance elapsing moments of ever-changing Nature rather than the idea of Nature as a perennial reality, then Donne's poetry has a better claim to be called baroque than Spenser's, Webster's plays than Marlowe's, and Bacon's prose than Ascham's or Hooker's. To the new age, so often sceptical, tentative, and self-conscious in its exploration of hidden motives, a new style was necessary, a style that could express the mind as it was in movement, would record the thought at the moment it arose in the mind.[2]

This is not the right time to quibble over the meaning of the word 'baroque'. The writer of the above lines clearly considers the term as a useful label, one in fact that he does not completely adopt as his own, and, in 1945 (at the time of publication of *Elizabethan and Jacobean*), had the concept of Mannerism been as readily available as it is today, it is permissible to surmise that F.P. Wilson might perhaps have preferred it to the term 'baroque'. What is important is that the new style was no longer content with a number of rhetorical practices that F.P. Wilson refers to as 'amplifications and formal figures' and further, as 'the round-ness of the Ciceronian period wheeling its way to a long foreseen conclu-sion'. These techniques were deemed incompatible with the intellectual and aesthetic demands of the new outlook.

If this mutation is accepted as an overall phenomenon on the terms by which it is described to us, a parallel can be traced between the situation of literature in late sixteenth-century England and Italian art at the beginning of the Cinquecento. Michelangelo, Pontormo, Rosso, Parmigianino and others were reacting against the domination of a style which thwarted any expression of an individual manner (all classicism tending to iron out difference), but above all against a style which immo-bilized the representation of moving reality in the intolerably unchang-ing and reassuring features of eternity. In England, during the 1590s, poets like Donne, playwright-poets like Shakespeare, Jonson, Chapman and Marston, and prose-writers like Bacon were attempting in their work to renew methods. They were turning away from the varieties of rhetoric that had been fashionable until almost their own time (Euphuism, Petrarchism, Ciceronianism and the dramatic aesthetics of Kyd and Marlowe), since these techniques no longer seemed appropriate to the need for more critical attitudes, a heightened awareness of the tumultuous, unpredictable movement of thought and an increased desire to explore the complex interrelationships between individuals, as well as between individuals and the outside world. Like the Italian painters who rejected the exclusive domination of the style imposed on them by the High Renaissance, the above writers' refusal of these types of rhetoric was not only a sign of a taste for novelty *per se*, but also a sign that, at a deeper level, there was a more acute, and often more painful, perception of the precariousness and complexity of the world.

F.P. Wilson speaks of a 'sceptical' age, but the meaning of the word has to be defined. Montaigne, Bacon, the so-called metaphysical poets and, more generally speaking, the Jacobean writers did not, by and large, adhere to any kind of metaphysical scepticism. In spite of the upheavals and uncertainties arising from the New Science, they still saw the world as ultimately bound up with the divine scheme of things even if the ways of God were becoming more and more difficult to scan. Rather, the nature of their scepticism was epistemological. They were imbued with a sense of the contingency of earthly things and of the relativity of opinions and knowledge: hence a frame of mind prone to doubt and questioning, but also to an unconditional surrender to dogma in everything outside the scope of natural philosophy and secondary causes. This dichotomy, which was experienced in diverse fashion by individual minds, was obviously favourable to the emergence of Mannerism.

But there are limits to the parallels that can be drawn with painting. The classical art of the High Renaissance is fundamentally normative. The high degree of formal coherence achieved by its most distinguished representatives (Perugino, Leonardo, Fra Bartolomeo, Titian, Andrea del Sarto in particular) largely results from their suppression of a number of figurative answers inherited from the past but still lingering on among certain painters of the early decades of the Quattrocento, nevertheless considered as innovators – artists such as Masolino, Uccello, Masaccio or Piero della Francesca. Compared with this 'open', experimental art situated at the crossroads of past and future, High Renaissance painting conveys a finished effect, as if entrenched in its certainties and stabilized in its methods. Yet a mere glance at Elizabethan drama written before the changes noted by F.P. Wilson had had any marked impact reveals an amazing diversity of form and technique. This is hard to reconcile with the idea of even a short-lived orthodoxy and a theretofore unsurpassed perfection of form, assessments that are generally associated with High Renaissance art. To cling but briefly to an analogy that is beginning to appear unsound, my first impression is that Lyly, Kyd, Peele, Greene, Marlowe and the early Shakespeare are more reminiscent of the pioneering Quattrocento painters than of the more impeccable artists of the following generation. Therefore, all things considered, it is better to abandon the concept of a High Renaissance as one which is not pertinent to the English context.

This means that the basic question remains unanswered. How can one explain how a dramatic output that had no real canon of form should have been affected by the reappraisal of ideas and methods that went on during the 1590s? What was it in the multifarious character of this drama that made reform so necessary? Where should one look for the model, the given style of reference, the guiding aesthetics without which, it is claimed, there can be no Mannerism? The answer has already been suggested in previous pages: the common denominator shared by literature and drama and facing Shakespeare at the outset of his career was the powerful influence of rhetorical formalism.

Rhetorical formalism is not a style in itself, but an important feature found in several styles and referring by implication to an identical idea of art. Muriel C. Bradbrook notes that the main problem pre-Shakespearian dramatists had to face was essentially one of technique: how were they to give a truly dramatic form to material that the Middle Ages had made into plays, using a structure more akin to narrative than to fully fledged dramatization?[3] Rhetorical formalism developed out of a need to raise drama to the rank of a noble art combining moral profit, aesthetic pleasure and entertainment. My aim in linking together two terms normally used separately is to insist on the correlation between discourse as such, *elocutio* which belongs to rhetoric in the strict sense of the term, and the other levels of composition, *dispositio* and *inventio* which concern the organization of the text into sequences and of the action into episodes, as well as characterization, thematic selection etc. The idea is that the principles governing the organization of the sentences are, to a large extent, similar to those actuating the construction of the whole work. A few examples will illustrate certain aspects of this homologous process.

The dominant trait of Marlowe's rhetoric is a division of the discourse into syntactical and rhythmic units that are relatively independent of each other. The tirade almost always advances incrementally, unit being added to unit, through which a series of constants and variations is established. This produces the effect of a language that is entirely controlled, that unfolds methodically and that is enumerative rather than discursive:

> FAUST How am I glutted with conceit of this!
> Shall I make spirits fetch me what I please,
> Resolve me of all ambiguities,
> Perform what desperate enterprise I will?
> I'll have them fly to India for gold,
> Ransack the ocean for orient pearl,
> And search all corners of the new-found world
> For pleasant fruits and princely delicates;
> I'll have them read me strange philosophy,
> And tell the secrets of all foreign kings;
> I'll have them wall all Germany with brass,
> And make swift Rhine circle fair Wertenberg;
> I'll have them fill the public schools with silk,
> Wherewith the students shall be bravely clad;
> I'll levy soldiers with the coin they bring,
> And chase the Prince of Parma from our land,
> And reign sole king of all our provinces.
>
> *Doctor Faustus*, i, 77–93

It is a method which is wonderfully appropriate to incantation or invocation; it is perfect to express reiterative or culmulative thought, but it is
hardly suitable for conveying the innumerable shocks that thought is heir
to during the gestation period – the association of sudden, strange or
chaotic ideas, contradictions, hesitations, corrections, flashbacks etc.
Nevertheless, at the denouement of the tragedy, when Faustus is racked
with anguish at the prospect of imminent death and damnation,
Marlowe breaks the formal stiffness of the syntactical pattern, thereby
giving the character's speech a halting, gasping rhythm which allows an
effect of spontaneity to prevail over mechanical response:

> See, see, where Christ's blood streams in the firmament!
> One drop would save my soul, half a drop: ah, my Christ!
> Ah, rend not my heart for naming of my Christ!
> Yet will I call on him: O, spare me, Lucifer!
> Where is it now? 'tis gone: and see, where God
> Stretcheth out his arm, and bends his ireful brows!
> Mountains and hills, come, come, and fall on me.
> And hide me from the heavy wrath of God!
> No, no!
> Then will I headlong run into the earth:
> Earth, gape! O, no, it will not harbour me!
>   xix, 146–56

But moments like these are exceptional. When Tamburlaine's raving
has reached its peak, he still expresses himself in a style redolent of
rhetoric:

> See, where my slave, the ugly monster Death,
> Shaking and quivering, pale and wan for fear,
> Stands aiming at me with his murdering dart,
> Who flies away at every glance I give,
> And, when I look away, comes stealing on!
> Villain, away and hie thee to the field!
> I and mine army come to load thy bark
> With souls of thousand mangled carcasses.
> Look, where he goes! but, see, he comes again,
> Because I stay! Techelles, let us march,
> And weary Death with bearing souls to hell.
>   *Tamburlaine the Great* (Part 2) v, iii, 67–77

The construction of these plays is still mainly dependent on a division
into tableaux as was the practice in the medieval theatre or in medieval
art in general. Indeed, Marlowe's plays recall an important aspect of
Gothic or pre-Renaissance painting, which is the panelling of the subject

into several scenes that are treated almost as independent entities whose overall meaning derives from a continuous perception or page-by-page reading of the parts. The Siennese painters of the Trecento come to mind, especially Duccio and Simone Martini, but the practice lived on into the following century, particularly in paintings by Gentile da Fabriano such as the *Presentation at the Temple* in the Louvre and even in the work of Uccello, in the predella of the *Profanation of the Host* at the Palazzo Ducale in Urbino, judged by Francastel to be a regression in the representation of space. Uccello was keenly aware that the unification of space through a single perspective is perfect for the dramatization of a special moment in the action, but ill-suited to the narration of a story. The construction of 'space' in Marlowe's plays is reminiscent of the discrete, cumulative vision of Gothic art, where, in the words of Arnold Hauser, 'it is always the principle of expansion and not of concentration, of co-ordination and not of subordination, of the open sequence and not of the closed geometric form, by which it is dominated'; and he goes on to draw a parallel with the theatre: 'the drama strives to make the episodes as complete as possible and prefers, instead of the concentration of the action in a few decisive situations, frequent changes of scene, of the characters and the motifs'.[4] The processional mode thus seems to reiterate on a larger scale the structure of the sentences themselves. Both proceed by adding one separate entity on to another, while the characters are created according to a linear or sedimentary process, as, one by one, new situations give rise to new types of behaviour and expand the previous psychological image.

But rhetorical formalism possesses other facets. When studying the rhetoric of Kyd in *The Spanish Tragedy*, Jonas A. Barish noted that the antitheses and the see-saw symmetry of the discourse reflect the structure of the plot, as well as the relationships between the characters. One of Barish's examples is the well-known episode where Horatio and Belimperia talk of their love, while Balthazar and Lorenzo spy on them, commenting on the situation in their asides:

> BAL. Oh sleep, mine eyes: see not my love profan'd;
>   Be deaf, my ears: hear not my discontent;
>   Die, heart: another joys what thou deservest.
> LOR. Watch still, mine eyes, to see this love disjoined;
>   Hear still, mine ears, to hear them both lament;
>   Live, heart, to joy at fond Horatio's fall.
> BEL. Why stands Horatio speechless all this while?
> HOR. The less I speak, the more I meditate.

BEL. But whereon dost thou chiefly meditate?
HOR. On dangers past, and pleasures to ensue.
BAL. On pleasures past, and dangers to ensue.
BEL. What dangers and what pleasures dost thou mean?
HOR. Dangers of war, and pleasures of our love.
LOR. Dangers of death, but pleasures none at all.
BEL. Let dangers go; thy war shall be with me,
      But such a war as breaks no bond of peace.

                                              II, ii, 18–33

Barish mainly focuses on the first two speakers' opening lines which he glosses thus:

Each speaker pursues a formula of systematic invocation, directing his eyes, ears and heart in turn to react to love, to sorrow and to joy. But the two speeches are also antithetical, and Lorenzo's forms an answer to Balthazar's. Balthazar invites his faculties to abandon their function, to wrap him in insensibility and death. Lorenzo, following the same grammatical scheme, instructs his senses to redouble their activity.[5]

To make the analysis complete, I would add that the rest of the passage is equally remarkable in the use of parallelism and antithesis, for complicity in love is counterbalanced by complicity in hate. The two lovers are on stage, before the audience's eyes; the two spies are almost invisible, in the gallery above. The dialogue between the lovers is partly interrogative and partly affirmative. Thematically, the pleasures of love are opposed to the perils of war, the past to the future, until the metaphorical rehandling of the warrior theme (love as a peaceable duel, a commonplace of courtly literature) allows Bel-imperia to resolve the contradictions by dismissing all reference to danger. This rhetorical sleight of hand, which is instrumental in introducing a happier atmosphere and acts as a prelude to the amorous jousting beneath the arbour, does not banish the real danger: the interspersed remarks of Balthazar, and Lorenzo are reminders of their lurking presence and they place the love-talk in a cruelly ironic perspective. Thus confined in rhetoric's rigid mould, the episode acquires the stylized, graphic and almost abstract beauty of a line drawing, which is not incompatible with a degree of theatrical efficiency, providing, that is, that the rhetoric is not camouflaged on stage under the guise of naturalness or spontaneity.

There is no need to insist on the extreme formalism of Lyly's drama. One especially noteworthy point is the extent to which the distinctive characteristics of Euphuistic prose (antithesis, assonance, alliteration) reveal a tendency to conceive of and represent situations, characters and themes in a binary mode. With the exception of *Mother Bombie*, influenced by the methods of the New Latin Comedy with a splendidly built plot which feeds expectancy about the denouement, the action in Lyly's other plays moves forward smoothly and without suspense in a series of tableaux which are composed, broken up and recomposed like the figures in a well-ordered ballet. The regular course of the action is enlivened solely by the sparkling wit of the repartee. The dialogue carries the action along under the stylized garb of fashionable conversation which reaches the highest pitch of formal perfection. The disorder of real life vanishes behind the ordered rhythms of word-play, as if human relationships were being channelled into the structured forms of a debate, with the confrontation between love and honour, love and chastity, good government and the pitfalls lying in wait for the ruler etc. This composition for concertante voices, which is a sort of *disputatio* acclimatized to the atmosphere of courtly entertainment, harmonizes well with the tendency to create parallel situations by analogy or contrast, and to group together the characters by affinity or opposition. The debate of ideas is not only the thematic frame or ideological reference of the play, it also cements together the various episodes in the action.

These authors' shared preference for rhetorical formalism in its many varieties should be understood as the expression of a wish for order, of a desire for permanence and stability and of a highly exacting artistic vision. The technical responses differ according to the dramatist, the genre chosen for the play and the nature of the subject-matter. It will be seen once again that rhetorical formalism was too diverse to constitute one particular style, but sufficiently recognizable to have served as a point of reference for the Mannerist experiments to come.

What about Shakespeare at the beginning of his career? Towards 1592, although the date is uncertain, he used his budding talents to write comedies and he contributed *The Comedy of Errors*, a play derived from *The Menaechmi* and *Amphitryon* by Plautus, to the repertory of his company. The work was probably staged at Gray's Inn towards the end of December 1594, after the epidemic of the plague in London, and according to Leo Salingar it is the first play written in English that complies with the artificial order, 'beginning at a high point of action, relating antecedent events in the course of the action, and pursuing a unified plot to a climax of "rediscoveries"'.[6] Had Shakespeare seen *Mother Bombie*, written about 1589? Whether he had or not, he adopted one of Lyly's innovations, which was to increase the number of masters and servants so as to obtain an effect of symmetry. He took the two masters from

Plautus (the Antipholus twins) and added the two servants, the Dromio
twins. On the other hand, very probably influenced by Gascoigne's
Supposes, another Gray's Inn entertainment whose first performance in
1566 Shakespeare could not have attended but which he had read, and
possibly also influenced by Plautus' *Rudens*, he expressed his difference
from Lyly by inserting the classical motif of errors into the romantic and
pathetic story of a family scattered after a shipwreck and brought
together again at the denouement.

In *Love's Labour's Lost* (1593?), there is a resemblance to Lyly in the concertante structuring of the action and in the play's overall atmosphere.
The amorous adventures of the King of Navarre and his companions of
Academe are set against a backcloth of debate between Nature and
Artifice. In opposition to the laws of Nature, the young lords and the
King swear they will give up love and devote themselves to the more
austere pleasures of scholarship for a limited period of time. The failure
of this madly juvenile undertaking is Nature's answer to a perverted idea
of Culture. Since they are unable to resist the attractions of love-talk, the
young folk hotly pursue the rhetoric of pretty phrases, until they come to
realize that affected language hampers the expression of true feelings
and so the natural achieves its revenge over the artificial. Following on
from the masque that marks Artifice's final assault comes the discomfi-
ture of the suitors, who have been deceived by the superior artfulness of
the young ladies, also in disguise. When they return to their senses, they
confess their love for each other, but it is too late since a painful fact of
Nature, the death of the King of France, the Princess' father, suddenly
breaks into the artificial world of the court of Navarre. This recall to
reality means that the hoped-for engagement will be postponed for a
year, during which time the thoughtless suitors will be able to redeem
their errors through the trials inflicted upon them, thereby proving their
constancy in love. There is one character, Berowne, who is more perceptive than the others, and he advances the debate between Nature and
Artifice by condemning the errors to which he himself has yielded. As
for Holofernes' heavy pedantry and Don Adriano's grotesque bombast
(other variations on the theme of artificious rhetoric), neither survives
the raillery of Costard and Moth. The play-within-the-play, 'The Nine
Worthies', casts out the demon of grandiloquence from the young lords
by objectifying it as a thing to be ridiculed. When writing *Love's Labour's
Lost*, in which rhetoric is brought to the acme of brilliance but also ineffi-
ciency, Shakespeare may be thought to be inflicting on himself the same
kind of therapy as that undergone by his characters.

Turning to the Chronicle Plays, written at the same period, one can observe a comparable blending of imitation and innovation. E.M.W. Tillyard has shown the great importance of what he himself calls 'formalism' and 'stylisation' in the shaping of the first tetralogy of history plays.[7] He puts their presence down to the lingering influence of the medieval Moralities dramatizing the eternal conflict between good and evil; the truth of these remarks should be expanded by insistence on the idea that reading history from a dualistic viewpoint was an equally important preoccupation of the early Renaissance, using a binary scheme in order to come to terms with such an abundance of historical material and to structure it so as to produce a coherent, intelligible vision, which, in addition, would be ideologically efficient. Referring to plays, such as *Titus Andronicus* and *Richard III*, that relate more closely to the tragic mode, one could quote example upon example of formalism from the work of Kyd: Titus' long complaints in monologue, the stichomythia of the wailing exchange between Queen Margaret and Queen Elizabeth in *Richard III* (Act IV, scene iv), the parallel speeches of Richard and Richmond before the Battle of Bosworth (V, iii) and, in the same scene, the speeches of the ghosts directed first at Richard, then at Richmond.

However, it is perhaps in *Romeo and Juliet* (*c.* 1595) that Shakespeare is most systematic in creating symmetry of presentation. In his Introduction to the play Brian Gibbons explains how Shakespeare brought changes to his sources to make them fit in with his initial purpose.[8] The insertion of comic episodes corresponds to the wish to enhance and tinge with irony both the lyrical atmosphere and the climate of violence surrounding the main action. The dramatic interest is divided between the discord separating the two families and the troth being plighted between their offspring; this bipolarity of structure reflects the tragic divorce between public life and private life whilst underlining, by antithesis, the individual's duty to maintain a necessary correspondence between the reasons of the heart and the reasons of the community. The choice of some of the minor characters depends on a desire to create a play of contrasts and similarities: Benvolio, who embodies goodwill and level-headedness, is opposed to Tybalt, who is violent and rash; each is related respectively to the Montagues and the Capulets by a similar though inversely symmetrical family tie – Benvolio is Montague's nephew while Tybalt is Lady Capulet's. The Nurse's rude pleasantries enhance Juliet's youthful delicacy; Mercutio's cheerful raillery is a foil to Romeo's dreamy melancholy. The situation of Paris, who loves Juliet unrequitedly, is put in parallel with Romeo's initial situation as Rosaline's unhappy admirer. When the two young men become rivals in love, Romeo embodies disobedience to the laws because of love, whereas Paris offers the perfect image of a suitor who is right in every way. Some situations recur at regular intervals: Prince Escalus first appears in Act I, scene i, where he attempts to safeguard civil peace; he speaks a second time in Act III, scene i, where he draws attention to the harm done by discord and pronounces the sentence of banishment on Romeo for having slain Tybalt; lastly, he points out the lessons to be learnt from the tragedy in the denouement (v, iii). These three ritualized speeches personify citizenship reminding the protagonists in the drama how harmful law-breaking is to the whole community.

There are two decisive episodes built on an almost identical pattern: in Act II, scene v, Juliet is informed by her Nurse, who bears a message from Romeo, that their marriage ceremony is to be held secretly in Friar Lawrence's cell, while in Act III, scene ii, it is again the Nurse who informs her of Tybalt's death and her husband's banishment. In the first instance, the Nurse postpones the announcement of the good news out of mischief (in keeping with the traditional roguishness of servants) and in order to increase her mistress' joy by keeping up the suspense; in the second instance, she makes Juliet fear the worst (Romeo's death) before undeceiving her in the hope of alleviating her grief.

But of course Shakespeare was not the only dramatist of the younger generation to yield to the 'Pleasures and Perils of Rhetoric' as described by Barish. Was it because *The Case is Altered* (1597?) made too obvious use of theatrical conventions later regarded by Jonson as outmoded, that he decided to omit the comedy from the 1616 Folio? Jonson was probably unwilling to allow the scrutiny of his contemporaries and posterity to be brought to bear on one of his early plays that was too remote from his mature style and that did not seem worth rehandling, unlike *Every Man In His Humour*. *The Case* is a Plautine comedy, but one which has been enriched, or encumbered, with a typically Elizabethan type of rhetorical formalism. In it, Jonson uses a mixture of two different plots: the first, taken from *Aulularia*, is satiric and burlesque, with the miser Jaques de Prie as its main character; he disguises himself as a beggar, hoarding a stolen treasure, which is taken from him, only to be returned at the denouement. The other plot, taken from *The Captives*, is a romantic one: it springs from the abduction of Camillo, the son of Count Ferneze, kidnapped when a child and then brought up by Lord Chamont under the name of Gasper. The second plot dramatizes the life of Paolo, Camillo's brother, as a captive in France, and leads to the mutual rediscovery of the two young men and their father in Milan. The coexistence of these two plots within a single play could have endangered the unity of action. Jonson's answer was taken directly from the methods tried out by Lyly and Shakespeare, which consisted in increasing the number of symmetrical situations. Hence he doubled the motif of separation and rediscovery by extending it to Rachel de Prie, who is no other than Isabel, abducted long ago from her father, Lord Chamont (he does not appear on stage), by Melun, alias Jaques de Prie. This is the selfsame Jaques who has stolen a large sum of money from his former master. The denouement allows the spectator to witness two main rediscovery scenes, between Ferneze and his son Camillo on the one hand, and between Chamont (Lord Chamont's son) and his sister Isabel on the other. But closer inspection reveals that the structural pattern based on the loss and recovery of a precious possession generates two other situations: added to those already mentioned are the rediscovery by Ferneze of his other son, Paolo, as well as Jaques' rediscovery of his treasure. Chamont generously gives it up to him in his delight at Isabel and Paolo's union in addition to his own engagement to Ferneze's daughter, Aurelia. It is almost superfluous to say that an extremely enjoyable counterpointing effect is achieved through these four rediscoveries, brought about by three unmaskings when Camillo reveals that he is Gasper, Rachel discovers that she is really Isabel and Jaques admits that he is Melun.

Jonson, however, takes his liking for symmetry into another area: one after another, several characters fall in love with the ravishing Rachel, which is another means of linking the two plots. Crowning the pursuit of different objects is the pursuit of the same object – woman, the object of desire. Love spreads from one to the other like a chain reaction when each lover confides in another character who cannot wait to fall in love himself and act in his own interest: Paolo is betrayed by Angelo, Onion by Christophoro, Christophoro is betrayed by Ferneze, who sees Rachel as a consolation for his widowhood and the loss of his two sons. Recurrent situations that are structurally similar, although with contrasting atmospheres, are a sure source of comedy. Here one need only compare Paolo's chivalrous declaration of love with the burlesque treatment of Onion's courtship of Rachel.

The language too is marked by formalist attitudes. Jonson has not yet realized the advantages to be gained from changes of syntax, dissymmetry of construction, modifications of rhythm and startling lexical combinations, all of which characterize the quick verve of his mature style.

Compared to Volpone's tirades that seethe with explosive energy, Jaques' long monologues with their binary structure are laborious, alliterative and syllogistic:

> So now enough my heart, beat now no more;
> At least for this afright. What a cold sweat
> Flow'd on my brows, and over all my bosom!
> Had I not reason? to behold my door
> Beset with unthrifts, and my self abroad?
> Why Jaques? was there nothing in the house
> Worth a continual eye, a vigilant thought,
> Whose head should never nod, nor eyes once wink?
> Look on my coat, my thoughts; worn quite threadbare.
> That time could never cover with a nap,
> And by it learn, never with naps of sleep,
> To smother your conceits of that you keep.
> But yet, I marvel, why these gallant youths
> Spoke me so fair, and I esteemed a beggar?
> The end of flattery, is gain, or lechery:
> If they seek gain of me, they think me rich,
> But that they do not: For their other object:
> 'Tis in my handsome daughter, if it be.
>
> 11, i, 1–18

This is how Jaques introduces himself on stage and the part quoted here is a mere third of his opening tirade.

Independently of the circumstances of the action, Paolo's speech has been treated to a grandiloquence which is ill-suited to the character's youthfulness. There is no intended irony in Jonson's choice of a precious and sometimes Euphuistic style for Maximilian, the general of the Milanese army, especially as he is neither a pedant nor a courtly flatterer, but a soldier who is rather staid and wise. It is interesting to see Jonson at the outset of his career believing he has hit the right tone just by having his character speak a language that respects the conventions of the 'noble' style, while failing to take stock of its artificial and affected tones.

I have tarried too long over *The Case* and a comparison with *Romeo and Juliet* may well come as a surprise, but the fact is that, in spite of glaring differences, the two plays are equally hallmarked with the characteristic rhetorical formalism prevailing at the time. The main impression given by this type of drama, although here and there examples will be found which invalidate the generalization, is its undemanding use of relatively simple, clearly drawn characters, with uncomplicated psychological motivations, with no blurred outlines or grey areas, and of fairly unequivocal ideological themes. When the characters experience an inner conflict, the terms of the alternative are easy to grasp. When in the grips of a powerful, unreasoning passion, they shoulder their destiny with so much determination that very little room is left for hesitation, doubt or the pricks of conscience. Underlying this drama is perhaps a faith in the truth of logical discourse, an optimistic conviction that the rhetorical design conferring clarity and coherence upon words, as well as order and shapeliness upon works, is a replica of the Grand Design of all things at a material and spiritual level.

But as Shakespeare gradually awoke to the ambiguousness of the real – and the dramatization of this ambiguousness is what is best in his work – he became less and less willing to use ready-made schemes which trammel thought and language. From this point of view *The Merchant of Venice* is a play at a crossroads. It is still clearly structured according to a binary process: the topographical opposition between Venice and Belmont generates a bipolarity of theme. Venice is the mecca of mercantile capitalism, with trading as its acceptable face and usury as its unacceptable – though tolerated – face. The affluence of the merchant class is shown to have negative side-effects such as parasitism and dissoluteness as seen in Salerio, Solanio and Gratiano, minor characters none the less typical of Venetian society. There is much feasting in Venice and the squandering of food is emblematic. In Shylock, the theme appears in bestial, anthropophagous form of which the pound of flesh is, as it were, the sublimated metaphor. But on the other side of Venice's crude hedonism is the puritanism of a city whose conduct is dictated by rigid, punctilious legalism.

Belmont, on the other hand, has all the enticing charm of a poeticized rural retreat opposed to the city of business. The ordeal of the three caskets devised by Portia's deceased father invites the spectator to let his fancy stray into a world of fairy-tale where the suitors for the love of an unattainable lady undergo initiatory ordeals in order to become the worthy recipient of her favours. Belmont is one side of Venice's fantasy life, Shylock is the other: in the very heart of the city, his presence circumscribes a sort of space which is both real (the ghetto) and mythical; Shylock is the mirror that Venice has provided itself with so that it can see itself from a convenient distance in the otherness of the alien Jew, authorized to live among ordinary citizens, but without merging his identity with theirs. Like and unlike them in equal proportion, he is the darkened reflection of their own baseness.

Opposed to the uncertainties of the *laguna* where fortunes are made and unmade, and to the feverish bustle of commerical activity at the Rialto, stands Belmont on its elevated site, the security of the *terra firma*, withdrawn from the vagaries of the winds, the waves and speculation. It is a sheltered haven for music and love, the seat of the beloved lady and the meeting place of lovers. Opposed to Venice's crude pleasures are Belmont's nobler delights of love and art. In the leaden casket, Bassanio discovers a miniature of Portia and he enthuses over the painter's skill, while gallantly observing that the 'counterfeit' does not meet the original.

But what is especially noticeable is that this diptych also suggests the disquieting idea that the two places are also complementary, as if Shakespeare were stressing the oppositions only in order to show how very relative they are. Antonio and Bassanio are undoubtedly the best that Venice can offer: one is a merchant, yet all his fortune is at sea; the other is a soldier, but one impoverished by ungrateful traders and politicians. Antonio cultivates friendship, while Bassanio is on the look-out for a good match to satisfy his desires and retrieve his fallen fortunes. Their hearts are in the right place and this quality makes both of them natural sojourners in Belmont. When the time to choose comes, Bassanio selects the right casket and thus reveals his wisdom and generosity. We are now quite sure that this young man, who has gained our immediate affection as a warm friend and a penniless soldier in spite of his fortune-hunting, is worthy of Portia, because he knows that loving means giving as well as taking. In this he resembles Antonio, who sacrifices his wealth and almost his life to his friend's happiness, in return for which Bassanio introduces him to Belmont where Antonio, full of mixed joy and sadness at his friend's nuptials, learns that three of his argosies, thought to be lost, have come home to port. Skilful use of Venetian law has allowed the merchant's life to be saved and now Providence restores his fortune – and what better place than Belmont to receive the news of such a happy conclusion?

Concerning Portia and the nobler values of Belmont that she embodies, it is surprising to see how easily she adapts to the legalistic quibbling and pettifoggery of the Venetian courtroom. The fact is that Portia is not only a creature of a magic dream world, she is also Shakespeare's version of a medieval prototype, actually dating back to earliest times and embodying the Shrewd Woman, who reappears as Helena in *All's Well That Ends Well*. In the name of Venice's hard laws, Portia takes Antonio to the very brink of the grave; only then does the chicanery of the grossly unjust discrimination between Jews and Christians allow her to save his life *in extremis*, so that she can turn her legalistic weaponry against Shylock himself. After the initial plea for mercy, to which the Jew turns a deaf ear, comes the indictment of the plaintiff, at the close of which it is Shylock who ends up facing death. By merely taking part in the trial, disguised as Balthasar, Portia is condoning the unjust justice of Venice; but although she makes use of the legal possibilities of the system, including the most questionable among them, she does so mainly to remind all who hear her that charity and forgiveness cannot be dissociated from true justice. We have here the budding stages of a theme that Shakespeare developed more completely in *Measure for Measure*.

Even Shylock is clothed in ambiguity. Although so heinous, he is not Evil incarnate. His peculiar status as both an alien and a resident of Venice makes him an eminently perverse reflection of Venetian society, but he is also the scapegoat chosen by Venice to fulfil a need. Deservedly despised for his disreputable, though necessary, profession, he is wrongly scorned because of his 'race'. Shylock is a disgraceful and indispensable cog in the machine of mercantile capitalism. His symbolic function is just as important as his economic role as usurer. Hence, because he is a Jew and wicked by definition, he represents the surest foil to the virtues boasted of, but not practised by, the Venetian Christians, apart from the eponymous merchant. Shylock is an image of baser humanity fabricated by the Christians, one bereft of spirituality through failure to acknowledge the Redeemer. In the famous speech 'I am a Jew. Hath not a Jew eyes?' (III, i, 52–62), Shylock claims the right to be recognized as a man among men. Yet the vocabulary constantly refers to man's physical nature, based on a purely biological view of the human being, making Shylock reflect both his unspirituality and Venice's materialism of which he is also a product. But at this most basic level, the only one at which Shylock is capable of placing himself, how can anyone fail to see that acceptance of the equality of 'races' is necessarily founded on this pathetically grotesque awareness of biological sameness? It is indeed one of the not insignificant paradoxes of the play that such a hateful character as Shylock – whose hate is as immense as the humiliation he endures – should demand the right to revenge in the name of his very appurtenance to humanity: 'if we are like you in the rest, we will resemble you in that'.

The vocabulary of commerce and usury is again noticeable in its extensive penetration of the language of love, so much so that the same words are equally applicable to the financial transactions in Venice and to the amorous relationships in Belmont. This lexical ambivalence is perhaps the most obvious link between the two worlds. In the very first scene, Bassanio compares Portia's 'sunny locks' to a golden fleece, which he dreams of conquering like another Jason. When Bassanio leaves Venice-Argos for Belmont-Colchos, he goes in quest of 'fortune' in both the literal and figurative sense. It is no accident that, during his ordeal of initiation, he is called upon to choose between several caskets ranging from the most precious to the basest. Happily Bassanio is not a carrier of Venice's selfish greed. Unlike his rivals, Morocco and Aragon, who want to possess without giving or risking anything (the bearing of these two foreigners in Belmont duplicates Shylock's acquisitive attitude in Venice), Bassanio moulds his behaviour in love on the way Antonio conducts his business, handing over and risking what he has, in obedience to the motto engraved upon the leaden casket: 'Who chooseth me must give and hazard all he hath'. Having won the contest in which he has invested money lent by Antonio, Bassanio carries off the 'prize' and becomes the happy owner of Portia and her wealth. When Gratiano expresses his good wishes for the happiness of the lovers and announces that he too intends to marry, he defines the plighting of their troth as a commercial transaction to the advantage of both parties: 'The bargain of your faith' (III, ii, 194). Love is also a capital, ventured day after day, like the wealth of the merchant-adventurer, but when this capital is managed in a spirit of reciprocal generosity it yields a dividend of bliss. As in the *Sonnets* with their ready use of an economic register, Shakespeare plays upon the ambivalence of words, as if to reconcile, at least verbally, two types of activity often thought to be mutually exclusive.

Incomplete as it is, this commentary none the less gives a glimpse of the method used by the dramatist. He erects distinctions, underlines differences and carefully signposts the field of action, whereupon he immediately confuses the issue. Before the Problem Plays, *The Merchant* is no doubt the work that most clearly displays a Mannerist delight in ambiguous situation, equivocal discourse and ambivalent behaviour, but this mischievous game-playing occurs within a dramatic and ethical framework formed by the opposition of good and evil. I do not hold with the view expressed by W. Sypher that 'the moral premises behind *The Merchant of Venice* . . . are all obscure and debatable'.[9] In the dichotomy between Venice and Belmont, two systems of values are opposed. The fact that there may be some degree of osmosis or ironic interaction between them does not mean that the two systems should be confused.

Act v of *The Merchant* opens with Lorenzo and Jessica's love-duet by moonlight, beneath the trees. This short dialogue of about twenty-five lines is a delightful exercise in rhetorical formalism, where each response reiterates the refrain 'In such a night' seven times over, and repeats the same syntactical structures, apart from a few variations, as well as the same rhythmic patterns. Even though the atmosphere and figures of speech are different to those used by Kyd in the arbour scene in *The Spanish Tragedy*, the two pieces resemble each other in their metronomic regularity. At first sight, there is no indication of any ironic or parodic purpose. Shakespeare is using a traditional form of *badinage* love-talk in which sentimental duetting takes on all the piquancy of a verbal duel. Yet in Kyd, this type of formalized scene is but an extreme manifestation of a general tendency, observable in the work as a whole. In Shakespeare, on the contrary, a scene like this immediately stands out as exceptional. The purpose of such lyricism is, of course, to extol Belmont's atmosphere which is so propitious to the untroubled outpourings of mutual love. However, Shakespeare's choice of a style, which forms such a striking contrast with the general trend of the work, including the declarations of love of Bassanio and Portia, means that the scene is isolated in its apartness, so that it is highlighted for what it is – a recital for two voices which momentarily suspends the course of the action, or , to put it another way, a ritual ceremony in homage to love. Yet the charm is not protracted beyond what is necessary. The last act of the play begins in moonlight, lulled by the music of the spheres and other music, yet it ends in ribaldry and references to cuckoldry, a salutary reminder that marriage means wedding and bedding, rather than star-watching: it is this which places the love-duet, retrospectively speaking, but only retrospectively, in an ironic perspective.

As rhetorical formalism was gradually declining as a desirable mode of dramatic expression and construction, isolated instances of its presence were turned to special and carefully localized effects. Shakespeare is lavish in his use of conspicuous rhetoric whenever he wishes to endow particular episodes or speeches with a special resonance, be it ceremonial, archaic, magical or parodic. It is a resonance found in the abdication scene of Richard II, at Rosalind and Orlando's marriage, in Brutus' speech to the Roman citizens, in Helena's miraculous healing of the King of France, and even in Hamlet's scholarly disputation 'To be, or not to be'.

When Falstaff plays the King to Prince Hal in *Henry IV, Part I* (II, iv), the fat knight's Euphuistic speech connotes majesty, but it is of such a histrionic kind that it brings out the derisive purpose of the play-acting. In the same work, Shakespeare makes Hotspur sound like a character in

Marlowe in order to show up the soldier's heroic mettle, but also to indicate the anachronistic nature of the feudal values he embodies. In *Henry IV, Part 2*, the mighty lines' pastiche acquires a burlesque tone in the mouth of a character as unglamorous as Pistol.

The initial function of rhetorical formalism was to pattern out dramatic discourse in a harmonious way. At this later stage, it was advertising itself as a coded language and boldly asserting its own artifice. Throughout his career, Shakespeare retained his fondness for bipolarity of theme, symbolized notably by contrasts of place such as Westminster opposed to Eastcheap, the court to the Forest of Arden, Rome to Egypt, Sicily to Bohemia, or Milan to the Bermudas, although these oppositions are never homologues of the conflict between good and evil. While it is true that Shakespeare did prolong the ethical debate that had been such a strong structuring principle in the not so distant medieval Moralities, yet he did so in his own way, not, fundamentally, in the name of a philosophy of moral relativism but mostly as the result of an increasingly sophisticated theatrical practice. The fact of staging characters meant to be credible as human beings and of dramatizing some imaginary experience (but one embedded in the complexity and contingency of individual and collective existence) implies that words and deeds should be inserted into a more or less problematic space, with good and evil often meeting and meshing, shifting places or combining. The formative straitjacket of rhetorical formalism used in the early plays had, therefore, to be loosened to accommodate a certain degree of ambivalence necessary to a more convincing representation of human action and language. This is why Shakespeare gradually did away with the rigid patterning which impoverished the vision of the play, ridding it of the systematic oppositions, the see-saw structures and the term-to-term correspondences. It took an artist who had achieved fuller command of his skills and one who had freed himself from excessive concern for order and proportion to reach this goal. We know that Mannerist experiments demand a very high degree of craftsmanship.

Sonnet 76 contains an allusion to 'new-found methods' and 'compounds strange' used by rival poets, and Shakespeare ascribes these innovations to the vagaries of fashion and a taste for ostentation that he himself has eschewed:

> Why is my verse so barren of new pride?
> So far from variation and quick change?
> Why with the time do I not glance aside
> To new-found methods and to compounds strange?

And he goes on to justify the immutability and simplicity of his own style with reference to the constancy of his theme:

> O, know, sweet love, I always write of you,
> And you and love are still my argument.[10]

Yet it may be that the persistently interrogative tone of the first quatrain half-betrays a longing, or at least an awakening of interest. The thematic and stylistic evolution of the *Sonnets* and the plays shows that Shakespeare did not long remain indifferent to the possibilities of the new style. Towards the end of the century, he adapted for the stage some of the 'methods' and 'compounds' that John Donne had experimented with a few years previously in his poetry.[11]

But having reached the point where the constraints of rhetorical formalism were overcome in Shakespeare, it is worth returning briefly to Jonson. The reason is that Jonson too was striving to free the theatre from the trammels of convention; his ambition was to replace rhetorical phrasing with a new style that would give an illusion of spontaneous utterance, and to replace the artificial plots derived from Latin comedy and encumbered with the parallelisms and counterpointing of Renaissance formalism with an action that would develop more naturally through peripeteia interconnected by thematic contiguity rather than by mechanical causality. However, Jonson was to veer away from and even turn his back on Mannerism because, unlike Shakespeare, he was a radical in his reforms and a dogmatist in his methods.

In *Every Man In His Humour* (1598), Jonson shed certain conventions such as the doubling of analogous situations and symmetrical groupings of characters. Though the play still contains two gulls opposed to two wits, this arrangement scarcely affects the structuring of the action. The characters pursue their chartered course in an almost autonomous fashion; their paths cross, diverge and intersect on several occasions, but without giving rise to parallel situations. The central presence of Brainworm, the schemer, is not enough to unify the action into a single plot. It is more like a set of journeys in which the characters peregrinate from one spot to another, suggesting similarities with picaresque narrative. Their course is marked out by the threads of multiple plots spun and woven by Brainworm's inventive genius. The play is not a comedy of intrigue articulated around a central motif, but a series of sequences designed to illustrate dynamically the 'humour' of each character – Bobadill's cowardly boasting, Kitely's morbid jealousy, Stephen's touching silliness, Matthew's affected melancholy and Brainworm's irresistible compulsion to mystify others. In writing this play, Jonson discovered or rediscovered that plot is not the sole 'mover' in a comedy.

In *Every Man Out of His Humour* (1599), he went one step further and reduced the role of the plot even more, while giving exceptional prominence to the systematic display of individual eccentricities. Methodical exposure of behavioural disorders became the mainspring of the action, at the expense of cleverly contrived imbroglios and an ingeniously managed unravelling of complications. Jonson's main preoccupation was to track down the aberrations affecting the moral well-being of individuals and society, and to use satire not as a side-effect but as a means to structure the action. This is why Jonson turned to the methods of *Vetus Comoedia*, as his mouthpiece, Cordatus, explains to Mitis before the beginning of the play itself. *Every Man Out* introduces itself immediately as an experimental work which might startle the spectator, as Cordatus warns: 'how it will answer the general expectation, I know not!' The unfolding of the action depends on the condition that the characters must give free rein to their humours before they can recover from them. The main, if not the sole, purpose of the encounters that take place or the relationships that are formed is to symptomatize each disease and then foster the recovery of the subject's health. Even if there is a shadowy plot towards the end when Malicente manages to cure Deliro and Fallace simultaneously through a cleverly arranged combination of circumstances, this concession to classical comedy is not truly representative of Jonson's new method, one that he was to use again in two other 'comical satires', *Cynthia's Revels* and *Poetaster*, written between 1599 and 1601.

When Shakespeare partially repudiated rhetorical formalism, it was, I think, in response to a desire to do justice to the complexity and ambiguity of things. Jonson's similar reaction pushed him in a different direction, towards an art of caricature in an attempt to cleanse morals and manners. Caricature presupposes a restrictive, over-simplified and exaggerated vision of reality; it washes its hands of nuances or ambiguities. Shakespeare's approach is all-inclusive; his eye probes all around the object, catching its multifarious facets in a prismatic vision, setting each single point of view against the many, revealing the fragility of appearances, and paradoxically allowing glimpses of a reality that extends far beyond the reflections we receive of it and the interpretations we give of it: 'There are more things in heaven and earth, Horatio/Than are dreamt of in your philosophy'. Jonson, on the other hand, only works away at surfaces that are visible to the naked eye;[12] he looks at things frontally and his view, which is two-dimensional and unwavering, comes from the fixed standpoint of comic satire. The only aspects of reality that Jonson retains are the few that are pertinent to his design; he focuses on what he wants, and magnifies it into a startling, often grotesque, and dreadfully one-sided image of tremendous effectiveness. It is pointless, therefore, to seek any kind of 'deeper level' in Jonson's theatre, if what is meant by this is the suggestion of a grey area, like a halo of implicitness surrounding words and deeds. The stage presence of Jonson's main characters is as powerful as that of Shakespeare's, but it is of a different kind. Unlike the great Shakespearian figures that create the illusion of living a life of their own outside the stage microcosm, even the most memorable of Jonson's characters, such as Volpone, Mosca, Sir Epicure Mammon, Morose or Zeal-of-the-land Busy, seem to use up their whole stock of existence on stage. The glass that Jonson holds up to nature is not Shakespeare's many-sided mirror, but a thick lens that enlarges and distorts, one suited to the observation of 'the time's deformity/ Anatomiz'd in every nerve and sinew' as Asper puts it in *Every Man Out*. No ambiguity can be tolerated if the anatomy lesson is to be understood by the public.

The method expounded and applied dogmatically in the comical satires is distanced in *Volpone* (1609) and Jonson's other major comedies written between 1609 and 1614 (*Epicoene*, *The Alchemist* and *Bartholomew Fair*). These plays show a return to unified action and plotting in the style of the New Comedy, partially replacing the previous experiments in kaleidoscopic image-making. But even in these plays of a more classical stamp, it is aberrations of behaviour which generate the plot. Later on, in *The Staple of News* (1625) Jonson experimented even more boldly with a three-tier synthetic approach, choosing the outward form of the comedy of intrigue but using the humours in a way reminiscent of the comical satires, and mingling with the 'humorous' characters allegorical figures harking back to the medieval Moralities. This hybrid species might at a pinch be seen as a Jonsonian variety of Mannerism. Like certain Mannerist paintings, the play exhibits a 'discord of parts' in that the symbolism of the allegorical parable has difficulty rubbing shoulders with the realism of the satire and the suspense of the comedy of intrigue. Yet in actual fact there is no trace of Mannerism in this assemblage of incongruous parts because the meaning of the message in Jonson's work is clear and readable at first sight. Though the dramatist juxtaposes different perspectives, he never confuses the issues. No matter what methods are used, whether in combination or separately, it is always clarity that prevails. Jonson's belief in the ethical and cathartic function of the theatre meant that he had a moral and aesthetic duty to produce a coherent and immediately decipherable picture of the deviations he was condemning. This conviction may well have been the most powerful antidote of all against Mannerism.

Lyly extols an ideal of harmony that he wants to see reflected in his Euphuistic prose, a dream world of absolute consonance. Jonson wields his scalpel towards deviance, through a world of pathological aberration that is just as unreal and contrived as Lyly's. Both writers inhabit a universe that is stable, ordered and predictable, whereas the Mannerist artist labours under no banner, except perhaps the need for free play of mind in order to test the validity of Horace's paradox 'rerum discordia concors' and to try out, half-seriously, half-jokingly, what disconcerting effects may be drawn from it. It is when an artist 'is capable of being in uncertainties, mysteries, doubts, without any irritable reaching after fact and reason', when, in short, he is imbued with the 'Negative Capability' that Keats attributes to Shakespeare,[13] and when he uses his art to make us share in it, that he can be said to come closer to the Mannerist frame of mind.

CHAPTER 4

Julius Caesar *and 'dramatic coquetry'*

In the second volume of his book on Shakespeare's histories, Professor Paul Bacquet rightly insists on the pedagogical function of the Chorus in *Henry V*. The role of the Chorus, he argues, is more systematically developed in this play than in any other of the same period, and serves to guide the spectators through the play's various episodes and also to encourage them to perform an act of 'collective imagination' without which there would be no dramatic illusion.[1]

It seems to me that the Chorus' repeated plea to the audience to compensate mentally for the material limitations of stage production serves another equally indispensable, if less obvious, purpose, which is to secure the audience's adherence to the play's ideological message. In Shakespeare's view, the people assembled in the playhouse would be all the more willing to accept that a few square metres of boards in the centre of that wooden 'O' might represent the battlefield of Agincourt if they could be made to feel party to the glorious national epic that was being played out before them, for them and, up to a point, thanks to them. Whatever their social rank, cultural origin and religious or political allegiance, the members of the audience – possibly viewed by the dramatist as the epitome of British society or perhaps a peace-time reflection of the King's army – were urged to unite in a shared feeling of patriotic fervour. The special theatrical strategy geared to such an uncommon goal was to enlist them in the actual making of the show so that this rare moment of dramatic experience might also be one of ideological consensus.[2]

1599 is also, in all probability, the year of *Julius Caesar*, another history play but one with no Chorus to sustain the audience. Here the spectators are left to themselves and it is up to them alone to construe the meaning of what they see and hear on stage, not such an easy task, as we shall see. British history is no longer at stake. However decisive the murder of Caesar may have been in changing the face of the planet, this momentous event still concerns the ancient world. Ideologically, the play does not require the same emotional commitment from the audience and its progress does not depend on the same type of dramaturgic collaboration. It is enough for the audience to behave 'normally' – to consent to the usual suspension of disbelief expected at the theatre – to preserve the chances of minimal dramatic illusion.

Like *Richard II*, *Julius Caesar* is the story of a conspiracy undertaken in the name of the common weal. But Richard was king, a sacred figure, and his deposition and murder were impious acts. Like Richard's, Caesar's power is legitimate, but, contrary to what he would have the citizens of Rome believe, it is not of divine origin. His murder, therefore, is not technically a sacrilege, except in the minds of those who made him into a god in his own lifetime. Richard was an unworthy ruler and his replacement by Bolingbroke could appear as a measure of public salvation, a morally reprehensible but politically desirable usurpation despite the civil disorder it was bound to kindle. The answer to the question of whether the kingdom gained or lost from this change in dynasty is long in coming: the problem of monarchical legitimacy in the face of reasons of State and the dilemma between the sacred and the political haunt the end of *Richard II*, the whole of *Henry IV* (*Parts 1* and *2*) and occasionally surface again in *Henry V*. It is only the latter play that turns the scales in favour of the house of Lancaster. As to whether the violent overthrow of Caesar proved beneficial or detrimental to Rome, neither *Julius Caesar* nor *Antony and Cleopatra* – the sequel to the former play inasmuch as it dramatizes events subsequent to Caesar's death – offers the least clue. Though the Elizabethans knew, as well as we do, that the fall of Caesar was to give rise to the empire heralded by Octavius' glorious principate, Shakespeare remains conspicuously silent about this, focusing instead upon the convulsions attendant upon the murder, iniquitous proscriptions, the rivalry within the triumvirate, the war against the conspirators and the discords between Brutus and Cassius. Neither in Octavius' final speech nor elsewhere in the play is there a hint that good may eventually come from evil. The crucial issue of whether Caesar's blood was shed for the good or the ill of Rome is deliberately left pending. In *Julius Caesar*, Shakespeare highlights the event and its immediate consequences, thus enclosing the action within the impassable boundaries of an intensely dramatized present. Thus isolated from past and future, the facts confronting us cannot be fitted into a long-range vision that would give them meaning and relevance in terms of a country's destiny. Ideologically, the spectators of the play are well and truly alone.

Following close upon *Henry V*, *Julius Caesar* is yet another exploration of the hero figure. That Shakespeare was turning to Plutarch (via Sir Thomas North) after he had just brought to an epic finale the cycle of plays devoted to national history shows clearly that the theme of the great man still interested him. If antiquity was to supply a hero as prestigious as Henry, the choice naturally lay between Alexander and Caesar.[3] The circumstances of Caesar's assassination, the ensuing civil war and the conspirators' defeat offered excellent material for yet another history play structured around three dramatic moments: the hatching of a conspiracy, the execution of a murder and the meting out of retribution to the guilty. Not only could Shakespeare once again furnish the stage with vivid tableaux such as Caesar amid his court, Brutus deliberating with his conscience, Caesar stabbed to death at the foot of Pompey's statue, Brutus' and Antony's celebrated speeches at the market-place or the conspirators' suicide at Philippi, but he could also easily work these spectacular scenes into a unified drama, patterned on the old, still successful formula of the revenge tragedy.

More decisively, perhaps, Shakespeare's preference for the story of Caesar's life accorded well with the direction he was working in after the completion of his two historical tetralogies, namely towards a more curious probing into the complexities of the human mind and soul and a more realistic rendering of the often chaotic life of consciousness together with a more critical appraisal of man's 'greatness and nobility', a trend that *Hamlet* and the dark comedies were soon to exemplify. Shakespeare knew how controversial and enigmatic Caesar had appeared, both to his contemporaries and to succeeding generations. Borrowing from Roman antiquity, he no doubt felt free from the ideological constraints that inevitably impinge on the representation of national history. Furthermore, the story of Julius Caesar offered the advantage of including not one but two heroes in whom greatness and weakness intermingle, thus providing the dramatist with the exciting possibility of counterpointing two forms of heroism, each one marred with its own shortcomings: in Caesar, the glory of the conqueror and statesman tarnished by excessive pride; in Brutus, the integrity of the true republican led astray by political blindness. This dualistic vision, sanctioned by Renaissance historiography, whereby assessment of both personages could only be a qualified one, fitted exactly with Shakespeare's project. In many respects, the subject of Caesar's downfall at the hands of patriots who were diversely (and some of whom were dubiously) motivated carried enough ambiguity to lend itself to Mannerist treatment.

There was yet another advantage which, from a non-Mannerist per-spective, would have seemed more like a drawback: no episode of ancient history was better known and more loaded with moral and polit-ical glosses than Caesar's rise and fall. His destiny had long been food for thought on the vagaries of Fortune and the ironic proximity of the Capitol to the Tarpeian Rock, revealing the dark face of greatness and the often conflicting demands of civic duty and friendship. Reflecting upon his choice, Shakespeare may well have felt that he was coming too late and that all had been said on the subject. Telling the story of Julius Caesar and of Brutus and his associates could only be a retelling. Substantially altering the facts of history was out of the question, and therefore innovation had to be confined to matters of form. It was as if, from the start, Shakespeare found himself in the position of a composer having to write variations on a canonical theme, a situation of relative constraint or conditional freedom most favourable to a Mannerist approach. When an artist has no other choice but to reproduce what C.G. Dubois calls 'une thématique magistrale' (a set of themes sanc-tioned by the authority of masters) he or she must gear his or her inspira-tion to 'the multiplying of forms and proliferating of variations'.[4] This incidentally sheds light on the old concept of refurbishing erstwhile suc-cesses according to current fashion; what has perhaps too often been taken for sheer opportunism on the part of authors in need of popularity may well evince – in some cases at least – a Mannerist propensity for sub-versive allegiance. Is it by accident that *Hamlet* (which is regarded by many as a Mannerist play, if not the epitome of Mannerist dramatic art) proceeds from an *Ur-Hamlet*? If this theory holds true, *Hamlet* can be seen as Shakespeare's personal variation upon the traditional formula of the revenge tragedy. Whether *Julius Caesar* was inspired by an existing play or not is of little importance. Because of the exceptional popularity of the fable, it is History itself, as constituted by the gradual sedimentation of the commentaries, which serves as reference or model. Addressing a subject like this with its compulsory figures (almost in the choreographic sense of the term), Shakespeare was practically forced to seek originality of treatment. More specifically, it is in the Mannerist presentation of the characters that Shakespeare's art is most innovative.

What I designate here as a Mannerist trait, Ernest Schanzer calls 'dra-matic coquetry'. This facetious and telling expression denotes the method whereby the dramatist manipulates our response to the main characters 'playing fast and loose with our affections for them, engaging and alienating them in turn'.[5] Though a similar technique is at work in several other plays, it is never more systematically used than in *Julius Caesar*. Schanzer has studied in great detail how a succession of images, in turn positive and negative, disconcerts the spectator to the extent that he or she can no longer situate the characters on a scale of moral values. Since Caesar and the conspirators can gain our sympathy or antipathy only transiently and incompletely, the murder itself appears in an ambiguous light. If it is true that Caesar's murder was indeed a political error, was it also a morally reprehensible act? According to Schanzer, this is the central question posed by the play, one that Shakespeare is careful *not* to answer.

The presence of Mannerism is indicated not by Caesar, Brutus, Cassius and Antony (to mention only the major characters) being alloys of good and evil: this ambivalence is supported by history and can be thought of as inherent to all credible portrayals of human nature. This might even be another example of rhetorical formalism with character-istic effects of binary opposition and symmetrical balancing. That each character should view himself and others from an angle entirely his own is not particularly relevant to Mannerism either. It is not surprising that Caesar as seen by Cassius should not be a faithful mirror image of Caesar as seen by Brutus, even less so by Antony, not to mention Caesar seen by himself or by the audience. All plays and novels containing several characters consist of such sets of mirrors in which images are thus reflected and interconnected. It is through such reverberations that identities are formed. But Mannerist art has the particularity of thwart-ing this image-making process by maintaining the characters on this side of a true identity. Mannerism discourages us from ever being able to organize into a viable entity – that is, a coherent and credible whole – the pieces of the puzzle scattered before our eyes. Mannerism strives hard to preclude the possibility of a global, unified perception.

Why, when looking at a Mannerist bronze by Giovanni Bologna, are we seized with a desire to inspect it from all angles? As we cannot turn it this way and that, why are we tempted to walk around it as if to discover yet another hitherto unsuspected angle? How is it that having to stand in front of Pontormo's *Deposition* or Michelangelo's *Last Judgement*, we com-mission our gaze, as it were vicariously, to wander over the composition? The answer is that in a Mannerist work where everything attracts the eye, nothing arrests it. No standpoint imposes itself as decisive in procur-ing the most satisfying vision, which hopefully might best reveal to us the work's 'truth'. What reasons are there to prefer confronting the statue frontally rather than obliquely? Each point of view appeals to our eye and momentarily frustrates it from the pleasure of discovering what the next point of view would disclose. Unlike classical characters, collected in almost all of their actions and speeches, at all times coextensive with themselves, their Mannerist counterparts are always presented incomplete; they sharpen our curiosity and direct it towards a hypothetical 'elsewhere', the hidden face of their being, in the illusory expectation of a revelation of the whole self.

Something analogous to this wandering gaze occurs in *Julius Caesar*. I shall not restate Schanzer's excellent analyses showing how the characters are split into successive images, either flattering or derogatory, but equally credible. Dramatic coquetry is a dynamics of ambiguity, in that it arouses excitement and disappointment in turn: we believe we grasp the 'truth' about a character (on which the meaning of his action depends), only to realize immediately afterwards that it was premature to stop at what was only an aspect, a facet among others. When Caesar dies, we still do not know what we should 'really' think about this immensely proud character who swings from the grotesque:

> Danger knows full well
> That Caesar is more dangerous than he.
> We are two lions litter'd in one day,
> And I the elder and more terrible.
>
> II, ii, 44–7

To the sublime:

> constant as the northern star,
> Of whose true-fix'd and resting quality
> There is no fellow in the firmament.
>
> III, i, 60–2

Caesar is warm with his friends:

> Good friends, go in, and taste some wine with me;
> And we, like friends, will straightway go together.
>
> II, ii, 126–7

His irresolution verges on caricature:

> Caesar shall forth. The things that threaten'd me
> Ne'er look'd but on my back.
>
> II, ii, 10–11

> Mark Antony shall say I am not well,
> And for thy humour I will stay at home.
>
> II, ii, 55–6

> Give me my robe, for I will go.
>> ii, ii, 107

But he is stoical at the thought of his own death:

> Cowards die many times before their deaths;
> The valiant never taste of death but once.
> Of all the wonders that I yet have heard,
> It seems to me most strange that men should fear,
> Seeing that death, a necessary end,
> Will come when it will come.
>> ii, ii, 32–7

His self-centredness is exorbitant:

> Decius, go tell them Caesar will not come.
> DEC. Most mighty Caesar, let me know some cause,
> Lest I be laugh'd at when I tell them so.
> CAES. The cause is in my will: I will not come;
> That is enough to satisfy the Senate.
>> ii, ii, 68–72

But it is matched by equally uncompromising self-abnegation:

> What touches us ourself shall be last serv'd.
>> iii, i, 8

Caesar is superstitious:

> Forget not, in your speed, Antonius,
> To touch Calphurnia; for our elders say,
> The barren, touched in this holy chase,
> Shake off their sterile curse.
>> i, ii, 6–9

Except however when he himself is concerned:

> What say'st thou to me now? Speak once again.
> SOOTH. Beware the ides of March.
> CAES. He is a dreamer. Let us leave him. Pass.
>> i, ii, 22–4

His grasp of human psychology is remarkable and likely, one would think, to caution him against 'dangerous' persons:

> I do not know the man I should avoid
> So soon as that spare Cassius. He reads much,
> He is a great observer, and he looks
> Quite through the deeds of men. He loves no plays,
> As thou dost, Antony; he hears no music.

Seldom he smiles, and smiles in such a sort
As if he mock'd himself, and scorn'd his spirit
That could be mov'd to smile at any thing.
Such men as he be never at heart's ease
Whiles they behold a greater than themselves,
And therefore are they very dangerous.

I, ii, 197–207

Yet his superhuman stature – notwithstanding his physical disabilities – puts him above the fears of common mortals:

I rather tell thee what is to be fear'd
Than what I fear; for always I am Caesar.
Come on my right hand, for this ear is deaf.

I, ii, 208–10

In addition to the images Caesar projects of himself there are those given by the receivers, namely the characters who look at him and judge him. Brutus, like the Plebeian Tribunes, sees in Caesar a potential tyrant:

a serpent's egg,
Which, hatch'd, would, as his kind, grow mischievous.

II, i, 32–3

The one difference is that Brutus loves Caesar ('I love him well', I, ii, 81). Though Brutus detects in Caesar a weakness for honours ('He would be crown'd', II, i, 12), he sees him above all as a reasonable man in control of his passions:

I have not known when his affections sway'd
More than his reason.

II, i, 20–1

For Cassius, on the other hand, Caesar is a clay-footed giant:

A man no mightier than thyself, or me,
In personal action, yet prodigious grown,
And fearful, as these strange eruptions are.

I, iii, 76–8

A 'colossus' who destroys all hope of honour in his fellow citizens:

Why, man, he doth bestride the narrow world
Like a Colossus, and we petty men
Walk under his huge legs, and peep about
To find ourselves dishonourable graves.

I, ii, 133–6

His tyranny, more moral than political, teaches the Romans servility in defiance of their ancestral values:

> our fathers' minds are dead,
> And we are govern'd with our mothers' spirits;
> Our yoke and sufferance show us womanish.
>
> I, iii, 82–4

The one fleeting image of Caesar given by Antony while the former is alive is that of an authoritarian father figure who knows how to be obeyed:

> When Caesar says, 'Do this', it is perform'd.
>
> I, ii, 10

Yet he is someone to whom Antony can freely express his disagreement:

> Fear him not, Caesar, he's not dangerous.
>
> I, ii, 193

After the death of Caesar, Antony's words depict him as a man who could inspire the strongest friendship:

> That I did love thee, Caesar, O, 'tis true!
> If then thy spirit look upon us now,
> Shall it not grieve thee dearer than thy death,
> To see thy Antony making his peace,
> Shaking the bloody fingers of thy foes.
>
> III, i, 194–8

He is one whose nobility was incomparable:

> Thou art the ruins of the noblest man
> That ever lived in the tide of times.
>
> III, i, 256–7

His loss is felt with pain:

> for mine eyes,
> Seeing those beads of sorrow stand in thine,
> Began to water.
>
> III, i, 283–5

Such effusiveness, the sincerity of which cannot be doubted (unlike Antony's carefully studied posturing during his speech to the citizens at the market-place), evokes the figure of a friend, an aspect authenticated by Brutus himself:

I slew my best lover for the good of Rome.

III, ii, 46

On the negative side of things, the toadying of Caesar's entourage corroborates Cassius' claim that the Romans are overshadowed by Caesar and have abdicated all republican pride. So even Cassius' discourse on Caesar, biased as it is, and dictated, as we know it to be, by hatred and envy, holds elements of truth.

Of all the images that Caesar reflects, and they are diverse and numerous since no one is exposed to the others' gaze as much as Caesar, none is conclusive. The 'truth' about Caesar cannot be obtained by sorting out the true and false images, those which apparently bring us closer to the 'real' Caesar and those which do not. The truth about Caesar is to be found in every single reflection from these multifaceted mirrors. This helps to understand why the Mannerist method renders obsolete the traditional and rhetorical opposition between appearance and reality, between the mask of the public figure and the face of the private person. As Raymond Willems has neatly written:

It would be vain to look for the 'true' Caesar behind the mask of the mythical Caesar. Caesar is not an impostor. He plays a role, of course, but it is his own role. He simply tries to be himself, not to give an embellished image of himself. His play-acting does not therefore tend towards duplicity, but towards the unity of his self. When he proclaims 'I am Caesar', it is not vain boasting. The phrase is the expression of the terrible effort he must make to stick to his character. Hence his almost incantory repetition of his own name which has become like a talisman.[6]

Why introduce this notion of tending towards 'the unity of the self'? It is because the self is not of the order of the given, but the ever-receding horizon of a never-ending quest, the forever disappointed promise of an illusory cohesion between disparate images.

After this dizzying kaleidoscopic review of the most telling images relating to Caesar, I hesitate to extend it to other characters. Suffice it to say that dramatic coquetry is not confined to Caesar alone. It is a deliberate stand on dramaturgy, a departure in the art of drawing characters and bringing them to life on stage. Shakespeare is Mannerist in so far as he constantly eludes the spectator's expectation of characters clustered around a key image. Like Mannerist painters or sculptors, he repudiates all sense of hierarchy in viewpoints, thus holding up disparity and off-centredness as the structural principles underlying his treatment of characters.

The corollary of this is that the actions themselves are irremediably ambiguous, the best example being the murder of Caesar. Shakespeare does not choose between the two conflicting images of the murder: Brutus' image of murder as sacrifice and Antony's image of butchery. History chooses for him and gives Antony the advantage over Brutus in the contest between images. It is clear that Antony has carried the day when the sacrificial and emblematic blood in which the conspirators have ritually bathed their hands and swords becomes the blood of the massacre, which murderous envy has caused to flow:

> Look, in this place ran Cassius' dagger through:
> See what a rent the envious Cassius made:
> Through this the well-beloved Brutus stabb'd;
> And as he pluck'd his cursed steel away,
> Mark how the blood of Caesar follow'd it,
> As rushing out of doors, to be resolv'd
> If Brutus so unkindly knock'd or no.
>
> III, ii, 176–82

Henceforth Antony's image of Caesar's death has supplanted Brutus' in the eyes of the citizens. Shakespeare had no other choice but to ratify the verdict of history, but this does not mean he had to *justify* it. It is not because the image propagated by Antony proves more credible to 'the masses who make history' and more profitable to those who are its privileged actors that Brutus' contrary image is invalidated. In an attempt to make ethics coincide with politics, it has been argued that Brutus' staged ceremony following the assassination of Caesar is a murderer's contrivance, designed to shelter his sensitivity from the unbearable horror of the collective crime, a ritual seen as the dressing up of bad faith.[7] I do not share this view. Here Willems is worth quoting again:

To take appearances in hand is not necessarily to use them to deceive. Brutus is concerned about controlling them because he knows they are misleading. He wants to prevent his act from being misunderstood. From this perspective 'this shall make/Our purpose necessary' is only apparently paradoxical. According to Brutus' logic, it is the manner of killing Caesar which will give his act its true meaning. If he can convince the other conspirators to consider the murder as a sacrifice, then it will indeed be a sacrifice.[8]

In the ontological world of Mannerism, truth is a useless hypothesis, only representation matters. The Mannerist artist does not conceive of his or her work differently from the way Brutus looks upon his act: only the manner carries meaning.

If truth is reducible to a vertiginous parade of images which correct, contradict and complement but in no way *cancel* each other out, what is more tempting than to give oneself over to the impressions of the moment, since each moment expresses a truth? Mildred E. Hartsock thinks that the play is constructed in such a way as to place the spectator in a situation analogous to that of the Roman crowd at the market-place: 'We are fully committed at every point in the play to *someone*. Ironically, we have something in common with the Roman mob: we believe what we hear as we hear it, only to be involved in one emotional or intellectual partisanship after another.'[9] This opinion should be qualified, or the Mannerist game of dramatic coquetry will be over-simplified. Shakespeare is more subtle, more authentically Mannerist, less of a crude hoaxer than Hartsock supposes. We know that he is careful to ensure that no image can be purely and simply accepted or rejected. Coquetry or flirtatiousness is the art of not taking advances or rebuffs too far, lest the game come to a halt. This is why no character in the play inspires either love or hatred. The Mannerist artist takes care not to play on extremes of emotion, his or her range is voluntarily limited. He or she expects connivance more than participation from the audience, an attitude that is more playful than sentimental, more intellectual than emotional. Baroque characters – say Othello, Lear or Macbeth – violently catch hold of us for better or worse: Mannerist characters intrigue the audience more than inflame them. Even when the Mannerist hero is endowed with a strong presence both textually and scenically (as is the case with Caesar and Hamlet), he is always held at a distance, like an object of curiosity meant to be considered with a careful and critical eye. This is why the pleasure obtained from a Mannerist work always has a streak of narcissism about it, as if much of the enjoyment comes from detecting the irony of the message.

At two decisive moments – before his departure to the Senate and before the murder – Caesar indulges in a fit of self-aggrandizement, almost disowning his human nature, first through an animal metaphor (the image of the two lions already mentioned), and then through a cosmic simile which develops into a whole tirade:

> But I am constant as the northern star,
> Of whose true-fix'd and resting quality
> There is no fellow in the firmament.
> The skies are painted with unnumber'd sparks,
> They are all fire, and every one doth shine;
> But there's but one in all doth hold his place.

So in the world: 'tis furnis'd well with men,
And men are flesh and blood, and apprehensive;
Yet in the number I do know but one
That unassailable holds on his rank,
Unshak'd of motion; and that I am he,
Let me a little show it, even in this,
That I was constant Cimber should be banish'd,
And constant do remain to keep him so.
III, i, 60–73

T.S. Dorsch rightly sees in this speech an outburst of pride caused by
the servility of Metellus and Cassius, come to plead the cause of Publius
Cimber. But such arrogance, he claims, triggers so much antipathy
among Caesar's entourage and the audience that the forthcoming
murder appears almost justifiable.[10] I do not find this psychological interpretation of causes and effects entirely convincing. If this be pride, it is
the legitimate pride of a monarch, something that an Elizabethan audience would not consider as grossly 'extravagant' as we do today.
Shakespeare is not trying to justify the murder beforehand by making
Caesar especially odious. A more plausible explanation that does justice
to Caesar's self-coined image of superhuman infallibility is that
Shakespeare is here presenting the murder as a truly political option
rather than the outcome of accumulated personal grudges or resent-
ments. Richard Marienstras' comment on this episode is very much to
the point: 'this political murder, this sacrifice, the fall of this star, for one
moment appears as an attempt to replace an inhuman cosmic order by
an order of another nature, governed by the will of men and by social
ethics founded purely on contract'.[11] The irony, therefore, is not exactly
where Dorsch believes it to be found. It stems from the fact that it is
Caesar *himself*, in his use of cosmic imagery to illustrate his 'constancy',
who confirms the need for the conspirators to rid themselves of that
inhuman authority of superterrestrial nature. In a pagan context, where
the monarch's power does not proceed from God (meaning the Judaeo-
Christian God), it is by no means impious to prefer a contract to an order
founded on transcendence, which, in any case, is not of divine essence.
By comparing himself to the pole star, the fixed point *par excellence* and
keystone of the cosmos, Caesar had no notion of the extent to which he
was playing into the conspirators' hands: this concept was precisely what
they wanted to destroy.

As for the mini-parable of the two lions, through which Caesar
expresses his contempt of danger, it shows almost in caricature how

arrogance can sink into ridicule; danger is first the object of an unspeci-
fied personification ('Danger knows full well . . .'), then what might pass
as a fairly bad flash of wit ('Caesar is more dangerous than' Danger itself)
becomes a grotesque metaphor – Caesar and Danger are two lions 'lit-
ter'd in one day', but Caesar is 'the elder and more terrible' of the two.
Calphurnia is right: excessive self-confidence causes her husband to
rave. When Caesar presents himself as a fierce, invulnerable being, he
only succeeds in prefiguring what could appear as a form of senility.
When he proclaims himself as 'constant' as the pole star, he unveils the
inanity of such pretensions when they are embodied in a mortal being. A
few stabs will suffice – and what conspirator does not think of this when
listening to Caesar – to turn this figure of immortality into a 'bleeding
piece of earth'. Similarly, it is when Brutus professes honesty most vehe-
mently that he is the least convincing:

> There is no terror, Cassius, in your threats;
> For I am arm'd so strong in honesty
> That they pass by me as the idle wind,
> Which I respect not.
>
> IV, iii, 66–9

Such Caesar-like grandiloquence sounds strained and suggests that
Brutus, like Caesar, has to struggle to live up to his own legend. These
characters are engaged in the construction of their own myths. In everything they say and do, in the day-after-day management of the images
they wish to convey of themselves, they have to take into account what
history and legend have already made of them.

But in this play that is fraught with ambiguity, are there any moments
when we are tempted to commit ourselves unreservedly to a character, if
only for the time he speaks? At the market-place, before the crowd,
Brutus expounds his reasons for having killed Caesar, with the vigorous
clarity of his Lacedaemonian style. We might almost be convinced, thus
imitating the citizens, as Hartsock would have it. Unlike Antony's succeeding oration, Brutus' speech strikes us as being basically honest, the
opposite of manipulation. Yet one sentence at the end throws everything
into doubt:

> The question of
> his death is enroll'd in the Capitol; his glory not
> extenuated, wherein he was worthy; nor his offences
> enforc'd, for which he suffered death.
>
> III, ii, 38–41

Brutus blames Caesar for errors *already* committed and turns the murder into a punishment, in blatant contradiction to the preventive murder theory he had developed in Act II:

> And since the quarrel
> Will bear no colour for the thing he is,
> Fashion it thus: that what he is, augmented,
> Would run to these and these extremities.
>
> II, i, 28–31

What can justify this double language? Why does Brutus change from sacrificer to avenger or righter of wrongs? Is there a version of the murder for private use, his own and his associates', and another for public use, that of the Plebeians, whom the first version had no chance of convincing? What spectators would want to identify with this credulous, changeable and over-emotional crowd who is debarred from knowing the ins and outs of the affair?

The market scene is placed right in the middle of the play; it does indeed have an emblematic value, though not perhaps the one suggested by Hartsock. My hypothesis is that Brutus' and Antony's orations are theatrical pieces; the tribune is their stage and the Roman citizens are their spectators, a feverish, fascinated and easily manipulated audience, the very opposite of the sort of audience that Shakespeare would have wished for his own play. Through an act of negative symbolization strategically performed at the very core of *Julius Caesar*, Shakespeare treats his own audience to a show of irony aimed at a category of spectators he esteems incapable of reacting suitably to the subtleties of Mannerist theatre, and this brings me back to my starting-point which was the playwright's attitude to his audience. In *Henry V*, Shakespeare expected from them a sustained collaboration in the drama; he asked them to provide thought-out and voluntary support from the heart and mind, unlike the irrational, inconstant, follow-the-leader attitude of the Plebeians enslaved to their urges of the moment. Conversely, it is a totally receptive, totally free, totally critical audience that is needed for *Julius Caesar*, where ambiguity reigns, where dramatic coquetry feeds theatrical pleasure. But what use is to be made of such liberty and lucidity? To indulge without illusion in the Mannerist game of engagement and disengagement and to eschew the trap of images no further than the game requires, Shakespeare wants his audience to be astute enough to appreciate the ambivalence of words and situations, civilized enough both to understand the value of poetry and, unlike the Roman frenzied mob, not to kill the poet.

CHAPTER 5

Hamlet: *optical effects*

At the turn of the century, shortly after the Lord Chamberlain's company had taken possession of the recently built Globe theatre, a new play came out which had every reason to intrigue the playgoers who were tolerably well informed of the London productions of the previous decade. As a modernized version of an old success and a refashioning of the traditional revenge play, Shakespeare's *Hamlet* was likely to appear to the more discerning as an innovation within the framework of tradition. Though such an unwonted avenger as Hamlet had never been seen on an English stage before, the subject-matter itself was familiar enough and the figure of his kingly father, armed from head to foot and crying out for vengeance from under his helmet, must still have been present in many a memory. In the preceding decade, an earlier version of the same story had been staged several times, originally at the Theatre, where the actors of Lord Strange and the Lord Admiral were currently perform- ing, then at the Newington Butts theatre in 1594 and finally at the Theatre again when it was revived by the very same actors – the Lord Chamberlain's – who were soon to pride themselves on a *Hamlet* of their own, a play written by one of their fellow members, possibly the most successful playwright of the day. Once again, Shakespeare took up the challenge and breathed new life into fairly hackneyed material, a task that had to meet the usual requirement of respecting the broad lines of the old story whilst bringing into it enough novelty to satisfy a widely shared craving for change and justify the rewriting of a popular play.[1] To cling too closely to the old Kydian formula would have turned away from the Globe the most avant-garde part of the audience and made them easy prey for those 'little eyases' who then officiated in the more fashion- able private theatres; on the other hand, to ridicule tradition as Marston had done, or was soon to do, in *Antonio's Revenge*,[2] would have alienated the more popular and more conservative section of the audience that Shakespeare was equally anxious to please. Once again, the playwright

87

was left with no other choice but that of imitating with a difference, a strategy especially propitious to Mannerist experimentation.

The main pitfall besetting an approach to *Hamlet* from a Mannerist standpoint is a tendency to overemphasize the play's Mannerism, either by focusing too narrowly on what W. Sypher has termed its 'devious, oblique and seemingly improvised structure',[3] or by portraying the eponymous hero as the archetypal figure of Renaissance Mannerism, a Rosso- or Pontormo-like neurotic, an 'ever irresolute and sexually ambivalent introvert, always acting in contradiction with the demands of logic, decency and moral duty'.[4] The trouble with G.R. Hocke's definition quoted above, and other similar psychological inventories listed out of context, is that they can be reversed point by point with an equal claim to credibility. So what is the use of taking the opposite stand? Although Hamlet invites questioning from his entourage about 'that within [him] which passes show', and tantalizes those sent to spy on him with his 'mystery', should we not know better than poor Rosencrantz and Guildenstern? Should we not realize that Hamlet has no secret for *us* or that his secret, if any, lies not in the dark abyss of psychology but in the language that clothes him as a fascinating theatrical creation?

Unencumbered by any concern about a Mannerist framework, Harold Jenkins feels free to discern great coherence of development in the play. Admittedly, it unfolds 'in a leisurely, meditative fashion' mainly through an abundance of monologues, seemingly casual conversations and numerous digressions, but Shakespeare, Jenkins insists, 'holds in assured grasp the many threads of his complicated plot'.[5] To assess the play's Mannerism, one must start by acknowledging the author's masterful control of his material. Globally speaking, the play's narrative follows the three-tier Kydian pattern of revenge: first the crime or its disclosure, which causes an intense emotional shock and subsequently motivates revenge; then the identification of the guilty party, either after an investigation conducted by the potential avenger or his allies, or owing to a combination of circumstances, fortuitous or provoked; and finally, the peripeteia attendant upon the revenge proper, possibly with the murderer's counter-offensive following the exposure of his guilt and preceding the simultaneous deaths of the avenger and his adversaries. In contrast to *The Spanish Tragedy*, the initial murder in *Hamlet* takes place before the play starts, but from the moment Hamlet learns of his father's death his situation is analogous to that of Hieronimo discovering his son hanged. For some time, Hieronimo remains in the dark as to the identity of the murderer, whereas Hamlet is informed straight away of his uncle's guilt; but this difference has no significant impact on the story's development since both the Ghost's revelations and Bel-imperia's letter provoke similar reactions of scepticism, calling for further investigation and checking. In both plays, obtaining the truth is the focal point of the action. The letter found on Pedringano's body may well be a poor invention compared to Hamlet's superb staging of the 'Mousetrap', but the two episodes serve the same purpose, which is to confound the guilty party. This is followed by the adversaries' confrontation in mortal combat. Lorenzo suspects Hieronimo of knowing the truth and succeeds in barring his access to the King, thus forcing him to plan his own wild form of justice for want of a legal procedure. In *Hamlet*, Claudius' failure to have Hamlet put to death in England gives the Prince yet another reason to execute his long-planned revenge. A comparison between the two plays reveals their similitudes and differences. In the second half of *The Spanish Tragedy*, the emphasis is definitely on Hieronimo's diabolical ingenuity in framing a stratagem designed to compensate for his inability to have recourse to regular justice. In *Hamlet*, in which Claudius contrives a second plot against Hamlet's life, this time with the help of Laertes, the emphasis is on Hamlet's relative 'innocence' (at least as regards Claudius himself, since Hamlet has mistakenly killed Laertes' father) and on the King's ingrained Machiavellianism. We remember Hieronimo as a cruelly hurt and frustrated father, whom grief drives to madness and inhumanity. We remember Hamlet as an equally hurt son, quite as much determined to avenge himself, but in a way that does not impair his mental balance and moral integrity. Claudius recognizes in him the quality he lacks most: 'most generous and free from all contriving' (IV, vii, 134). As a murderer through blunder and an avenger through filial obligation, Hamlet does honour to his humanity. Aided by circumstance and sustained by his deep-seated disgust at having to play the detested part of an executioner, Hamlet eventually, almost accidentally, takes his revenge without tainting his soul in some base ambush. Despite this noteworthy difference, which contributes not a little to Shakespeare's highly original treatment of the revenge motif, the denouement of both plays conforms to tradition: the avengers die carrying out their vengeance whilst the guilty are unwitting parties to their own destruction.

In *The Spanish Tragedy*, causality of events is flaunted ostentatiously and regulated with mechanical precision. Andrea has died in combat at the disloyal hands of Balthazar, the Viceroy of Portugal, and his ghost, for this reason, cries out for vengeance; Bel-imperia wants to avenge her

dead lover and considers using the services of Horatio, with whom she
has become enamoured; Lorenzo favours the prospect of having his
sister married to Balthazar and feels deadly jealous of Horatio, who
shares with him the honour of having captured Balthazar on the battlefield; Horatio's murder is therefore the outcome of two vengeances,
Balthazar's and Lorenzo's, and the murder itself is the trigger of
Hieronimo's vengeance, spurred on by the suicide of his wife. In *Hamlet*,
chain reaction is also to be found, as befits the genre. Hamlet's need to
obtain evidence more palpable than the Ghost's allegations, and to carry
out his investigation without being suspected, accounts for his strategy of
feigned madness and, in turn, determines, at least partially, the break
with Ophelia. But Ophelia's undiscriminating obedience to her father,
together with Hamlet's disgust at his mother's hasty remarriage, play
their role as secondary causes. In *Hamlet*, causality is not dependent on
purely practical necessities. The character's idiosyncrasies and circumstances adjacent to the main plot are determining factors. For example,
the play-within-the-play initiated by Hamlet and Polonius' accidental
murder feed the King's suspicion; but Gertrude's love for her son,
Claudius' love for Gertrude and the people's love for Hamlet force the
King to plot Hamlet's death outside Denmark. Another consequence of
Polonius' murder and Ophelia's ensuing madness is Laertes' legitimate
desire for vengeance. However, his innate rashness and moral deficiency
demote him from the status of an avenging redresser of wrongs to that of
a revengeful accomplice to Claudius, committing him to an act of foul
play.

When the time comes for Shakespeare to unravel the play's complicated plot, he stages a pattern of retribution as neat and faultless as that
of *The Spanish Tragedy*. It befits the laws of the genre and the demands of
poetic justice that Hamlet should kill the King, guilty of having poisoned
Hamlet's father intentionally and his mother accidentally. Similarly,
Laertes kills Hamlet, guilty of having accidentally killed Polonius and
indirectly caused Ophelia's death. The Queen, guilty of incest through
her second marriage, dies at the hands of the man who is partly responsible for her sin, and Laertes, guilty of having betrayed Hamlet's trust by
joining forces with the play's villain, dies at the hands of his former
friend.

In addition to the firm and cogent structuring of the revenge story,
recurrent scenes in the same vein tie up the episodes into a coherent
whole and help the audience to keep their bearings. Hamlet's soliloquies
are a case in point. The spectators await and expect them almost at

regular intervals as privileged opportunities for them to deepen their relationship with the hero. When they disappear at the end of Act IV, they are replaced by dialogues between Hamlet and Horatio which fulfil the same purpose. Thematic similitudes have been noted between the four important monologues distributed throughout the play according to a chiasmic pattern: the first ('O that this too too sullied flesh'), in I, ii, and the third ('To be or not to be'), in III, i, are concerned with melancholy and suicide; the second ('O what a rogue and peasant slave am I'), in II, ii, and the fourth ('How all occasions do inform against me'), in IV, iv, are devoted more specifically to Hamlet's sense of guilt at his own inaction. At the other end of the spectrum in terms of stage occupation, there are three collective scenes placed equidistantly in the play and showing Hamlet confronting the whole court of Elsinore at strategic moments: Act I, scene ii, sketches the nature of the relationships between uncle, mother and son, the protagonists of the family triangle; Act III, scene ii, establishes Claudius' guilt, at least in the mind of Hamlet, through the stratagem of the 'Mousetrap', and Act V, scene ii, witnesses Hamlet's revenge and the general retribution through the final duel. These are public scenes, largely ceremonial in tone, counterbalancing and off-setting private sequences located in the more confined spaces of the palace, during which passions are given freer rein. Such public scenes, while exemplifying the spurious majesty of Claudius' court, mark out the trajectory of the main plot by periodically summoning to a central area the characters engaged in momentarily scattered actions.

But Shakespeare's technique of variation upon a theme within a controlled pattern of change and continuity is best shown in the handling of Hamlet's feigned madness. I shall not trace its development through the whole play, but content myself with the sequence comprising, say, the cellarage scene (I, v) and the nunnery scene (III, i). In the cellarage scene, following Hamlet's first encounter with the ghost, he formally acquaints Horatio and Marcellus with his decision 'to put an antic disposition on', as occasion requires; but he does so after having first perplexed his companions with 'wild and whirling words', as if he wished to try out on them a sample of his future feigning, or as if the idea of mock madness was itself consequent upon an actual, if transient, eclipse of reason owing to the emotional shock he has just undergone. Shortly after the beginning of Act II, Ophelia informs her father of Hamlet's strange behaviour towards her in a piece of vivid description placing Hamlet's 'ecstasy' in the context of their love relationship. The next scene shows that Hamlet's 'transformation' has become public knowledge, causing enough disquiet in Claudius and Gertrude to make them call for an immediate investigation, an espionage mission entrusted to the officious care of Rosencrantz and Guildenstern. Then, in a speech parallel to Ophelia's narration, but now spoken by Polonius, Hamlet's mental derangement is publicly diagnosed as frustration in love. With Hamlet's reappearance on stage in the course of this long scene (II, ii), and through his mad but 'pregnant' words to Polonius, the conventional image of the lunatic lover is soon superseded by the equally conventional image of the court jester, a hitherto unexplored manifestation of Hamlet's antics. Once he is left alone with the King's informers, Hamlet sheds his guise of madness, soon to take it up again when Polonius returns, this time assuming the expected pose of the despairing lover, as if to confirm the old man's diagnosis and further justify the need for a confrontation with Ophelia. Prior to the nunnery scene, which is designed partly to offer a live representation of Hamlet's madness after it has been prefigured through Ophelia's previous narration, Rosencrantz and Guildenstern are shown reporting to the sovereigns on their mission (III, i), but far from clearing up the enigma of Hamlet's conduct, they make it even more opaque by substantiating both the hypothesis of genuine confusion and that of 'crafty madness':

> ROS.   He does confess he feels himself distracted,
>   But from what cause a will by no means speak.
> GUILD. Nor do we find him forward to be sounded,
>   But with a crafty madness keeps aloof
>   When we would bring him on to some confession
>   Of his true state.
>
> III, i, 5–10

Thus, in the context of court and state affairs, we see emerging anew an image of Hamlet's ambiguous madness, one that had been glimpsed only fleetingly in the context of Hamlet's companionship with Horatio and Marcellus during the cellarage scene, and then abandoned. Finally, in the nunnery scene at the close of our sequence, the very same suggestion of ambiguity is taken up again, to receive yet another contextualization and to be poignantly dramatized as Hamlet casts, or feigns to cast, upon Ophelia and woman in general the real disgust he feels for his own mother.

Sketchy and incomplete as it is, since the theme of madness extends far beyond Act III, scene i, this survey demonstrates how very carefully Shakespeare establishes, at all stages, the various registers on which Hamlet's simulation, or pseudo-simulation, operates and the various circumstances attendant upon its manifestations. This goes to confirm Jenkins' appreciation of the play's total coherence. Nothing could be further from the truth than to see in *Hamlet* signs of disorder or care-lessness. It is precisely because Shakespeare knew what he was heading for, within the received pattern of the revenge tragedy, that he could afford to take perhaps the longest way round to the expected denoue-ment. Sureness of direction allows for leisurely wandering in the course of the journey. If there is Mannerism in *Hamlet*, it is to be found in the alliance of true logic and apparent whimsicality, in an aesthetics of cal-culated negligence, reminiscent of Montaigne's *Essays* or possibly of Castiglione's *sprezzatura* applied to the art of play-making.

DEFLECTION

By punctuating the story-line with episodes of madness, Shakespeare reassuringly keeps his audience aware of one of the play's major themes. But by submitting madness to such a diversity of viewpoints, he also creates an impression of surprise that may at times verge on puzzlement. Watching or reading *Hamlet* for the first time, one is liable to feel that variety and variation somehow obscure the play's unity of purpose and sense of direction. A spectator or reader of *Hamlet*, immersed in an unin-terrupted flow of signs, finds some of them difficult to decipher; and when taken up by the pleasure of successive discoveries, any prolifera-tion of side episodes or overemphasis on detail may blur the general outline of the plot, however coherent and apparent it may seem to anyone who can take a bird's-eye view of the play.

In *Hamlet*, the axes of theme and plot converge on the hero's final revenge. But whereas Kyd signals the unravelling of the plot from afar and, as the action proceeds, closes the side-doors until *only* one exit remains, Shakespeare is much less directive. He opens lateral perspec-tives, thereby uncovering unexpected viewpoints, as it were 'amusing' the audience with a magnified detail, so that we momentarily lose sight of the vanishing-point towards which we are slowly but surely progress-ing without yet knowing the way or the distance. Montaigne does the same. The ultimate goal of his meandering, he warns us, is a better knowledge of the human self, but what wanderings and ramblings it takes to approach this ever-receding horizon! With Montaigne and Shakespeare, one must often consent to waste one's time – or, rather, to take one's time – and believe that a detour is preferable to a straight route. Polonius teaches Reynaldo, whom he is sending to Paris to keep an eye on Laertes, the art of spreading false rumours to know the truth, a well-known police method. There is no doubt some whiff of Mannerism in this strategy, expounded in deliberately metaphorical language as if to allow the description to apply equally to the Mannerist artist and diplomat:

> And thus do we of wisdom and of reach,
> With windlasses and with assays of bias,
> By indirections find directions out.
>   ii, i, 64–6

Eventually Hamlet avenges himself and is killed, but what itinerary are we to take to reach this destination? We *know* that Shakespeare has mapped it out for us, but we do not always see what lies ahead. The play's visibility is low. Montaigne, Shakespeare and most Mannerist artists favour a certain degree of myopia in the spectator/reader, with our eye on the captivating detail rather than on the whole that we take in only from a distance. A particular gesture may be drawn with graphic precision and endowed with considerable dramatic power at the very moment it is performed and yet receive little or no intelligibility from its immediate context. It is as if Mannerist art strove to occult the processes and progressions, the whys and wherefores, to confront us with a naked gesture, motiveless in appearance, seemingly untimely or gratuitous: the curiously tense hand of a Florentine aristocrat portrayed by Bronzino; the curiously limp hand of the personage who should be holding the body of Christ in Rosso's *Deposition*; Hamlet's hysterical hilarity in the cellarage scene – Mannerism is unsurpassed in slackening the link between sign and referent, thereby extolling the sign that has become an end in itself, an object of curiosity, the emblematic figure of the world's arbitrariness.

The technique used by Shakespeare to produce this kind of effect has been well studied in Susan Snyder's *The Comic Matrix of Shakespeare's Tragedy*.[6] The optical concept of 'deflection' serves to define a method whereby discontinuity is introduced into a given sequence to create a hiatus between cause and effect, beginning and completion. Thus duration is splintered into a succession of instants and instantaneousness enhanced at the expense of the passing of time. Snyder compares two series of events situated between Act ii, scene ii, and Act iii, scene i. The first series is taken from the First Quarto, which is presumably a memorial transcription of a performance, whilst the other comes from the Second Quarto and the First Folio, which are supposed to be closer to the original text. What emerges from the comparison is that the order of the episodes in the First Quarto respects the logic of the narrative, as this is what the mind memorizes most easily. On the other hand, in the Second Quarto and First Folio the order of succession is split in an unnatural manner, as if Shakespeare had set up 'deflectors' in certain places in order to prevent incipient action from developing and ending normally. In the First Quarto, Polonius' announcement that he has smelled out the cause of Hamlet's madness, and his plan to eavesdrop, together with the King, on Hamlet and Ophelia are quite naturally followed by the nunnery scene fittingly introduced by Hamlet's soliloquy 'To be or not to be'. Succeeding these two consecutive episodes is another homogeneous narrative cluster of several episodes: Rosencrantz and Guildenstern investigating Hamlet's madness; Hamlet's welcome to the strolling players, still in the presence of the King's informers; his idea of the 'Mousetrap'; the informers' report to the King and their announcement that Hamlet intends to have a play acted before the court, and finally the performance of 'The Murder of Gonzago'.

Turning now to the Second Quarto and Folio versions, one is faced with a more sophisticated, not to say Manneristic, method of storytelling. The sequence opens with the King's project to have Hamlet spied upon, but at this point a deflector diverts the action from its expected course to introduce Polonius expounding his own theory and tactics. But then another deflector postpones the implementation of Polonius' scheme until Rosencrantz and Guildenstern are back from their unsuccessful mission of espionage. The action is further deflected when the long-expected encounter between Hamlet and Ophelia (the nunnery scene) is inserted between the announcement of the forthcoming play and its actual performance.

On a larger scale, it is the same technique of deflection which, in my view, accounts for the intermittent incursions into the domestic and – at the beginning at least – basically comic world of the Polonius family. Though there is nothing particularly Mannerist about this regular alternation of scenes, motivated by a need for comic relief and ironic counterpointing, the fact remains that if one considers dramatic action outside the thematic kinship of the two plot-lines, one is struck by the non-pertinence of the Polonius family episodes to the central tragic motif. It is the death of the father, not the break-up, however cruel, between Hamlet and Ophelia, that casts brother and sister into Hamlet's tragic orbit. By heedlessly adventuring outside the comic space where he belongs, and then meeting his death at the Prince's hands, Polonius precipitates Laertes and Ophelia into the vortex of the tragedy. Until this gory error occurs, the Polonius sequence, however thematically relevant, appears to be little more than a diversion from the play's main line of action.

The hero's exile for two-thirds of Act v is an act of deflection of comparable magnitude, allowing the sub-plot to migrate into the central zone of the tragedy. In the absence of Hamlet, who is the play's principal avenger, Shakespeare engineers a mechanism putting Laertes in the position of second avenger; this is effected through Ophelia's madness and subsequent death, Laertes' return home and his complicity with Claudius. Two letters precede Hamlet's reappearance, one to Horatio, relating the boarding of the pirate ship and promising more sensational news, and one to Claudius, informing him that Hamlet has landed on the Danish coast. Yet, on his way to the court of Elsinore, Hamlet stops off at the graveyard and there, instead of the expected seafaring tale, we are treated to a philosophical meditation on death, the Grand Leveller, and the vanity of earthly things. It is only after Ophelia's burial and the scuffle around her grave between Hamlet and Laertes that Hamlet, at long last, reveals what happened at sea in a conversation with Horatio.

The above remarks help us to grasp what is meant by 'low visibility'. In *Julius Caesar* the segmentation of characters precludes all judgement on them other than fragmented and provisional assessment. In *Hamlet* another form of dramatic coquetry consists in using certain situations from sequence A as deflecting screens interposed between other situations in sequence B, a technique that obstructs our vision of what looms ahead, thereby arousing in the mind of a frustrated audience a sense of suspense and a compulsion to speculate on what lies behind the screen. In true Mannerist fashion, this device tends to diffract attention from Hamlet's revenge, the official centre of interest, to peripheral but more intensely captivating motifs.

But the most efficient agent of deflection is none other than Hamlet himself. Of all his roles, that of deflector is perhaps his most constant. In traditional plays of revenge, avenging oneself does not consist of killing one's enemy by accident or at the last resort, but in patiently and adroitly concocting one's revenge, often with the consummate expertise of an artist. Hieronimo, Barabas and Vindice exult in their hour of triumph. At the conclusion of John Webster's *White Devil*, Lodovico stands back and contemplates his work with the proud contentment of a painter – a tenebrist – laying down his brushes: 'I limb'd this night piece and it was

my best'. There is nothing like this in *Hamlet*. Not that our avenger is
incapable of plotting successfully: he has 'The Murder of Gonzago' performed before the court, thereby catching the conscience of the King,
and he forges a document to send his two seafaring companions to their
deaths in England. But, in the first case, Hamlet wants to know the truth,
whilst, in the second, he wants to save his life. Never does it occur to him
that he might obtain his revenge by trickery. In one of his self-accusing
monologues, Hamlet, who takes such extreme pleasure in exercising his
brains, reproaches himself for leaving his reason inactive:

> Sure he that made us with such large discourse,
> Looking before and after, gave us not
> That capability and godlike reason
> To fust in us unus'd.

IV, iv, 36–9

But at the very moment when he seems to behave like all the avengers
in the repertory, crying out, 'About, my brains' (II, ii, 584), which should
trigger the plotting of his revenge, he is struck with paralysis. That which
Hamlet is capable of doing when actuated by the need to discover the
truth or save his life, he is incapable of when he has to muster patience
and method to organize the death of his enemy. The elimination of
Rosencrantz and Guildenstern is proof enough that Hamlet does not
leave his reason 'unus'd' for long, but through an ironic displacement –
another case of deflection – his easy-won success with mere executants
amplifies his incapacity to strike at the head. Hamlet offers two contradictory explanations for his inhibition: 'bestial oblivion', which abolishes
thought and, on the other hand, an over-niceness in exercising thought:
'some craven scruple/Of thinking too precisely on th'event'. But his
actual conduct points to the contrary: not only does he not forget, but he
can, on certain occasions, put in enough thinking to prove an efficient
schemer. At no moment does he question the moral validity of
vengeance, nor does he feel squeamish about performing it; but rather
he wants it entire, destructive of body *and* soul (III, iii, 93–5). But Hamlet
knows that vengeance conceived as a methodically planned action
monopolizes thought in the service of this one cause. He knows that a
responsible avenger must consent to be single-minded, a monomaniac,
and this is too much to ask of Hamlet, the humanist, the man of the
world, the fine flower of the nobility of heart and mind. He is, *par excellence*, a man of shifting ideas, of alert awareness perpetually solicited by
the diversity of the world. How could he possibly renounce world-

embracing thought and the society of his fellow men where thought is
constantly refreshed? No obligation, however sacred, can be worth sacrificing the restless vigilance of a searching mind; no cause can justify the
mutilation of the spirit. It is not for want of temptation, but Hamlet
holds fast. Here perhaps resides the special heroism of the Mannerist
hero: preserving, at all costs, a maximum receptivity to the stimuli of
material and spiritual experience.

Before encountering his father's ghost, Hamlet has two obsessions:
disgust at the world, generated by disgust at his mother, and a suicidal
tendency. What vision of things could be simpler and more attractive
than one of universal and irredeemable corruption?

> O that this too too sullied flesh would melt,
> Thaw and resolve itself into a dew,
> Or that the Everlasting had not fix'd
> His canon 'gainst self-slaughter. O God! God!
> How weary, stale, flat, and unprofitable
> Seem to me all the uses of this world!
> Fie on't, ah fie, 'tis an unweeded garden
> That grows to seed; things rank and gross in nature
> Possess it merely.
>
> I, ii, 129–37

Structurally, setting aside content, Hamlet's frame of mind recalls that
of the traditional avenger, possessed with the all-absorbing idea that
vengeance is all, even at the cost of death. At this stage of his immaturity
and inner unawareness, Hamlet's first impulse following the Ghost's revelations is, typically, to inflict upon himself a type of brainwashing in
order to eliminate all trace of past (and henceforth useless) experience
and rid thought of all the clutter of debris in order to make room for the
Idea of Vengeance in sovereign purity:

> I'll wipe away all trivial fond records,
> All saws of books, all forms, all pressures past
> That youth and observation copied there,
> And thy commandment all alone shall live
> Within the book and volume of my brain,
> Unmix'd with baser matter.
>
> I, v, 99–104

It is as if Hamlet is now tempted into the suicide of consciousness in
order, he thinks, to be worthy of the task awaiting him. But nothing is
more adverse to his nature than maiming the integrity of his consciousness, as the remainder of the monologue reveals. Like a model scholar,

Hamlet has brought his writing 'tables' with him, but to record what? Some exhortation to act, some practical detail to remember? By no means. Merely a maxim of the kind he has just repudiated, stating that one may smile and be a villain. At the height of avenging exaltation and against his resolution of a second before, Hamlet cannot resist an aphorism (a banal one, but there is a beginning to everything) on being and seeming. This digression has a precedent; when Gertrude reproaches her son for 'seeming' to refuse the law whereby 'everything which lives must die', he answers by evading the point, as if to corner her on her unfortunate choice of the verb 'to seem': 'Seems, madam? Nay it is. I know not "seems"' (I, ii, 76); whereupon Hamlet's art of irrelevance occasions a speech on the deceptiveness of appearance:

> 'Tis not alone my inky cloak, good mother,
> Nor customary suits of solemn black,
> Nor windy suspiration of forc'd breath,
> No, nor the fruitful river in the eye,
> Nor the dejected haviour of the visage,
> Together with all forms, modes, shapes of grief,
> That can denote me truly.
>
> I, ii, 77–83

It becomes easier now to see how Hamlet's mind works. If it is true that awareness is necessarily predicative of something, in Hamlet this something is always manifold and multiform. Although disqualified as an efficient avenger, he is qualified as a thinker and metaphysical poet because of his ability 'to live in divided and distinguished worlds and to pass freely to and fro between one and another, to be capable of many and varied responses to experience, instead of being confined to a few stereotyped ones'.[7] It is the irresistible emergence of different viewpoints in Hamlet's consciousness which accounts for his bifurcations of thought and behaviour. It may well be that Hamlet's 'double awareness', as Snyder aptly calls it, proceeds from a mode of thought attentive to and critical of its own functioning. It is the double awareness of a dual personality in the grips of the most passionate and peremptory conviction:

> Bloody, bawdy villain!
> Remorseless, treacherous, lecherous, kindless villain!
>
> II, ii, 576–7

Yet it is a conviction fated to be superseded a few seconds later by the recognition that this 'certainty' based on the testimony of a ghost of dubious nature might be unfounded:

> The spirit that I have seen
> May be a devil.
>
> II, ii, 594–5

But the victories of a lucid and self-questioning mind are not secured once and for all. At the end of the long second scene of Act III, Hamlet is jubilant because the 'Mousetrap' has worked perfectly and the little parable in action (the recorders' scene) which he has concocted for Rosencrantz and Guildenstern has brought it home to the two spies that surveillance must cease. Hamlet exults at having unmasked his enemies. But why must this jubilation resound with the savage and ghoulish tones that accompany the most frenzied imprecations of villains?

> 'Tis now the very witching time of night
> When churchyards yawn and hell itself breathes out
> Contagion to this world. Now could I drink hot blood,
> And do such bitter business as the day
> Would quake to look on.
>
> III, ii, 379–83

Passion has overcome reason. But when, in the following scene, Hamlet chances upon Claudius kneeling at prayer and so could quench his blood-lust, reason returns in strength, not to neutralize violence but to keep it in store for a better occasion when it will be utterly destructive:

> Up, sword, and know thou a more horrid hent:
> When he is drunk asleep, or in his rage,
> Or in th'incestuous pleasure of his bed,
> At game a-swearing, or about some act
> That has no relish of salvation in't.
>
> III, iii, 88–92

Passion still prevails but supported by a surfeit of reasoning, a perverted exercise of the reason which presumptuously and almost impiously casts its calculations into the hereafter. Wishing to act for eternity, Hamlet does nothing and blinds himself to the demand and meaning of the present moment, as if he were oblivious of his wonted lucidity which had enabled him to distinguish so punctiliously between appearance and reality. It does not even occur to him that Claudius kneeling may not be Claudius praying, even less Claudius in a state of grace, as evidenced by the concluding couplet of the King's confession:

> My words fly up, my thoughts remain below.
> Words without thoughts never to heaven go.
>
> III, iii, 97–8

It is no mean stroke of irony to have the 'words without thoughts' of the unrepentant murderer equal in inefficacy the over-thoughtful words of the avenger.

When, in the next scene, Hamlet thrusts his rapier into the arras and Polonius' body, he appears to have lost his head. After surfeit comes dearth of thought. Not so long before, Hamlet was assuming the prerogatives of God, pronouncing upon the salvation or the damnation of souls; a moment later, he is plunging recklessly into irresponsibility and we see him become the play's second murderer, after Claudius. After a missed opportunity comes a blunder: 'I took thee for thy better' (III, iv, 32).

So within a short period of time, Hamlet goes through three different states, each marked by an eclipse of reason. He yields in succession to passion, ratiocination and then pure reflex. These sudden and fleeting changes of direction delineate a zigzagging course, which could be seen as the theatrical equivalent of the *contrapposto* which gives Mannerist figures their characteristic contortions. The apostrophizing attendant upon Polonius' murder – 'How now? A rat! Dead for a ducat, dead' (III, iv, 22) – recalls the wild words in the cellarage scene, 'Well said, old mole, canst work i'th'earth so fast?' (I, v, 170), with similar animal imagery, nervous outbursts and grotesque gesticulation.

In the eighteenth century, an era of reason and sentiment alien to the aesthetics and spirit of Mannerism, audiences laughed at Hamlet's madness as a clever hoax practised on his entourage, while the Romantic era no longer dared to bank so unreservedly on Hamlet's mental health and tended to clothe the pensive Prince in the garb of the tenebrous 'poète maudit' whose sombre, enigmatic genius often courted insanity. Glancing back to Robert Burton's view that 'Folly, melancholy, madness are but one disease',[8] and having renewed acquaintance with Mannerism, we may now regard Shakespeare's portrayal of Hamlet's 'madness' as a masterly cultivation of ambiguity. Let us examine the very first words that Hamlet addresses to the King, prior to his decision to feign madness:

> KING But now, my cousin Hamlet, and my son –
> HAM A little more than kin, and less than kind.
> KING How is it that the clouds still hang on you?
> HAM. Not so, my Lord, I am too much in the sun.
>
> I, ii, 64–7

They are barely distinguishable from this other retort to the King, which we know from Hamlet himself to be intentionally 'mad':

> HAM. They are coming to the play, I must be idle.
>   Get you a place.
>
> Enter King, Queen, Polonius, Ophelia, Rosencrantz,
> Guildenstern, and other Lords attendant, with the King's Guard
> carrying torches.
>
> KING How fares our cousin Hamlet?
> HAM. Excellent, i'faith, of the chameleon's dish. I eat the air,
>   promise-crammed. You cannot feed capons so.
>
> III, ii, 90–4

From Aristotle to Tesauro, through Marsile Ficino, Giordano Bruno and Robert Burton himself, it is agreed that madmen are especially gifted in the use of metaphors, word-plays and paradoxes, since, like poets, they can glimpse into the secret kinship of disparate objects.

When Hamlet apologizes to Laertes for his conduct at Ophelia's funeral, he pleads madness:

> What I have done
> That might your nature, honour and exception
> Roughly awake, I here proclaim was madness.
>
> V, ii, 226–8

Here madness is no contrivance, but a lapse into self-forgetfulness triggered by Laertes' immodest display of grief:

> But I am very sorry, good Horatio,
> That to Laertes I forgot myself.
>
> V, ii, 75–6

To Hamlet, to be mad is to be beside oneself, but to Laertes, the King and the Queen, who have been witnesses to another form of madness, Hamlet's behaviour inevitably points to true insanity. Hamlet's madness, which Shakespeare continues to exploit up to the very end (see Hamlet's whirling words to Osric before the duel) is fraught with the most intriguing ambivalence: without any doubt a disguise, but also a natural disposition, a psychic response consecutive to an initial trauma and perhaps a self-imposed, if precarious, adjustment to an unbearable environment. Whatever it is, Hamlet's madness reveals the working of the Mannerist technique of deflection. Imperceptibly, one form of madness drifts into another. The rationale of disguise is lost sight of, so that the audience are increasingly confronted with a seemingly gratuitous and 'disinterested' madness. It is as if madness, originally conceived as part of a strategy of deception, was pursuing a life of its own, almost deprived of relevance to action, to become a curiosity in its own right, designed to arouse perplexity at the expense of other sources of interest.

Before *Hamlet*, madness on stage was either feigned or real, and the two conditions could coexist but never be confused within the same play, as in *Titus Andronicus*. With *Hamlet*, madness becomes problematic. Starting from an initially simple and popular motif which he found in such works as *Orlando Furioso*, *The Spanish Tragedy* or *Tamburlaine the Great*, Shakespeare reworked it into an enigma open to the speculation of a questioning audience. Rosso had done something of the same when taking the canonical motif of the dead body of Christ as a pretext for research into the erotic potentialities of the male figure, yet without denying the sacredness of the subject or sacrificing the conventions of traditional iconography. The price to be paid for the intellectual sophistication of Mannerist theatre is a diminishing of its emotional potential. Hamlet himself is too equivocal a character, too disturbingly intriguing, to be as deeply moving as other Shakespearian characters of comparable magnitude. Even more than the fragmented figure of Caesar, Hamlet sheds light on the futility of attempting to achieve a full grasp of a Mannerist character, and this is all the more frustrating for the audience as no other figure has been or was to be so fully hyperbolized as Hamlet. Inevitably, for many critics and spectators, the Prince has often seemed to overshadow the Poem, and it is true that, however rich and varied the play-world may be, it looks shrunken and stale compared with Hamlet's inner world over which he reigns as 'a king of infinite spaces'. Despite his physical frailty, Hamlet recalls those Michelangelesque figures whose repressed strength is squeezed into a constricted space. Careful as we should be not to hypostatize the hero, we cannot help feeling that Hamlet, as a dramatis persona, has been so designed as to fill the void left by the off-centring of revenge, in an attempt to recentre the play around the eponymous figure.

REFLECTION

Deflection of interest from plot mechanisms results, though indirectly, in an over-focusing on the character of Hamlet, more on what he is than on what he does. But Shakespeare goes one step further: to complement the Mannerist process of deflection, he deploys another technique whereby reflecting mirrors, artfully placed around the central figure, produce a hyperbolic image of the hero. These 'reflectors' are situated in Hamlet's entourage, characters that enhance him as an exceptional individual by means of a set of contrasts and similitudes; contrasts with the negative images that such characters as Polonius, Rosencrantz, Guildenstern or Osric project of themselves and contrasts-plus-similitudes with the mixed images deriving from other characters like Horatio, Fortinbras and Laertes.

But before discussing this other aspect of Shakespeare's optical strategy, I must pause and observe that, even before Hamlet's singularity finds expression through his relations with the other characters in the play, it is inscribed, as it were, in his genetic heritage. At the centre of the father-mother-uncle triangle, Hamlet is endowed with traits that make him the most composite and thoroughly human creation in the play. Hamlet twice compares his father to Hyperion (I, ii, 140; III, iv, 56) and, through lavish mythological references, he likens him to a god:

> See what a grace was seated on this brow,
> Hyperion's curls, the front of Jove himself,
> An eye like Mars to threaten and command
> A station like the herald Mercury
> New-lighted on a heaven-kissing hill,
> A combination and a form indeed
> Where every god did seem to set his seal
> To give the world assurance of a man.
> III, iv, 55–62

And yet the human nature of the dead father is not overlooked: 'A was a man, take him for all in all' (I, ii, 187). By virtue of his divinity, his sire could direct the winds of heaven not to visit his Queen's face too roughly. But his all-too-human failings are also amply demonstrated: the Ghost speaks of 'foul crimes done in my days of nature' (I, v, 12), and Hamlet himself recalls in what conditions death came upon him: 'grossly, full of bread/With all his crimes broad blown, as flush as May' (III, iii, 80–81).

Opposite this half-godlike, half-human creature stands another double, Claudius, half-man and half-beast, whose dual nature is reflected in the hallmarking image of the satyr (I, ii, 140). Taken together, the two brother kings reconstitute the mythical wholeness of man, partaking of divinity and animality. As for Gertrude, Hamlet's mother and old Hamlet's 'most seeming virtuous queen', who passes so easily from Hyperion to a satyr, thus falling from empyrean heights to a 'nasty sty', she embodies, as it were dynamically, the contiguousness of love and lust. It is no surprise therefore that Hamlet, who was born from 'lust, though to a radiant angel link'd' (I, v, 55), should articulate and epitomize the paradox of man's nature, 'in apprehension how like a god', but 'the paragon of animals' (II, ii, 306–7), beset at times by beastliness 'If his

chief good and market of his time/Be but to sleep and feed' (IV, iv, 34–5).
Thus burdened from birth with the ambivalence of the human condition, Hamlet feels entitled to speak on behalf of mankind, which he does
more unreservedly than any other Shakespearian character. But on the
other hand, Hamlet has a painful sense of his election to an accursed and
formidable mission which isolates him from his fellow men:

> The time is out of joint. O cursed spite
> That ever I was born to set it right.
>
> I, v, 196–7

The paradox is that Hamlet is closer in affinity to the Elsinore of after
the crime (after the Fall), with its subtleties and opaqueness, than to the
prelapsarian Elsinore of his father, in which simplicity and transparency
prevailed. He feels nostalgia for the absolute, but thrives upon the contingency of modern times. His 'duplicity' is all the more striking as, with
the possible exception of his own family, he is surrounded by compara-
tively simple reflectors.

Polonius and Osric are among the simplest of all. Polonius shares with
Hamlet a university education and a taste for words and theatre. But
whereas Hamlet displays a refreshingly inventive and searching mind,
Polonius is entangled in manic and verbose pedantry and exemplifies the
fossilizing effects attendant upon a fixed idea. But Shakespeare is more
subtle here than might appear at first sight. Polonius is not infallible, and
this gives greater credibility to his character. To Ophelia, he acknowl-
edges that what he has mistaken for the wayward flirting of a fickle
prince is heartfelt passion:

> I am sorry that with better heed and judgement
> I had not quoted him. I fear'd he did but trifle
> And meant to wrack thee.
>
> II, i, 111–13

Yet to someone like Polonius, who must needs cling to some certainty, it is
unthinkable to be mistaken twice. Polonius has by now exhausted his
capacity for change and error and, against all comers, he remains comically obstinate in his interpretation of Hamlet's madness:

> But yet, do I believe
> The origin and commencement of his grief
> Sprung from neglected love.
>
> III, i, 178–80

As for Osric, who would not be out of place in a Jonson or Middleton
comedy, he summarizes the degeneracy of manners at the court of

Claudius. Under the late King, it was Hamlet himself, Ophelia laments, who embodied the complete gentleman:

> The courtier's, soldier's, scholar's, eye, tongue, sword,
> Th'expectancy and rose of the fair state,
> The glass of fashion and the mould of form,
> Th'observ'd of all observers, quite, quite down!
>
> III, i, 153–6

The calibre of Osric is all that Claudius' court can afford: and why should it be otherwise when Polonius is seen as the acme of moral and political wisdom and Rosencrantz and Guildenstern are entrusted with the service of the State?

Among these characters enhancing Hamlet's moral and intellectual superiority through an exhibition of their own mediocrity, Rosencrantz and Guildenstern are situated half-way between the comic duo of Polonius and Osric and the serious triad of Horatio, Laertes and Fortinbras. In some respects, these birds of a feather belong to the comic side of Elsinore, and no sensible director would fail to bring out the humour latent in two of the play's most memorable lines:

> KING.   Thanks, Rosencrantz and gentle Guildenstern.
> QUEEN. Thanks, Guildenstern and gentle Rosencrantz.
>
> II, ii, 33–4

It should be noted, however, how insistently Shakespeare underlines the comradeship uniting Hamlet and his old schoolmates, and the warm welcome he gives them:

> My excellent good friends. How dost thou,
> Guildenstern? Ah, Rosencrantz. Good lads, how do you both?
>
> II, ii, 224–6

At this point, the image of Hamlet conveyed by such greetings is that of a young man ready to give himself up to simple, spontaneous and undissembling joy. To the King's informers, however, this expression of pleasure is tainted with calculation, as appears from the somewhat dour tone of their answer, 'As the indifferent children of the earth'. A little later, when Hamlet suspects that they have been sent to spy on him, he fervently appeals to their sense of mutual trust:

> But let me conjure you,
> by the rights of our fellowship, by the consonancy of
> our youth, by the obligation of our ever-preserved
> love, and by what more dear a better proposer

can charge you withal, be even and direct with me
whether you were sent for or no.

II, ii, 283–8

When at last the pair reluctantly own up, Hamlet charitably spares them
the humiliation of having to disclose the reasons behind their mission. It
is interesting at this stage to note how Shakespeare seems to toy with the
suggestion that friendship could still be possible, were they to renounce
their role as spies. The playwright often lingers in like manner on critical
moments or crossroads, when a mere word or gesture would suffice to tip
the scales decisively, as he knows that the pleasure of tragedy owes something to our regret at foolishly and irremediably lost opportunities. It is
perhaps a token of Hamlet's youthful idealism that he can imagine his
companions capable of living up to his own sense of friendship. Fealty to
the impulses of the heart rather than to the demands of service is rather
more than can be hoped for from docile, almost faceless servants of the
State. With its over-studied imagery, Rosencrantz's tirade to the King,
following the recorders' scene, sounds like a recital by rote from the royal
catechism:

> The cess of majesty
> Dies not alone, but like a gulf doth draw
> What's near with it. Or it is a massy wheel
> Fix'd on the summit of the highest mount,
> To whose huge spokes ten thousand lesser things
> Are mortis'd and adjoin'd, which when it falls,
> Each small annexment, petty consequence,
> Attends the boist'rous ruin.

III, iii, 15–22

Close upon this profession of faith, Claudius is shown ironically tormented by his crime. In sharp contrast with the commonplaces of
rhetoric, there is Hamlet's painfully urgent demand for a purification of
the body politic. With their mutilating notion of man as a political
animal, Rosencrantz and Guildenstern cannot ascribe Hamlet's melancholy to any other cause than frustrated ambition, to which Hamlet
opposes 'the heart of my mystery' (II, ii, 256), claiming for himself and
for every man the right to secrecy and integrity of the soul. But when the
threats against Hamlet become more pressing, other images file past
before the audience's eyes, ranging from Hamlet's prophetic insight into
the two schoolfellows, 'Whom I will trust as I will adders fang'd' (III, iv,
204–5), to expressions of brutal explicitness:

ROS.   Take you me for a sponge, my lord?
HAM.   Ay, sir, that soaks up the King's countenance,
       his rewards, his authorities.

IV, ii, 13–15

Added to this is Hamlet's customary pose as witty, enigmatic court jester when questioned about Polonius' body:

ROS.   My lord, you must tell us where the body is
       and go with us to the King.
HAM.   The body is with the King, but the King is not
       with the body. The King is a thing –
GUILD. A thing, my lord?
HAM.   Of nothing. Bring me to him.

IV, ii, 24–9

The last allusion to Rosencrantz and Guildenstern, in the course of Hamlet's narration of his sea adventures to Horatio, conveys yet another facet of Hamlet, one of self-assurance and serenity, as far removed from vain cruelty as from cheap sentimentality:

HOR.   So Guildenstern and Rosencrantz go to't.
HAM.   Why, man, they did make love to this employment.
       They are not near my conscience, their defeat
       Does by their own insinuation grow.

V, ii, 56–9

But Hamlet's choice reflectors are understandably the characters to whom he can legitimately be compared. Fortinbras and Laertes belong to the triad of the father-avenging sons. At the beginning of the play, Fortinbras is described as a sort of seditious, undisciplined Hotspur, but the old King of Norway, his uncle, soon brings him back to his senses and turns him into a wholly admirable princely figure. Old Hamlet has defeated the Poles 'on the ice' and Fortinbras is set upon beating them on their own home ground. Hamlet's conscience is pricked when witnessing the gallantry and selfless zeal of Fortinbras, his readiness to risk all when honour is at stake, but once again Shakespeare complicates the issue. At the very moment when Hamlet accuses himself of 'bestial oblivion', a few hints of corrosive irony creep into his eulogy of the rival prince, as if to undermine the validity of the distinction between valour and cowardice:

Examples gross as earth exhort me,
Witness this army of such mass and charge,
Led by a delicate and tender prince,
Whose spirit, with divine ambition puff'd,
Makes mouths at the invisible event,

> Exposing what is mortal and unsure
> To all that fortune, death, and danger dare,
> Even for an eggshell.
>
> IV, iv, 46–53

In a seemingly half-conscious attempt to debunk what he otherwise admires, Hamlet finds unexpected support from the Captain, a hardened soldier, who bluntly admits the futility of certain military conquests:

> Truly to speak, and with no addition,
> We go to gain a little patch of ground
> That hath in it no profit but the name.
> To pay five ducats – five – I would not farm it;
> Nor will it yield to Norway or the Pole
> A ranker rate should it be sold in fee.
>
> IV, iv, 17–22

When Hamlet maintains that 'Rightly to be great' is 'to find quarrel in a straw', there is no reason to assume that he is only paying lip-service to Fortinbras' greatness, but why dwell so insistently, in the closing lines of the monologue, on the price to be paid:

> The imminent death of twenty thousand men
> That, for a fantasy and trick of fame,
> Go to their graves like beds, fight for a plot
> Whereon the numbers cannot try the cause,
> Which is not tomb enough and continent
> To hid the slain?
>
> IV, iv, 60–5

In true Mannerist fashion, two conflicting images of Hamlet, both endowed with equal credibility, are seen to fade into each other, the first featuring Hamlet as a self-humiliating hero *manqué* and the next one revealing him as a lucid debunker of military glory.

On the surface, the play's denouement is straightforward. Hamlet prophesies Fortinbras' accession to the Danish throne and gives him his 'dying voice', and the latter delivers a funeral oration in praise of the dead Prince. But one detail is worthy of attention: Fortinbras is not present at Hamlet's death, which Shakespeare shrouds in majesty and tenderness:

> HOR. Now cracks a noble heart. Good night, sweet prince
> And flights of angels sing thee to thy rest.
>
> V, ii, 364–5

Fortinbras does, however, hear Horatio reel off his account of the events that have shaken Elsinore:

> So shall you hear
> Of carnal, bloody, and unnatural acts,
> Of accidental judgements, casual slaughters,
> Of deaths put on by cunning and forc'd cause,
> And, in this upshot, purposes mistook
> Fall'n on th'inventors heads.
>
> v, ii, 385–90

Not only is the name of Hamlet not quoted, but Horatio's version excludes any possibility of heroism. Yet, somewhat unexpectedly, but with the mute assent of the spectators in the audience, who know what Hamlet was like, Fortinbras does homage to his kingly qualities:

> For he was likely, had he been put on,
> To have prov'd most royal.
>
> v, ii, 402–3

In implicitly recognizing that Hamlet's greatness was of a different nature, though no less estimable than his own, Fortinbras puts the finishing touch to an image outlined well before, that of Hamlet's kingliness. But what are these qualities that would have made Hamlet 'most royal'? Neither Horatio nor Fortinbras is in a position to answer this question, because Hamlet's greatness cannot be measured by their criteria. For this reason, 'The soldiers' music and the rite of war' bestowed on such a noble, yet unwarlike, character are not to be dismissed as a matter of mere decorum or a fitting end to a conventional denouement. Rather they are to be seen as the last stroke of an all-pervasive irony, since such a ceremony was never so well deserved, while at the same time so deeply stamped with derision.

By a curious process of transference, which once again points to Shakespeare's art of variation upon a theme, Laertes inherits Fortinbras' initial disposition and, in addition, the former's squad of rioters has been likened to the latter's gang of outlaws. But less has been made of the fact that Laertes' passionate abjuration of heaven and hell in the name of absolute revenge (IV, v, 131–4), recalls Hamlet's equally foolish, if less impious, desire to wipe his memory clear of all traces of human wisdom (I, v, 96–106). The timing, however, is most significant: by the time Laertes vents his destructive nihilism, Hamlet and Fortinbras have outrun this adolescent stage, so that the very negative image projected by Laertes enhances the positive development undergone by the others. When he becomes Claudius' associate in treachery and murder, the opposition is complete. Yet, paradoxically, Hamlet never feels closer to Laertes than when the distance between them is greatest. Laertes' intensely emotional response to the deaths of his father and sister is something with which Hamlet can sympathize. In Laertes he sees another side of himself, a youthful image of what he has been and might become again if provoked. The physical set-to and verbal exchanges in the confined space of Ophelia's grave translate visually the combined closeness and rivalry in love and grief of the two adversaries. In the next scene, Hamlet twice calls Laertes his brother (v, ii, 239, 249), as if symbolically to cancel out the mishaps which kept them from truly becoming brothers-in-law. So when Laertes, the 'false' brother, mortally wounds Hamlet in the ensuing duel, it is the final re-enactment on a figurative level of the literal fratricide with which the play opens and of its theatrical and deformed version ('The Murder of Gonzago') on which the play hinges. Hamlet is to Laertes what Claudius is to Hamlet, namely the murderer of the father; but Laertes is also to Hamlet what Claudius was to old Hamlet, namely the murderer of the brother, a belated impersonation of Cain. It can be argued that Claudius, by arming Laertes, takes on the main responsibility for the second murder after having assumed full responsibility for the first, and also that Hamlet and Laertes die forgiving each other, thus contravening the biblical image. But a given analogy may be only partially accurate and yet make its intended impact on the audience at the moment when it takes shape. Fortinbras' ambivalent heroism and Laertes' moral decline demonstrate the limits of conduct dictated by passion, whether it is disciplined as in Fortinbras or unbridled as in Laertes. Each of these characters mirrors one aspect of Hamlet's impulsiveness: Hamlet recognizes in them a feeling he has himself experienced, an urge for rashness and thoughtlessness to which it is tempting to yield when the mind's vigilance comes to flag.

The temptation of passion is diametrically opposed to the temptation of prudent rationalism embodied by Horatio. Hamlet may well find him admirable, but the comparison between the two friends always turns to Hamlet's advantage. Horatio is an overcareful deliberator:

> In what particular thought to work I know not,
> But in the gross and scope of my opinion,
> This bodes some strange eruption to our state.
>
> i, i, 70–2

But Hamlet's mind is of more generous proportions; his noble reason can accommodate strangeness and mystery because he knows intuitively that the world cannot be reduced to sheer rationality:

> HOR. O day and night, but this is wondrous strange.
> HAM. And therefore as a stranger give it welcome.
>   There are more things in heaven and earth, Horatio,
>   Than are dreamt of in your philosophy.
>
> I, V, 172–5

Against the wise man's reproach that thinking should not overstep certain boundaries ('Twere to consider too curiously to consider so', v, i, 199), Hamlet claims for himself the right to dream, speculate and allow the imagination to play on the confines of absurdity:

> Alexander
> died, Alexander was buried, Alexander returneth
> to dust, the dust is earth, of earth we make loam and
> why of that loam whereto he was converted might
> they not stop a beer-barrel?
> Imperious Caesar, dead and turn'd to clay,
> Might stop a hole to keep the wind away.
>
> v, i, 201–7

On two critical occasions, before Hamlet encounters the Ghost and before he fights the final duel, Horatio advises his friend to abstain from action; first because he is in danger of being driven mad, and then because of the danger of losing the combat. Horatio's maxim is non-commitment when the issue is uncertain. After the play-within-the-play, he sounds evasive on the subject of Claudius' guilt, leaving Hamlet alone with his belief:

> HAM. O good Horatio, I'll take the ghost's word for a
>   thousand pound. Didst perceive?
> HOR. Very well, my Lord.
> HAM. Upon the talk of the poisoning?
> HOR. I did very well note him.
>
> III, ii, 280–4

After hearing Hamlet's account of the ruse that enabled him to escape unharmed from the trap that Claudius had set him at sea, Horatio once again shies away from the question Hamlet is asking him:

> HAM.   is't not perfect conscience.
>   To quit him with his arm? And is't not to be damn'd
>   To let this canker of our nature come

In further evil?
HOR. It must be shortly known to him from England
What is the issue of the business there.

v, ii, 67–72

Whether on or off stage, Horatio's function seems to be primarily to enhance the hero's tragic solitude. When he does stand at Hamlet's side, it produces the strange impression that Hamlet is being revealed in dialogue with one side of himself, as if he were projecting onto Horatio his illusory longing for complete lucidity. When Hamlet weighs the pros and cons or when he shrinks from killing the King, on the pretence that the result obtained in the afterlife will not be the damnation of the King's soul which he so hotly pursues, he is giving voice to the Horatio-like part of himself. Hamlet may well envy his friend 'whose blood and judgement are so well commeddled' (iii, ii, 69), but where is the 'blood' in the Horatio that we know? Hamlet's praise of Horatio's temperance sounds more like the projected fantasy of an unattainable ideal than an accurate portrayal. Later on, through a beneficent sea change, Hamlet learns the positive value of rashness 'when our deep plots do pall' (v, ii, 9).

Horatio's refusal to act ends in a disinclination to live. If Hamlet had not entrusted him with the duty of bearing witness to what he has seen, Horatio would have committed suicide, thus surrendering to a temptation that Hamlet knows only too well. Hamlet saves his friend's life by making him the chronicler of his story. But did Hamlet know to what he was laying himself open? In view of the manner in which Horatio performs his duty, Hamlet's appeal to his friend appears in retrospect to be fraught with painful irony. Characteristically, the tragedy of Hamlet is presented as the outcome of a series of 'accidental judgements, casual slaughters, purposes mistook', but what else can be expected from 'reason' when it is left to its own devices? Horatio's impartial adhesion to facts proves notoriously incapable of making sense of history. By contrast, Hamlet's subjective faith in Providence confers significance upon 'the fall of a sparrow'. Horatio's presumptuous conviction that only the knowledge of cause and effect can justify action is mercilessly pitted against Hamlet's more humble and ultimately more efficient trust in opportuneness: 'The readiness is all' (v, ii, 218).

Whether rudimentary or complicated, transient or prolonged, each partial reflection of Hamlet helps to endow him with a strong stage presence. At the focal point where these images converge, Hamlet's consciousness is the inner area on which the play's most poignant drama is being played out. Discussing Hamlet's heroism, G.K. Hunter writes:

'The central focus which is lacking in *Julius Caesar* and *Troilus and Cressida* is here found in the mind of the prince; his self-consciousness (especially seen in the soliloquies) is the means by which Shakespeare is enabled to collate and compare modes of heroism which (objectively considered) are essentially disparate; for their fields of activity are here less important than the feelings about them in the central observing mind'; and Hunter further remarks that Fortinbras, Horatio and Laertes are 'figures whose meaning depends on their relationship inside the observing and discriminating mind of Hamlet himself'.[9] In this play, perhaps more obviously than in any other, the subjective viewpoint of the hero is given unusual prominence. Through his monologues, Hamlet is his own consummate reflector. Not only do these self-revelatory addresses to the audience provide a 'live' insight into Hamlet's consciousness but, in typically Mannerist fashion, they disclose his constant preoccupation with his role. Peter Ure has underlined the differences between Hamlet and other tragic heroes like Richard II, Richard III and Brutus.[10] These, he argues, have no difficulty in identifying with their roles to which they commit themselves wholeheartedly. Hamlet is just the opposite. However dedicated to his sacred duty as avenger, Hamlet never succeeds in making his role truly part of himself, accepting it as his *raison d'être*. He gauges its implications and confronts himself with his task, either despairing at his inability to fulfil or firing his imagination to live up to it. At last comes the time when he stops torturing himself while contemplating revenge as a coveted yet unattainable object; he then realizes that not all depends on him alone, that he is not at the centre of the universe (the graveyard scene is the deciding factor in this respect) and that, like everyone else, he is in the hands of Providence. At this point, revenge begins to resemble death:

> If it be now, it is not to come; if it be not
> to come, it will be now; if it be not now, yet it
> will come.
>   v, ii, 216–18

Hamlet's initial error was to believe that self and role must coincide, that he must become an avenger in conscience, like a débutant actor who fancies he has to 'live' his role, whereas he is simply asked to act it. For a long time Hamlet cherishes the fond hope of achieving a harmony within himself by reconciling being and acting, but *we* know that his true greatness resides precisely in that within him which precludes such easy identification.

Bronzino's Florentine aristocrats are supremely elegant and strained. It is plain for all to see that these enigmatic-looking figures are indeed posing for the painter, the viewers and perhaps posterity. Bronzino's talent lies in having recorded a trace of absence at the very core of this role-dictated presence. In order to sustain their ranks and roles, these personages have seemingly taken leave of themselves for the time it takes to pose, as if to signify that their roles, which justify their presence and convey to us the worldly ideals of the Medici court, can in no way pass muster for their inner selves. For this reason, Bronzino's portraits are not as straightforward as they appear, for in them established values and conventions are exposed as sheer exteriority. The lesson that these lofty figures silently proffer foreshadows Hamlet's affirmation: 'I have that within which passes show'. Hamlet is not an ordinary character in a play; he is an actor-character and the problem that he is faced with is basically one of acting: how should he act his part in the Elsinore scene? Hence his fascination for professional actors and the theatre. Far from recreating the character's dismantled unity, the monologues cast a fragmented image of Hamlet as an elusive, changing, hypothetical self, reluctant to commit himself and take up a position within the constraints of a role. When Hamlet at long last accomplishes his revenge, he neither gives up being himself nor identifies with his role. As if it were a Mannerist sleight of hand, the problem is dismissed at the denouement. Accidentally, almost casually, Hamlet chances to avenge his father after all, when Providence supplies the occasion, but Hamlet is spared to the very end the impossible task of being a true avenger or even contemplating himself as one.

THEATRE AS ANAMORPHOSIS

At the centre of the play, 'The Murder of Gonzago' is an emblem of the ambiguity of Elsinore and the theatre, two factitious places which share the Mannerist privilege of making things look what they are and what they are not. In the astonishing *trompe-l'oeil* set up by Hamlet, two images of the same crime are superimposed as through a process of double exposure. The first image reproduces Claudius' deed stage by stage, in accordance with the Ghost's allegations: the murder of the King in his sleep by means of poison poured into his ear, and the murderer's appropriation of the crown and the widowed Queen, with the notable difference that Lucianus, the villain in the play-within-the-play, is not Gonzago's brother but his nephew. Showing through the first image is a second one, identical to and yet different from the first, one which offers a premonitory vision of the nephew's vengeance upon his uncle. As a reproduction of the crime committed and an anticipation of the vengeance to come, the show is an artful blending of true and false, conferring on both protagonists double and contradictory identities; Gonzago stands both for old Hamlet, the late King, and Claudius, the present King, whilst Lucianus impersonates both Claudius, old Hamlet's murderer, and Hamlet, his nephew. The result of this optical manipulation is that the real Claudius and the real Hamlet, spectators at the show, are faced with imperfect doubles of themselves: Claudius lacks the innocence of old Hamlet to be able to identify completely with Gonzago; nor, as brother and murderer of the King, can he identify completely with Lucianus, a murderer like himself, but nephew to Gonzago. Similarly, Hamlet, as the son of the late King and innocent of his murder, is not inclined to see himself in Lucianus; but, as nephew to a murderous king who sooner or later must be put to death, Hamlet has some reason for viewing the play's murderer as a partial representation of himself, despite the fact that he has no relish for the means used by Claudius and Lucianus to assassinate the King. As for Gertrude, who is unaware of her husband's deed, she cannot remotely recognize herself as Baptista and this accounts for her innocent and ironic remark on the Queen's overemphatic protestations of fidelity. She might at the most feel somewhat uneasy when seeing how expeditiously a recent widow can break her vows, but the text offers no clue to confirm this supposition. It is as if Elsinore's deep-seated ambivalence has contaminated the theatre. Thematically, confusion between murder and revenge harks back to Pyrrhus' speech (II, ii), with its equivocal figure of the heroic avenger who is also a bloodthirsty barbarian. But what is new here, and unprecedented before *Hamlet*, is that in the near instantaneity of a carefully contrived theatrical gesture, Shakespeare abolishes time and confuses cause and effect, executioner and victim, crime and punishment.

This theatrical oxymoron or conceit in action is analogous to anamorphosis in painting. Thus, according to their respective positions, the various spectators of 'The Murder' do not see the same things. For Polonius, Ophelia, Gertrude and the courtiers, who are unaware of the King's crime, it is practically impossible to account for Hamlet's parodic quotation about 'the croaking raven [that] doth bellow for revenge' (III, ii, 248) following his injunction to the actor playing Lucianus that he must leave 'his damnable faces and begin'. If questioned about this incident, they would probably view it as yet another manifestation of

Hamlet's 'madness' or impute it to his petulance or whimsicality as director. Likewise, the King's hasty departure after the murder scene and Hamlet's anticipatory explanation of the next episode ('how the murderer gets the love of Gonzago's wife') could be ascribed by them to the King's indisposition (and the Queen does assume this), or at best to his impatience at Hamlet's unsavoury theatrical joke. To them, the grotesque image of a nephew enamoured of his aunt remains indecipherable. However, it all makes sense when considered from the positions occupied by Hamlet, Claudius, Horatio and the audience. Claudius identifies Lucianus' desire for Baptista as a recognizable, if distorted, image of his own desire for his sister-in-law, and Hamlet is able to see in the murder of Gonzago by his nephew a prefiguration of his future revenge. Metadramatically, the message put across by the play-within-the-play is clear enough: the mimesis of the theatre which makes for a certain degree of identification between audience and stage is inseparably linked to deception and distortion.

In *Hamlet*, with its mirror image achieved by the pivotal play-within-the-play, we are invited to watch theatre engaged in contemplation of its own mechanisms. It is perhaps the privilege of Mannerist art thus to give life, more vividly than other aesthetic modes, to the paradox that truth and falsehood are wedded and embedded in all artistic creation.

CHAPTER 6

When playing is foiling: Troilus and Cressida

When Hamlet welcomes the players in Elsinore (ii, ii), he asks one of
them to give him an insight into his acting skills; he does this less as an
audition (Hamlet's advice on the art of acting comes later during a
rehearsal of 'The Murder of Gonzago'), than to taste forthwith the pleasures of the theatre and to revel in listening to a 'passionate speech'.
Hamlet does not indicate the title of the play from which the extract is
taken, but we can guess that it concerns the sorrowful love of Dido and
Aeneas. In the part of the story which Hamlet knows by heart and which
he wishes to hear again, Aeneas re-enacts for the Queen of Carthage
one of the bloodiest episodes he took part in during the Trojan War: the
murder of King Priam by Pyrrhus, son of Achilles, as revenge for the
murder of Achilles by Paris. The tirade ends on the grief of Hecuba,
who was witness to the slaughter of her husband Priam.

   The dramatic and symbolic aptness of this passage is obvious,[1] but my
present concern lies elsewhere. Before declaiming the first lines himself,
Hamlet voices a judgement on the play in question, a judgement which is
in part personal and in part quoted from some judicious spectator of
whose opinion Hamlet approves (this is the well-known speech: 'I heard
thee speak me a speech once, but it was never acted', ii, ii, 430–44). Four
main ideas emerge from this comment:

(1) Hamlet's liking for the play – and more particularly for Aeneas' nar-
     rative – is not connected with his present situation. Hamlet already
     appreciated the play before the crime of Elsinore made him a poten-
     tial avenger.

(2) It would appear that Hamlet did not know the play from seeing it on
     stage. Moreover, there remains a doubt as to whether the play has
     ever been staged. Hamlet would not be able to judge the work as
     'excellent' if he had simply heard one speech (not necessarily this
     one) in private; we can therefore suppose that he read the play. This is
     apparently confirmed by his insistence on its style.

(3) This play was not successful with the general public, but was greatly appreciated by cultured people.

(4) Its qualities are: a well-thought-out plot; an art tempered by restraint, with no additions to 'make the matter savoury'; a healthy, unaffected art, more concerned with beauty than with prettiness.

The outline of an aesthetic position has thus been drawn up in a vivid style, that of the enlightened amateur (the opposite of Polonius' limp pedantry); it can be called 'classical' and ties in with Hamlet's idea of a good actor.

A little later in the same scene, when the actor begins the part of the story devoted to Hecuba, Hamlet starts when he hears an awkward expression – 'the mobled queen' – this goes to show that love of rhetoric and lofty style has not blunted Hamlet's critical vigilance. In the next act (III, ii), the rehearsal in the wings of 'The Murder of Gonzago' will be the occasion to make a speech about the art of acting; but, for the moment, the monologue on Priam's death gives rise to a comment on the art of writing for the theatre.

Turning to the Prologue of *Troilus and Cressida*, the play in which Shakespeare deals *specifically* with the Trojan War and of which Aeneas' story gave us a foretaste, it is noticeable how Shakespeare's use of the prologue testifies to a critical awareness regarding his art, as in the passage from *Hamlet* already mentioned. It is as if the dramatic representation of an action linked to the Trojan War or to its aftermath (like the story of Dido and Aeneas) makes the poet particularly sensitive to the problems of his art and induces a discourse in accordance with the classical ideal. This is not surprising, since Horace holds up Homer as an example in his *Poetic Art* and gives poets some advice from the method used by the author of the *Iliad*: start the story *in medias res* without going back to the beginning; have recourse to narration for everything which has to be told but which is not worth showing; eliminate the superfluous; mix fact and fiction and ensure a harmonious continuity between the beginning, the middle and the end. That is why, when Shakespeare tackled the same subject, the least he could do for fear of acting in defiance of the joint authority of Homer and Horace was to offer his audience a play that:

> Leaps o'er the vaunt and firstlings of those broils,
> Beginning in the middle, starting thence away
> To what may be digested in a play.
> Prologue, 27–9

Thus Shakespeare breaks with the method used previously in *Henry V*, the most recent of his war plays. In *Henry V* the Chorus implores the audience to agree to 'Turning th'accomplishment of many years/Into an hour-glass'; its function is to keep the audience's imagination alert, to help them 'leap o'er times' and transport themselves to different climes. Here, on the contrary, the role of the Prologue is limited, as its name suggests, to fixing the setting, creating the atmosphere and specifying the subject of the play; then it quite rightly disappears. As the play is supposed to place the audience in the heart of the important events right from the start, it is no longer necessary to provide a link between the episodes by means of a narrative external to the story. In *Troilus and Cressida* Shakespeare proclaims his intention no longer to use the sequential or processional method of the chronicle. We see him opt for the resolutely 'modern' method, at least as far as principles are concerned, of classical *dramatization* advocated by Horace, practised by Terence (of whom Horace speaks highly) and popularized by the Italian Renaissance theorists before being defended in England by Sir Philip Sidney. However, a close look at the play will demonstrate that respect of principles on the part of a Mannerist artist is more often than not accompanied by an approach which tends to empty them of their content.

Before examining the play, one should also consider the Epistle to the Reader printed on the second leaf of the 1609 Quarto (second state), because some of the arguments developed there are strongly evocative, through analogy or contrast, of certain remarks made by Hamlet. For example, the author of the Epistle prides himself on presenting the reader with a play which was 'neuer stal'd with the Stage', 'neuer clapper-clawd with the palmes of the vulger', nor 'sullied with the smoaky breath of the multitude'.[2] Like Hamlet, he draws on metaphors of taste, but with a contrary intention. Hamlet thought poorly of stylistic 'sallets', but the author of the Epistle praises Shakespearian wit, which, like salt, spices up the comedies, and particularly this one. The classical values of naturalness and restraint give way to the 'dexteritie and power of witte' as the most praiseworthy qualities, so that even 'the dull and heauy-witted worldlings . . . feeling an edge of witte set upon them, more then euer [they] dreamd they had braine to grinde it on'. Although contempt of the vulgar is common to the two texts, it is clear that in 1609 the earliest critic of *Troilus and Cressida* admired Shakespeare's work for reasons which are the opposite of those proffered by Hamlet in support of his admiration for the play from which Aeneas' story is taken. M.C. Bradbrook puts forward the appealing yet tenuous hypothesis that the play was conceived as much to be read as to be staged, which runs counter to current Shakespearian practice.[3] Without going to such extremes, it can be admitted that the length of the speeches, the importance attached to the discussion of ideas, the difficulty of the language and the relatively static nature of the action destined *Troilus and Cressida* for an audience capable of exceptional attention, able to appreciate the finer points of argumentation (especially when it is specious) without being put off by the subtlety of speech which is often ironic, sometimes bristling with witticisms and paradoxes. The Epistle in fact expresses one aspect of the work's novelty, its kinship both in spirit and form with the then trendy poetry that we have learnt to call metaphysical. To match a hypothesis with a hypothesis, let me put forward the idea that with a subject of such venerable prestige, Shakespeare was attempting a somewhat daring challenge: not to write the play that Hamlet admired with a touching nostalgia for the good old style, but to write the play that the Prince could have written himself, marked by the deleterious atmosphere of Elsinore, in times when the 'new Philosophy calls all in doubt', when ''Tis all in pieces, all coherence gone'. To attune the Trojan War sung by Homer and the love of Troilus and Cressida sung by Chaucer to a grating, refined modernity which no longer believes in the ideal of chivalry sums up the content of the artistic and ideological project which underlies this new Mannerist experimentation.[4]

THE PHONEY WAR

Troilus and Cressida is one of the rare plays by Shakespeare which to a large extent respects the rule of unity of time. As early as Act I, scene iii, during the debate between the Greek leaders, it is announced that 'tomorrow' will see the single combat proposed by Hector and on which the outcome of the war may depend. The same time indication is given during Act III, scene iii, when Thersites informs Achilles that Ajax has been chosen to face Hector. As for the combat itself, it takes place in Act IV, scene v; then Achilles and Hector arrange another single combat the day after, one which promises to be more bloody than the first. There is no break in time between the first two scenes of Act v and the preceding act; it is the evening of the same day; Hector is feasting with the Greeks while Troilus has been led to Calchas' tent where, unseen, he is witness to a love scene between Diomedes and Cressida. The following scene (v, iii) takes place the next morning; Hector is deaf to the pleas of Andromache and Cassandra and prepares himself for the combat with Achilles planned for the same day. The play ends with a series of very short, eventful scenes which finally present us for the first (and last) time with what looks like a battle. We see the confrontations between Troilus and Diomedes, Achilles and Hector, Menelaus and Paris; we witness the death of Hector, the consternation this produces within the Trojan ranks, Troilus taking control of the army and the dismissal of Pandarus. The whole series of war scenes therefore covers a period of no more than three days.

We reach the same conclusion when considering the love story. The first two scenes of Act i serve to present the two lovers separately. Their meeting takes place the next evening in Pandarus' house where they spend their one and only night together (iii, ii). In the morning they say their farewells; Diomedes comes to collect Cressida to take her to her father in the Greek camp (iv, ii, iii, iv); there follows the scene where Cressida allows the Greek leaders to kiss her (iv, v); after this, Cressida's betrayal in the presence of Troilus occurs in the evening of the same day. Clearly, Shakespeare removed all superfluous elements and confined himself to the indispensable episodes. The promise of the Prologue has been kept: from the outset, the audience is presented with a situation which is already advanced; this is true of the conflict between the Greeks and the Trojans, which has already lasted seven years, and also of the desire Troilus and Cressida feel for each other, which has already existed for a certain, non-specified time. In both cases the dramatist spares us the genesis of the events.

There is a concentration of space which corresponds to this concentration of time. The action takes place in four adjacent places: the Greek camp close to the walls of Troy, Priam's palace, Pandarus' house in the town and the neutral zone dedicated to warfare.

Lastly, the coexistence of two stories, one concerning love, the other war, does not interfere with the unity of action: the thoughts and scenes of love arise between the combats; Cressida is the object of bargaining between the two camps and rejoins Calchas, her father, who has taken refuge with the Greeks after sensing the fall of Troy. With its classical, tightened form, it is a work that marks a divergence from the previous plays dealing with historical subjects. Structurally, the play proves closer to comedy, despite everything in the story 'pulling' it towards tragedy or historical drama: the omnipresence of the war, Troilus' emotional wound and the death of Hector which preludes the fall of Troy.

How is it then that, despite this *objective* tightening of time which is attested by the time directions punctuating the text, the play is perceived by the audience – and even more so by the reader – as dragging on till it becomes almost unbearable? The Horatian precept of taking 'things in their middle' was based on the idea that the interest of a story does not lie essentially in the unveiling of the processes which lead to the event, but rather in the event itself, that privileged moment when past and present converge in the birth of an action which is strong enough to focus dramatic interest. Now, what do we see in *Troilus and Cressida*? By way of action, we have something more resembling inaction, waiting, a kind of factual void which marks a stagnation of history. Admittedly, the play takes us right into the heart of the subject and 'Leaps o'er the vaunt and firstlings of those broils', just as the Prologue warns us, but this 'heart' seems drained of all life-blood. The Prologue may well paint an enticing picture of decisive action of heroic grandeur:

> From Isles of Greece
> The princes orgulous, their high blood chaf'd,
> Have to the port of Athens sent their ships
> Fraught with the ministers and instruments
> Of cruel war.
> . . .
> Now expectation, tickling skittish spirits
> On one and other side, Trojan and Greek,
> Sets all on hazard.
>
> Prologue, 1–5; 20–2

But the play is constructed on the *absence* of what is expected, the absence of what is needed in terms of events and circumstances to enable the camps to do precisely what *is* expected, to stake all and brave destiny. *Troilus and Cressida* provides a new example of this 'subversive allegiance' which characterizes the Mannerist approach: the space–time framework is classical – a cultured audience would appreciate the homage to Horace and the modernist bias – but the action which comes within this framework does not fit the chosen format. Mannerist art has accustomed us to this kind of anomaly: contrived perspectives, figures represented in proportions incompatible with the postures they occupy within the com-position, or in positions unrelated to their role or their iconographic status, elements of architecture (pilasters, columns, pediments or con-soles) used in violation of architectonic logic.

Seven years of siege interrupted by a 'dull and long-continu'd truce' have placed the Greeks and the Trojans in an ambiguous situation where there is neither peace nor war. The impatience to vanquish which drove the 'skittish spirits' the Prologue speaks of has turned into a waiting for an opportunity which will unblock the situation – could it be the Trojans' decision to give back Helen? Or, on the Greek side, Achilles' decision to leave his tent and take up arms again, which would allow the glimmer of a hope of victory on the field? Shakespeare does not dramatize the culminating phase of a conflict, but the deterioration of a slack situation marked by the failure of those who want to revive the apparently interrupted course of history. For lack of a real battle which would end in victory or defeat – the only battle, at the end of the play, is inconclusive – each day which goes by provides one or two sorties on the battlefield. Armour is put on; it is then removed; the protagonists do not always feel like entering the lists. Made languid by love, Troilus decides to stop fighting for such a dubious cause: 'I cannot fight upon this argument;/It is too starv'd a subject for my sword' (I, i, 92–3).

Yet when the trumpets sound and Aeneas appears ('Hark what good sport is out of town today!' I, i, 113), he forgets his thoughts and returns to the fray. The day's combats and the return of those engaged in them are *entertainments*. Hecuba and Andromache go up the east tower so as not to miss a second of Hector's performance; and Pandarus, at the sight of these handsome warriors with their dented helmets, makes sure to arouse his niece's sensuality when speaking in favour of Troilus. The next day is a rest day for Troilus and Paris, and Pandarus visits the Paris–Helen ménage ('I would fain have armed today, but my Nell would not have it so. How chance my brother Troilus went not?' III, i, 132–4). After the sound of the fanfare, the combatants return to the fold. Helen follows her lover's advice and does Hector the honour of disarming him; and Troilus, conducted by Pandarus, goes to join Cressida. Later, in Act v, when Hector is readying himself to meet Achilles, he is astonished to see Troilus already prepared for battle; he asks him not to go, with the calm assurance of the professional whom duty calls once more:

> No, faith, young Troilus; doff thy harness, youth.
> I am today i'th'vein of chivalry:
> Let grow thy sinews till their knots be strong
> And tempt not yet the brushes of the war.
> Unarm thee, go; and doubt thou not, brave boy.
> I'll stand today for thee and me and Troy.
>
> v, iii, 31–6

To both sides, waging war is an everyday job; hence the recurrence of the word 'today' which punctuates the humdrum of daily tasks. The noisy adherence to the code of chivalry, with its rites and pomps and vanities, is balanced by the combatants' lack of faith in the justness of their cause. The hostility between the two camps finds no other expression than the devalued form of challenges issued periodically during diplomatic missions in the enemy camp or the inevitable bragging which at times verges on the grotesque:

> ACHILL. Tell me, you heavens, in which part of his body
> Shall I destroy him – whether there, or there, or there –
> That may give the local wound a name,
> And make distinct the very breach whereout
> Hector's great spirit flew? Answer me, heavens!
>   ...
>
> HECT.   Henceforth guard thee well;
> For I'll not kill thee there, nor there, nor there;
> But, by the forge that stithied Mars his helm,
> I'll kill thee everywhere, yea, o'er and o'er.
> You wisest Grecians, pardon me this brag:
> His insolence draws folly from my lips.
>
> IV, V, 241–5; 252–7

Hector is lucid enough to recognize the vanity of this little war of words and arms, and therefore exhorts Achilles to abandon his reserve:

> I pray you, let us see you in the field;
> We have had pelting wars since you refus'd
> The Grecians' cause.
>
> IV, V, 265–7

Ironically enough, Hector does not know that Achilles' taking up arms will be fatal for him; this valiant knight who spares the lives of his tired adversaries does not imagine that Achilles is less prone to fair play than himself and will take advantage of a moment when Hector has laid down his arms to have him killed by his Myrmidons. At this moment the war swings from the trivial towards the vile. On two occasions the combatants believe they have arrived at the crucial moment, but each time they are mistaken: the combat between Ajax and Hector comes to nothing and the reconciled cousins fall into each other's arms (III, v). As for the hopes of a fair combat between Achilles and Hector, they are soon destroyed by Achilles' decision to withdraw because of the oath which binds him to Hecuba and Polyxena (v, i). The audience has to wait till Patroclus is killed – an incident that Shakespeare leaves undramatized so as to emphasize its triviality – to see Achilles descend into the arena. Achilles is affected by the loss of his 'sweetheart' ('male varlet', says Thersites) and gives up his nonchalant Sybarite stand for deadly vengeance. Where patriotism has failed, a desire for vengeance succeeds.

In the same way, Troilus' feeling of humiliation after Cressida's betrayal sees an end to his intransigent attitude towards honour (cf. the debate scene with the Trojans, Act II, scene ii) and this transforms our exemplary knight into a cynical firebrand:

> TROIL. Brother, you have a vice of mercy in you,
> Which better fits a lion than a man.
> HECT. What vice is that? Good Troilus, chide me for it.
> TROIL. When many times the captive Grecian falls
> Even in the fan and wind of your fair sword,
> You bid them rise, and live.
> HECT. O, 'tis fair play.
> TROIL.   Fool's play, by heaven, Hector.
> HECT. How now, how now?
> TROIL.   For th'love of all the gods,
> Let's leave the hermit pity with out mother;
> And when we have our armours buckled on
> The venom'd vengeance ride upon our swords,
> Spur them to ruthful work, rein them from ruth!
> HECT. Fie, savage, fie.
> TROIL.   Hector, then 'tis wars.
>
> v, iii, 37–49

Hector himself, the pride of the Trojan nobility, gives in to an absurd, sordid desire: he catches sight of the magnificent armour of a passing Greek, pursues him like prey and kills him to obtain the panoply. He is not troubled in the slightest after this act of gratuitous bloody plunder, and lays down his arms to get his breath back:

> Now is my day's work done: I'll take my breath.
> Rest, sword; thou hast thy fill of blood and death.
>
> v, viii, 3–4

So it is a *doubly* disarmed soldier (morally and physically), a dishonoured warrior, that Achilles has his Myrmidons run though.

In a different way, the final scene exemplifies Shakespeare's Mannerist approach and his refutation of the ideas of grandeur and heroism mentioned in the Prologue. While behaviour was determined by the code of chivalry, the war scenes seemed unreal. As long as the combatants had no other reason to fight than the recovery or possession of Helen, the war needed the ceremonial of chivalry to mask the comic and cruel futility of the stakes (Thersites: 'All the argument is a cuckold and a whore: a good quarrel to draw emulous factions and bleed to death upon', II, iii, 74–6). As soon as personal vengeance comes into play and motivates actions (at least those of Achilles and Troilus), the conflict livens up; ritualistic violence gives way to unbridled violence. The final scene of *Troilus and Cressida* does not really resemble the denouement of a tragedy. A reputedly valiant but discredited warrior is speared to death by killers in the service of another warrior, who is also reputedly valiant but even more discredited: it is a false denouement for a false tragedy. The final episode in this play revives a smouldering flame instead of obtaining the appeasement which accompanies a more traditional tragic outcome when the sacrificial death of the hero consumes the last firebrands of a blaze he lit himself. But this disorderly, barbaric violence, earlier masked by the trappings of chivalry, now appears in a new, non-coded form which is both primitive and modern. The failure of Ulysses' scheme to have Ajax fight Achilles in single combat has caused the Greek rank and file 'to proclaim barbarism' (v, iv, 16–17). This over-crafty policy has defeated itself and discredited the very notion of policy. However, there is something still missing and that is heroism. The entire play strives endlessly to demonstrate its absence, to the point of making this emptiness the founding principle of the 'action'.

It is well known that Renaissance painters liked to include a mirror, or some other reflecting surface, in their compositions, to provide a partial or complete picture of what could not be seen, the other side of what was represented. In *Troilus and Cressida*, a similar mechanism shows us briefly the long-hidden face of war: when Hector robs the anonymous Greek of his gleaming armour, he discovers an already putrefied body. With its foreshortening technique, this allegorical vignette offers a condensed image of the play's progress. But a long time was necessary before the war itself disclosed its scandalous, repulsive nature, which Thersites had never stopped denouncing. Most of the play is taken up with describing a 'phoney war', with no glory or panache, a weary war which could well have ended comically in never-ending parley, verbal duels, failed tricks and interrupted or cancelled combats, had it not been for a late fortuitous motive of vengeance to save it from the constantly threatening peace. To push the point a little, I would say that this war fluctuates between old-time aerobics, sporting competitions and embassy dinners, before turning into a settling of scores between private persons.

TIME TRAPPED

As in certain Mannerist paintings, the characters in *Troilus and Cressida* float in a state of historic weightlessness, as if the passage of time had given way to an untiring reiteration of the present, cut off from both past and future. Such is the meaning of Agamemnon's remark to Hector:

> Understand more clear:
> What's past and what's to come is strew'd with husks
> And formless ruin of oblivion.
>
> IV, V, 164–6

Ulysses voices the same concern when he tries to encourage Achilles to take up with the present moment again:

> ACHILL.   What, are my deeds forgot?
> ULYSS.   Time hath, my lord, a wallet at his back
> Wherein he puts alms for oblivion,
> A great-siz'd monster of ingratitudes.
> Those scraps are good deeds past, which are devour'd
> As fast as they are made, forgot as soon
> As done.
>
> II, iii, 144–50

In the world of *Troilus and Cressida*, man, left to the contingencies of the present moment, has no hold over time; he is incapable of programming an action and planning its course. This is why Ulysses' stratagem to provoke Achilles' jealousy by having Ajax named champion of the Greek cause (through the use of a rigged draw) ends in failure. The same is true of Claudius' ruse to have Hamlet killed in England. In this respect, *Troilus and Cressida* prolongs Shakespeare's contemplation of the imponderables which foil 'our deep plots'. But Hamlet could, as a last resort, trust the urge of the moment, the impetuous act, once convinced that God and Providence give form and meaning to our actions, 'rough-hew them how we will'. This Christian certainty which comes to Hamlet late in the play is naturally refused to the pagan characters in *Troilus and Cressida*. True, Ulysses does use the word 'providence' in a speech to Achilles (III, iii, 195), but not in the sense of 'that divine providence' Hamlet sees at work in the fall of a sparrow. Nevertheless, the word does designate a 'divine' quality of government through which 'a watchful state' can pierce through the most private thoughts of its citizens ('plucking out the heart of their mystery', as Hamlet would put it). The religious connotation serves to deify an omniscient State, the secret dream of all intelligence services. Nor are the characters in the play granted the ancient belief in Destiny which governs the life of mortals. Nowhere is it suggested that Achilles and Hector will fulfil their destiny by breaking the rules of honour in the heat of the moment under the influence of their selfish instinct. Troilus does not put Cressida's betrayal down to fate, but to spiritual and moral chaos ('The bonds of heaven are slipp'd, dissolv'd and loos'd', v, ii, 155), thus confirming Ulysses' diagnosis formulated in his 'degree' speech. For a short moment Troilus foretells the military disaster, but when Aeneas accuses him of demoralizing the troops he disguises his meaning as a challenge (yet another) and takes refuge in the stereotyped formal language of an avenging imprecation. From the perspective of this play, present time is like Macbeth's notion of human existence: a sandbank surrounded by the unknowable. That is why Nestor, the voice of the past and comic 'has-been', speaks sterile words which are doomed to be the tautological gloss of the leaders' discourse. The past is powerless to guide the action and can at best support the present speech, supply it with examples and illustrate it by lending it some of its lustre. As for Cassandra, the voice of the future and the pathetic figure of the scorned prophetess, she has no chance of being listened to, not only because her speech is expressed in a divinatory form that makes 'reasonable' people reject it, but mostly because her claim that 'It is the purpose that makes strong the vow' (v, iii, 23) challenges the very dogma of honour on which Troy has built its ideology.

If love fails it is not because it is incapable of resisting the wearing effect of Time – the play's dramatic time is too short to allow Time to exert its corrosive effect – it is because Time is subjected to the fleeting present with no past or future. The vow of love and the act of sex are as transient as Achilles' deeds of war which Ulysses says are 'devour'd/As fast as they are made, forgot as soon/As done'. Troilus draws the same conclusion when he parts with Cressida:

> where injury of chance
> Puts back leave-taking, jostles roughly by
> All time of pause, rudely beguiles our lips
> Of all rejoindure, forcibly prevents
> Our lock'd embrasures, strangles our dear vows
> Even in the birth of our own labouring breath.
>
> iv, iv, 32–7

Within the very brief span of time allotted to the action, the love between Troilus and Cressida does not wane: it is consumed the moment it is consummated. Time is a thief in a hurry who packs his goods pellmell without knowing what he does (iv, iv, 40–1). Cressida's monologue at the end of Act I, scene ii, not only expresses the strategy of a cunning woman in love who hides her feelings and delays her admission to make the final surrender more precious; more deeply, it exposes the finitude of Time reduced to a moment, that is the finitude of love reduced to the act: 'Things won are done; joy's soul lies in the doing' (I, ii, 292). This intuition is reliable and is confirmed by a number of clues: the weariness which hangs over the lovers' conversation the morning after their night together, the speed with which Troilus takes his leave, the instructions which he gives to Aeneas, 'We met by chance: you did not find me here' (IV, ii, 73), and Cressida's vehement (too vehement) protestations in the farewell scene:

> Time, force and death
> Do to this body what extremes you can;
> But the strong base and building of my love
> Is as the very centre of the earth,
> Drawing all things to it.
>
> IV, ii, 104–8

As for Troilus' insistent (too insistent) calls ('Be true'), about twenty lines later during the parting scene, they are nothing but a gallant last stand, a vain attempt, perhaps without illusion, to give love duration regardless of the nature of things which Cressida alone apprehends correctly.

Psychological or ideological reasons can always be found for the reversals of attitude which punctuate the play: Hector's volte-face when he decides to keep Helen, Achilles' change of mind after the death of Patroclus when he goes back on his word given to Hecuba, Troilus' about-face when he reproaches Hector for his clemency, Hector's unwonted yielding when he gives himself up to covetousness. It is essential to realize that inconstancy, in whatever form, is inherent in *Troilus and Cressida*, which is held captive by the present; in this world an anachronistic system of values is supported by a great deal of talking, but finally collapses under the pressure of desire which wants immediate satisfaction. The most salient feature which distinguishes Troilus from Cressida is not that one is faithful and the other not; it is that Cressida unresistingly submits to the nature of things whereas Troilus deludes himself about reality (including the reality of his love) and chooses to retreat into an untenable belief which makes him doubt his senses and drives him to the verge of insanity:[5]

> O madness of discourse
> That cause sets up with and against itself!
> Bifold authority! where reason can revolt
> Without perdition, and loss assume all reason
> Without revolt. This is, and is not, Cressid.
>
> V, ii, 141–5

Therefore the use of dramatic time is in perfect harmony with the concept of Time expressed in the play. As far as the war story is concerned, the situation evolves in a succession of largely unpredictable moments against a background of daily routine. At the end of Ulysses' speech about the state of the army's morale, it appears necessary to restore discipline at all levels. Given Ulysses' report, we could expect measures to be taken to strengthen Agamemnon's authority and give him the means to force Achilles to obey orders; instead of this, Ulysses, who like a Jonsonian 'humour' is tormented by the need for trickery, proposes a morally dubious scheme which relies on Achilles' pride, the pernicious effects of which he has just denounced.

At this point it is no longer necessary to list all the events which deflect the planned actions from their course. *Troilus and Cressida* is not only a play where nothing happens; it is a play in which none of the things which are supposed to happen do happen. The love story consists of a few relatively static scenes or tableaux; they are quite distinct one from another and are inserted into the war story in such a way as to highlight the autonomy of each episode at the expense of the links which unite them. This method is fairly uncommon in Shakespeare's works and is reminiscent of the method Jonson experimented with in the comical satires; its effect is to concentrate the attention on the present moment much more than on the processes which induced it. Thanks to a thorough selection of the episodes, which eliminates the interstitial matter, the story of Troilus and Cressida is reduced to a few important monolithic scenes which correspond to the decisive steps in a love story.[6] From this point of view, the technique chosen for this story contrasts with that for the war story where, with the exception of the two debates which unfold on a purely discursive level, the absence of noteworthy events results in the audience dividing its attention between the minor events, whose aim is simply to maintain a certain amount of animation on stage: skirmishes between the two camps, Pandarus' visits to Paris and Helen, Agamemnon's and Nestor's to Achilles, Achilles' and Patroclus' distractions with Thersites, Ajax's bragging etc. The important point, however, is that the two methods serve the same purpose: they stress the moment to the detriment of the duration – the *insignificant* moment in the war story, the *decisive* moment in the love story.

The characters in *Troilus and Cressida* are the drop-outs of history. Some are forced to confront the absurdity of things; others belong to the unchanging world of the myth in which they are the unwitting actors:

PAND.   let all
constant men be Troiluses, all false women
Cressids, and all brokers-between Pandars.
III, ii, 200–2

The characters are stuck in an everyday world that has run short of history, or that has been cast beyond history into the timelessness of allegory or proverb; they are all prisoners of a palsied present, unable to place their actions within a time process. The play dramatizes the existential experience of the moment left to itself when Time is divested of its historical and metaphysical dimensions. Like many Mannerist paintings, *Troilus and Cressida* provides the image of a closed world in a closed form, a superbly described world, in its own desperate presence, fully and relentlessly exposed to view, with no area of shadow, no mystery, no background, no perspective.

COUNTERPOINT

Kenneth Muir has underlined a major point on which *Troilus and Cressida* differs from Shakespeare's other plays: the continually changing viewpoints, a 'shift of emphasis which makes the play so difficult to grasp as a unity'.[7] More recently, Philip Edwards expressed the same idea in terms which should hold the attention of anyone interested in Mannerism: '[the play] seems to circle about the Object, exchanging one valuation for another, and demonstrating their invalidity'.[8] The metaphor used by Edwards – probably with no 'Mannerist' intention – describes precisely the behaviour of a person contemplating a statue by Giovanni Bologna or Benvenuto Cellini which needs to be contemplated from different angles. The analogue in painting of what Panofsky calls 'multi-view' or 'revolving-view' sculpture would be an off-centre composition which destabilizes the attention to the extent that it sometimes imparts to it a centrifugal movement.[9] The study of *Julius Caesar* and *Hamlet* familiarized us with certain ways of transferring this principle, inherent in a large number of Mannerist compositions, to the theatre. However, Edwards is mistaken when he goes on to state that *Troilus and Cressida* is 'anti-art', or 'pre-art', or when he evokes Shakespeare's 'anti-formal ingenuity' in refusing to attribute a coherent form to an incoherent content under the pretext of showing life 'before the poetic imagination moulds it into meaningful shape'; the work is thus judged unsatisfactory because it includes neither resolution nor consolation. If we were to follow the critic's logic, the whole Mannerist movement would have to be denied the label 'art', since this trend rediscovers the incoherence of the world (temporarily overshadowed by the classicism of the Renaissance) in order to play with and enjoy it. Una Ellis-Fermor believed that the art of disharmony which is so present in *Troilus and Cressida* testified to Shakespeare's philosophical disarray.[10] Philip Edwards sees in this the sign of artistic disarray. And what if the answer lay elsewhere? Maybe in a desire to experiment, to see just how far the handling of a dramatic text could be pushed, with a wish to impose challenges on oneself, like taking as subject the Trojan War – the legendary prototype of a war for Shakespeare's contemporaries – and representing it through parody which would exclude not only glory but also war (as we imagine it) and which, on the other hand, would include a debunked and sordid image of Troilus and Cressida's love. The Mannerist hypothesis allows us to discard the two doubtful inferences of moral disillusionment and artistic weakness at a certain moment in the poet's life. It puts in their place a more plausible inference, and one which is corroborated by the development of Shakespearian art: that there was a period lasting a few years at the turn of the century during which the playwright devoted himself more intensely than at other times in his career to a search for themes and form; this would fit in between two phases of greater stability, that of the historical plays and romantic comedies on the one hand, and the tragedies on the other.

In *Troilus and Cressida* there is no hero with a centralizing and specular conscience who focuses on himself a large part of the dramatic interest and to whom the audience's attention is drawn as the point of convergence for the events and characters. In this respect *Troilus and Cressida* is closer to *Julius Caesar* than to *Hamlet*. The play is presented as an almost Jonsonian catalogue of attitudes in the face of love and war: none of these points of view is valid for long, either because its inadequacy is proved by contact with reality, or because it expresses itself through a comparison with another point of view which shows reality in another, but equally questionable, light. The systematic use of ironic counterpointing verging on automatism is a distinctive feature of the play. We have seen the consequences of Ulysses' impeccable diagnosis of the anarchy prevalent in the Greek army. This statement is not open to debate; it expresses the thoughts of everyone, both on stage and in the audience. There is no contestation either about the portrait of Achilles and Patroclus, who are symptomatic of an extreme form of evil. But the 'remedy' Agamemnon is waiting for will never be prescribed. The reality of the exterior world bursts onto the scene in the form of Aeneas, who

brings Hector's challenge. All efforts to solve the Greek problem as ratio-
nally as it had been raised are nipped in the bud by the demands of the
present moment and the obligation to meet them on the sole ground
available, the code of chivalry. Trickery now takes the floor and Ulysses
unveils another aspect of his character, that of the wily politician.

The warmongering of Troilus and Paris is based on specious logic,
that of assimilating the abduction of Helen to the choice of a wife, and
that of thinking that something only has a value as long as it is held in
high regard; this foolish belligerence is foiled by Hector's sensible speech
and the spectator can then hope that wisdom will win the day. But reason
is foiled in its turn by compulsory submission to a code forbidding loss of
face in the sight of the enemy, demanding solidarity towards one's brothers and impassiveness towards Cassandra's alarming predictions; and so
we have another volte-face.

To some extent the audience sympathizes with Troilus, who, like
Hamlet, yearns for purity and the absolute.[11] Troilus' tragedy is that
there is no 'objective correlative' to his idealistic dreaming: the war is
sparked off by a story of cuckoldry, and the love is tainted; Cressida is a
'daughter of the game' (according to Ulysses) and the whole affair grows
out of unhealthy soil ('I cannot come to Cressid but by Pandar'). The
young prince therefore has to project his fantasies against the background of unbearably sordid reality: he has to believe that Helen is 'a
theme of honour and renown' (II, ii, 200), that Cressida is 'a pearl' (I, i,
100) and that his desire is purer than religious devoutness, to the point of
making the gods jealous:

> Cressid, I love thee in so strain'd a purity
> That the blest gods, as angry with my fancy,
> More bright in zeal than the devotion which
> Cold lips blow to their deities, take thee from me.
>
> IV, iv, 23–6

The tutelary presence of Pandarus all through the love story, his role
as salacious go-between and voyeur, and his strongly materialistic
language all cast an ironic light on Troilus' lyrical effusiveness. But
Pandarus' point of view is not the only counterpoint to Troilus' attitude;
there is Cressida's down-to-earth behaviour, with her distinctive 'morality' where sincerity (she loves Troilus as long as he is close to her, and
suffers from their separation until she meets another man) rubs shoulders with cunning, where an almost touching meanness of the soul is
coupled with a badly concealed penchant for loose conduct.

Shakespeare deliberately places Pandarus' visit to the Paris–Helen ménage before the meeting between Troilus and Cressida, thereby giving an apparently trivial scene a *raison d'être* in the atmosphere it creates and in its position in the unfolding of the love story. To John Bailey the futility of the half-colloquial, half-fashionable language in this scene evokes a night-club.[12] R.A. Foakes is more receptive to the languid, vaguely lascivious atmosphere of their discussion and would happily situate it in a brothel.[13] The fact remains that this climate of daily lust affects our perception of the following scene, all the more so as Pandarus assiduously plays his role of go-between, showing off his merchandise to its best advantage and exacerbating his client's desire:

> I'll fetch her: it is the prettiest villain; she fetches
> her breath as short as a new-ta'en sparrow.
>
> III, ii, 31–3

Foakes is right, and the effects are used to prepare us for a second brothel scene, even if the lovers' banter and the exchange of vows are inspired by the verbal conventions of courtly Euphuism. As for the lovers' separation which causes Cressida so much heartache, it is preceded by a short exchange between Troilus and Paris, who uses words which are simple yet charged with irony (Paris pronounces them, unaware of their effect) to forestall the religious solemnity which Troilus would like to give to the farewell ceremony:

> TROIL.   Walk into her house.
> I'll bring her to the Grecian presently;
> And to his hand when I deliver her,
> Think it an altar, and thy brother Troilus
> A priest, there off'ring to it his own heart.
> PARIS.   I know what 'tis to love,
> And would, as I shall pity, I could help.
>
> IV, iii, 5–11

In the Greek camp, Thersites avails himself of universally destructive satire, which is sustained by the sight of human failings aggravated by war: Agamemnon's pompous majesty, Nestor's rambling wisdom, Ulysses' shrewdness, Achilles' proud nonchalance, Ajax's idiotic boastfulness etc. But Thersites' continual rantings and his all-too-expected soliloquies are juxtaposed with comic scenes which present the other side of that nobility of war which the Greek leaders display: the airs and graces that Agamemnon, Ulysses and Nestor adopt to excite Ajax into opposing Achilles and to turn his head with flattery (II, iii), and the show staged by Ulysses in which the Greek leaders disdainfully file past Achilles' tent in procession and thereby bring ridicule on themselves.

Examples of this kind are numerous, but enough has been shown to enable us to draw a conclusion already: there is no point of view which is not countered by the opposite point of view or confronted with different points of view which question and shed light on each other; there is no conviction or resolution which is not sooner or later repudiated by its author or belied by experience. Even Thersites' sweeping vision is not able to pass itself off as the most truthful representation of the war. The character is too contemptible: 'a rascal, a scurvy railing knave, a very filthy rogue' (v, iv, 28–9), or even 'bastard in valour, in everything illegitimate' (v, vii, 17–18), he says, including himself in his own derision. Thersites reminds us of the iconographic figure of the presenter or commentator in certain Mannerist paintings.[14] He is positioned on the edge of the painting, often in the foreground so as to be as close as possible to the people looking at the work; his function is to point to something which is happening right under our noses, to direct our eyes, or sometimes to deflect our attention. But Thersites is a grotesque presenter. He has an incomplete and biased vision of things owing to his status as professional scoffer similar to the stock fool. Thersites cannot guide our vision. When he criticizes Ulysses, it is the politician he is attacking; he ignores the wise man who measures the disastrous effects of anarchy (I, iii) and the ravages of Time (III, iii), and who predicts the fall of Troy. He sends Diomedes and Troilus away without pronouncing in favour of either of them, calling them 'wenching rogues'. He says almost nothing of Hector, because he cannot fit him into his vision of the world; when Thersites does speak of Hector, it is to curse the man who spares his life: 'a plague break thy neck for frighting me' (v, iv, 31). As for Pandarus' vision, which is only too prone to identify love with lust, it is no more reliable than Thersites', though, it must be said, it is not entirely wrong either.

One feature distinguishes the minor figures, such as Thersites, Pandarus, Agamemnon, Nestor, Ajax or Helen, from the more important characters, such as Troilus, Cressida, Ulysses, Hector or even Achilles. The behaviour of the first group is all of a piece and can be grasped in a second. The second group's behaviour is multifaceted, thus giving the illusion of change. In reality, however, these characters are as stable as the others; they do not really evolve; we do not see them forming or disintegrating before our very eyes, like Lear or Macbeth. In *Troilus and Cressida* the characters are still dealt with according to the

Mannerist method of ironic segmentation. Shakespeare portrays them in various, sometimes contradictory, positions. He catches an instantaneous, simplified gesture, then another, and another and so on. But at times the characters make two gestures simultaneously, which gives us the theatrical equivalent of the *contrapposto* or the serpentine line. Hector knows where the truth lies; he looks it in the eyes, but turns his back on it:

> Hector's opinion
> Is this in way of truth: yet ne'ertheless,
> My spritely brethren, I propend to you
> In resolution to keep Helen still.
>
>   II, ii, 189–92

Cressida goes through all sorts of contortions when she first meets Troilus in Act III, scene ii:

> Stop my mouth.
>   III, ii, 132

> 'Twas not my purpose thus to beg a kiss.
>   III, ii, 136

> CRESS. I have a kind of self resides with you,
>   But an unkind self, that itself will leave
>   To be another's fool. I would be gone:
>   Where is my wit? I know not what I speak.
> TROIL. Well know they what they speak that speak so wisely.
> CRESS. Perchance, my lord, I show more craft than love,
>   And fell so roundly to a large confession
>   To angle for your thoughts.
>
>   III, ii, 146–53

When she learns that they are splitting up, all she thinks of is crying, but the words she uses show that she is not overwhelmed with sorrow: there is nothing more studied than the indulgent and narcissistic image she gives of herself going through the ritual of despair in advance:

> CRESS.   I'll go and weep –
> PAND.   Do, do.
> CRESS. – Tear my bright hair, and scratch my praised cheeks,
>   Crack my clear voice with sobs, and break my heart
>   With sounding 'Troilus'.
>
>   IV, ii, 108–12

The feeling creates the show; the emotion is instantaneously translated into sound and vision. Cressida shares a highly developed sense of pose with the painted or sculpted figures in Mannerist art. Kenneth Palmer sees an 'emblematic pose' in Cressida's last appearance:[15]

> Troilus, farewell! One eye yet looks on thee,
> But with my heart the other eye doth see.
>
> v, ii, 106–7

But this narcissistic contemplation is also a feature of Mannerism, like Claudius' pose as he considers his bereavement and wedding 'with a defeated joy/With an auspicious and a dropping eye' (*Hamlet*, I, ii, 10–11) or Paulina's when she is torn between her pain as a widow and the joy at having saved the little princess from drowning: 'She had one eye declined for the loss of her husband, another elevated that the oracle was fulfiled' (*The Winter's Tale*, v, ii, 72–3). These images reproduce the structural figure of opposition so present in Mannerist art and which crystallizes poetically in the form of oxymoron. It is a double oxymoron, full of irony, which Paris expresses when he summarizes the welcome the Trojans gave Diomedes:

> This is the most despiteful gentle greeting,
> The noblest hateful love, that e'er I heard of.
>
> IV, i, 33–4

The implicit object of the satire is obviously the code of chivalry which forces unnatural behaviour upon the Trojans:

> AENEAS. And thou shalt hunt a lion that will fly
> With his face backward.
>
> IV, i, 20–1

Ajax, of course, has no need to take such contorted poses to appear unnatural. His oxymoronic nature – one hand and one leg Greek, the other hand and leg being Trojan – makes him one of the play's curiosities (IV, v, 125–6). Previously, Thersites had given a beastly definition of this compound of contraries: 'a very landfish' (III, iii, 262–3).

But *contrapposto* is not the only means of joining disparate realities. In *Hamlet*, the play-within-the-play fulfils this function perfectly. There is no such device in *Troilus and Cressida*. At certain moments, however, we can feel that the idea of exploiting the possibilities of the theatre in the theatre is present in the playwright's mind. In order to denounce Achilles' lack of respect for Agamemnon and Nestor, Ulysses describes him applauding Patroclus' imitations of the Greek leaders. But the story Ulysses tells includes description and direct speech and thus appears in its turn as a kind of one-man show, the imitation of an imitation in which

Ulysses plays several characters by himself. Through Ulysses' acting we can visualize Patroclus in his role of impersonator, Achilles in his role of exuberant spectator and Agamemnon and Nestor in their roles of ridiculous victims of the impersonation Ulysses re-enacts for them; we also see Agamemnon and Nestor as spectators of the unflattering image of themselves which this one-man playlet produces. In this way, thanks to the process of interlocking, our vision is enriched by the simultaneous disclosure of other points of view; the impression we have of Agamemnon and Nestor is supplemented by the caricature which Patroclus presents, and further enriched by the irony which a character as wily as Ulysses could not but add.[16]

In the last act, the seduction scene between Diomedes and Cressida opens up a triple perspective on Cressida's betrayal. It is a shattering reve- lation to Troilus; to Ulysses it represents the confirmation of his opinion of Cressida; to Thersites it is one more example of 'Nothing but lechery' in this base world. Three points of view and three psychological reactions are brought into view at the same time: Troilus' painful stupefaction, Ulysses' blasé indifference and cautious mistrust of any untimely inter- vention from his companion, and Thersites' bawdy, voyeuristic jubilation; these three scales of value are pitted against each other in a masterful way in order to give rise to the kind of exciting, incongruous situation favoured by Mannerist artists. Thus, in this play where there are no exalting deeds, the exaltation comes from elsewhere, from the kaleidoscopic stream of points of view, from their collision and juxtaposition which bring about a peculiar sense of animation, an intellectual restlessness which serves to counterbalance the immobility and scantiness of the action.

CONCLUSION

TROILUS. Words, words, mere words . . .
v, iv, 108

HAMLET. Words, words, words.
II, ii, 191

It is not possible to conclude this study of *Troilus and Cressida* without considering the verbosity of the language. It is as if the lack of action resulted in verbal hypertrophy. This inflation of speech goes hand in hand with inflation of the code of chivalry: both are a function of the disarray caused by the impossibility of efficient and lasting action on the stage of the world. The ritual and the rhetoric express the characters'

resistance – but also their powerlessness – when confronted with a drift-
ing world. There is a kaleidoscope of types of speech corresponding to
the kaleidoscope of points of view: the rhetoric of courtly love and
warlike enthusiasm on the part of Troilus; public eloquence on the part
of Agamemnon and Nestor; Hector's and Ulysses' discursive reason,
plus a touch of argumentative skill on the part of Ulysses and a dash of
honour and chivalry on the part of Hector; imprecation, abuse and
satirical portraiture on the part of Thersites. Looking closer, we can even
discover a rhetoric based on the love trade on the part of Pandarus and a
rhetoric of dissolute coquetry on the part of Cressida, not forgetting an
anti-rhetoric of verbal debility on the part of Ajax. But the Mannerism
does not lie in the fact that each character is given idiosyncratic language, for this is a question of decorum; Mannerism can be found in the
systematic exaggeration of individual features, with each of these idioms
designating itself as a rhetoric, or more exactly a parody, of the character's own speech. When Aeneas arrives as ambassador to the Greeks and
asks to see Agamemnon, he cultivates hyperbole to the extreme:

> I ask, that I might waken reverence,
> And bid the cheek be ready with a blush
> Modest as morning when she coldly eyes
> The youthful Phoebus.
> Which is that god in high office, guiding men?
> Which is the high and mighty Agamemnon?
>
> I, iii, 226–31

But by doing this he unwittingly reproduces a courtly style which is
already familiar to us:

> NEST.   With due observance of thy godlike seat.
>
> I, iii, 31

> ULYSS.   Agamemnon,
> Thou great commander, nerves and bone of Greece,
> Heart of our numbers, soul and only sprite,
> In whom the tempers and the minds of all
> Should be shut up, hear what Ulysses speaks.
>
> I, iii, 54–8

So Agamemnon can legitimately suspect Aeneas of intending parody:

> This Trojan scorns us, or the men of Troy
> Are ceremonious courtiers.
>
> I, iii, 232–3

In this aesthetics of excess applied to all the characters there is something which resembles a certain Mannerist trend exemplified by the engraver Goltzius; his figures were deformed by fantastic muscles out of all proportion with the characters' anatomy or postures, as if these monstrous bodies were besieged by an anarchic proliferation of muscle tissue. A similar phenomenon can be observed in *Troilus and Cressida.* Here speech frees itself of context; it expands disproportionately; it becomes a curiosity in itself, out of line with the situation which creates it and which it is supposed to recount. When Troilus exclaims, in an invocation to Apollo:

> Tell me, Apollo, for thy Daphne's love,
> What Cressid is, what Pandar, and what we.
> Her bed is India; there she lies, a pearl.
> Between our Ilium and where she resides,
> Let it be call'd the wild and wand'ring flood,
> Ourself the merchant, and this sailing Pandar
> Our doubtful hope, our convoy and our bark.
>
> I, i, 98–104

There is an 'overpoeticizing' of the speech which is justified by nothing in the actual circumstances, except perhaps an irresistible force of a fantasy going through Troilus' imagination at that moment. Moreover, as Arnold Stein points out, the process of metaphor is as contrived as it is suspicious.[17] We can feel Troilus' customary effort to make the sensual spiritual, although he cannot prevent the sudden evocation, both a little too explicit and too brutal, of the suggestive detail: 'Her bed is India'. As for the boat image applied to Pandarus and very much highlighted through the triad of nouns in the last line, it adds to the bed reference and impairs the romantic effect conveyed by 'pearl', 'India' and 'wandering flood'. A similar indication of suspicious zeal, as if Cressida wishes to overdramatize the unshakeable nature of her attachment, can be detected in her farewell speech already quoted (IV, ii, 104–8), in which she compares 'the strong base and building' of her love with 'the very centre of the earth / Drawing all things to it'.

Ulysses' degree speech, even when considered *in situ*, is almost an anthology piece. Stein points out a certain disproportion between the grandiose eloquence displayed by Ulysses, who calls on a set of themes from the cosmos, and the crucial subject which is never mentioned, the war with the Trojans. The omission of the referent 'war' isolates the speech from its historic and dramatic context; it creates a purple patch, an object of exhibition in praise of the man who produced it.

In a detailed study of language in *Troilus and Cressida*, T. McAlindon indicates another example of dissonance between speech and situation; it concerns Hector's speech in which he explains why he refuses to carry on fighting against Ajax (IV, v, 118–37), as well as his reply to the intervention of Ajax who is disappointed by the turn of events. McAlindon shows how the proliferation of words of Latin origin and neologisms based on Latin (*obligation, emulation, commixion, dexter, sinister, multipotent, impressure, mirable*) does not simply aim to reproduce the warlike bombast, but also to show the inadequacy of the speech to the circumstances: 'loud words which no seen or foreseeable acts can justify'.[18]

Likewise, Thersites' fanatical cynicism and the stream of abuse he spits out all the time bear no comparison with what he sees and what we see of his compatriots' behaviour. Thersites is 'lost in the labyrinth of [his] fury'; his speech has no real relevance to things; it generates itself and takes pleasure in contemplating its own performance; it also becomes an object of curiosity, an element in the general set-up of confrontation of different types of speech, counterpointing the love and chivalry speech, whose excess it mimics. When the battle of the leaders puts an end to the battle of words, Thersites proves no longer useful and appears only once more (V, iii) just before the death of Hector. Thersites is firmly anchored in a world where logomachy holds sway.

There is an arresting and meaningful detail when Ulysses asks Agamemnon for permission to speak and Agamemnon replies thus:

> Speak, Prince of Ithaca, and be't of less expect
> That matter needless, of importless burden,
> Divide thy lips, than we are confident
> When rank Thersites opens his mastic jaws
> We shall hear music, wit, and oracle.
>
> I, iii, 70–74

Why make an allusion to Thersites, thereby giving a succinct presentation of the character, in such a solemn context? Thersites has not yet appeared on stage; he plays a subordinate role and it is therefore surprising that at this moment he is in the thoughts of Agamemnon, the generalissimo of the Greek army. Agamemnon contrasts the content of two types of speech, not in terms of what they are, but in terms of what they are not, of what they could not be; this 'tortive' formulation is very much in character. But the contrast between Thersites and Ulysses introduces a touch of dramatic irony which the spectator will appreciate later. Without realizing it, Agamemnon challenges the usefulness of Ulysses' speech, since that of Thersites, whatever its content, symbolizes nothing but futility.

Words in *Troilus and Cressida* are ridden with impotence; they have no effect on the course of events and the amplification of speech changes nothing. Although Nestor deified Agamemnon ('thy godlike seat') and Aeneas followed suit ('that god in office'), Agamemnon's 'divinity' is not sufficient to make him recognizable by a visiting Trojan:

> AGAM.   What's your affairs, I pray you?
> AENEAS. Sir, pardon, 'tis for Agamemnon's ears.
>   I, iii, 246–7

Speech goes unheeded, even when it is a new, lively speech that sets itself against an overpowering fossilized speech. Cassandra is not only the unheeded voice of the future; she symbolizes the doomed fight between language and the nature of things. Hector's about-face is not only the expression of a choice in favour of chivalrous ethics against reason, it is the sign that the decision to act defies words, however convincing they might be. Troilus eventually understands the futility of words when they come from the mouth of Cressida who betrayed her vow:

> Words, words, mere words, no matter from the heart;
> Th'effect doth operate another way.
>   [Tears the letter.]
>   v, iii, 108–9

The word loses all credit once it has been repudiated; if adroitly manipulated, it can legitimate anything. Paris maintained that detaining Helen could remove the shame of her abduction; Diomedes does likewise: he maintains, in the presence of Paris, that Paris deserves Helen as much as Menelaus:

> He, like a puling cuckold, would drink up
> The lees and dregs of a flat tamed piece;
> You, like a lecher, out of whorish loins
> Are pleas'd to breed out your inheritors.
> Both merits pois'd, each weighs nor less nor more,
> But he as thee, each heavier for a whore.
>   IV, i, 62–7

It is always possible to play with words and make them say anything, because rhetoric is an exemption from commitment. But reversible speech does not suppress the war, with its deaths and its pathetic stakes; Diomedes knows this and soon moves on to more serious things, as if to show the inanity of his demonstration:

> hear me, Paris –
> For every false drop in her bawdy veins
> A Grecian's life hath sunk; for every scruple
> Of her contaminated carrion weight
> A Trojan hath been slain.
>
> IV, i, 69–73

Troilus, who does not have the cold lucidity of his rival, remains an adept of rhetoric to the end. How formally he concludes his speech after Cressida's betrayal:

> Instance, O instance! strong as Pluto's gates:
> Cressid is mine, tied with the bonds of heaven.
> Instance, O instance! strong as heaven itself:
> The bonds of heaven are slipp'd, dissolv'd, and loos'd;
> And with another knot, five-finger-tied,
> The fractions of her faith, orts of her love,
> The fragments, scraps, the bits, and greasy relics
> Of her o'er-eaten faith are given to Diomed.
>
> V, ii, 152–9

The balancing, the repeated exclamations, the ternary rhythm, the enumerative crescendo of the last lines and the base food image at the end which counterbalances the references to Pluto and to heaven – all this makes the conclusion the peroration of a speech. Troilus is lost in the labyrinth of his eloquence and gives himself over to the delights of the word. But a speech which is as passionate as this is surely a half-lie, as Ulysses intimates:

> May worthy Troilus be half attach'd
> With that which here his passion doth express?
>
> V, ii, 160–1

An ill-considered word is like a word renounced: it loses its credibility; nothing guarantees that it will be kept. When provoked by Achilles, Hector had let himself give a 'mad' pledge: 'I'll kill thee everywhere, yea, o'er and o'er'. His subsequent refusal to yield to Priam's request that he renounce the fight shows his determination to 'endeavour deeds to match these words' (IV, v, 258). But Hector dies at the hands of Achilles, the arch-renegade. He dies for having wanted, in his last moments, to restore the continuity between speech and action. Words let loose, words broken, hackneyed, dilated or distorted – the list of symptoms of this pathology of language is endless – are the visible signs of the evil prevalent in the micro-societies which Shakespeare depicts in his play. But it is not because evil is more widespread here than elsewhere that

Troilus and Cressida is more Mannerist than *Julius Caesar* or *Hamlet*; it is because its dramatic form is more propitious than others for the aesthetics of abnormality. Considered variously as a tragedy, a comedy, or a historical drama, *Troilus and Cressida* is precariously poised on the indistinct boundary where each of these genres drifts into what it is not. To summarize the play's Mannerism in brief, I would say that it consists in *foiling* expectation, at all levels of the play's structure.

In *Troilus and Cressida*, Shakespeare shows a playful detachment, which is always undervalued because the play is so sombre. But, as is said in the Prologue, we are not forced to like it:

> Like, or find fault: do as your pleasures are:
> Now good, or bad, 'tis but the chance of war.
>
> Prologue, 30–1

Things are uncertain as regards artistic preference as well. One may consider Shakespeare's taste dubious, not to say academic, when he tacks on to the play the incongruous dialogue of the Prologue and the Epilogue, of Heroism and the Pox. In *Shakespeare and his Predecessors*, published in 1896, F.S. Boas concludes his analysis of the play with these moving words:

The reader today mourns the degradation of the mediaeval romance of love and chivalry into a satire, however legitimate in itself, of the mediaeval ideals. It is turning the swords of the offspring against their mother's breast. And even if this be pardoned, we shudder, as an Elizabethan would never have done, at the spectacle of the god-like creations of the Greek Muse being dragged through the dirt . . . The feudal code of love and honour, artificial though it may be, deserves better than to be made the butt of savage scorn. Cervantes, within almost the same hour, had discovered a more excellent fashion of smiling it away.[19]

'As an Elizabethan would never have done . . .' Boas could not predict, at the end of the last century, that our era, hardened by other forms of destruction, would have sufficient iconoclastic taste and cynical detachment to appreciate the provocative and sometimes cruel games of Mannerism, *as an Elizabethan would have done.*

CHAPTER 7

Mostrar l'arte: All's Well That Ends Well *and* Measure for Measure

From the Forest of Arden, where the consort of voices and instruments are celebrating the wedding of loved ones, the reuniting of a father with his daughter and niece, the reconciliation of two brothers and the return of a prince to his estates, some minor, jarring notes reach our ears and add a touch of subtle irony to the triumphant tones of Hymen's choric song. Two weddings strike a somewhat discordant note: Phebe, faithful to her word (but dispossessed of her love since Ganymede changed back into Rosalind), marries Silvius, her long-rejected suitor, while Touchstone, once transported by passion, contents himself with Audrey, the country wench. After Jaques, the melancholy bachelor, has performed the ritual task of giving each Jack his Jill, he returns to the 'abandon'd cave' where, far from the festivities and the court, he will pursue his complacent meditation on the vicissitudes of the world.

Another denouement, another tune: *Twelfth Night* ends more humbly, on Feste's song full of longing for the good old days and regret over the endless rain. When Viola reveals her identity, Olivia realizes her error: the boy she loves is a woman. Believing him to be Cesario (alias Viola), she has promised herself to Sebastian – the male double of his sister Viola – and Olivia is now dumbfounded at the situation. 'Be not amazed – right noble is his blood', observes Duke Orsino to the girl who has always resisted his advances and now witnesses the sardonic revenge of unrequited love. Deceived to her advantage, but deceived nevertheless, Olivia has reason to pity Malvolio, for he experiences only shame and anger from having been so 'notoriously abused'. As for Orsino, who is bereft of any hope of obtaining the hand of Olivia, he yields to the love of Viola and is determined to 'share in this most happy wreck'; is this the wreck which cast brother and sister onto the shores of Illyria, or the wreck of his illusions? He will marry his page, once she has taken off her livery to don again the clothes of her sex.

What I find intriguing and attractive in these half-tone denouements

146

is not so much the image of blissful harmony thus outlined before us, as the lucid, amused look which the playwright casts upon his work. Good psychological and moral reasons can be found to explain why all ends well for some, less well for others and rather badly for yet others. A sense of justice (to each according to merit) is a great part of the contentment which we derive from comedy and which enlivens our existence for a while even after the show is over. But a voice from the back whispers that justice is not all, that it alone cannot settle everything and that in the theatre the return of concord is not quite as unerring as the return of spring after winter. This discreet voice, which sometimes belies our conviction of a justice operating from within or above, is the voice of the playwright confronting us with the necessities of art. Its message holds in two words: *comédie oblige*. This is why pursuing a happy end may justify compromises with or infringements of strict distributive justice. What is rightly considered an ethical requirement is also a professional obligation binding the author of comedies. There is no question of Phebe and Olivia going back on their word (despite their annoyance at having been deceived about the merchandise), of Sebastian taking offence at having been mistaken for his sister disguised as a boy, of Orsino going on courting Olivia. Without last-minute adjustments which do not always leave the characters' self-esteem totally unscathed, without providential reunions and saving conversions, without the artifice of the theatre, it would be less easy to overcome the destructive forces which divide not only people from each other, but also individuals within themselves. Like all great art, the art of Shakespeare hides nothing of the conventions which sustain it. On a square of boards – his Prospero's island – the playwright exerts demiurgic powers, but these are shown for what they are: a form of magic woven from cords scarcely more difficult to handle than those of the puppet-master.

MANNERIST HAPPY-END, OR THE POWER OF ART

All's Well and *Measure for Measure* go to unprecedented lengths in unveiling the artificiality of the dramatic machinery. When Mannerist painters elongate their figures regardless of verisimilitude and the Vitruvian canons, when they ride roughshod over Alberti's perspective, employ rare or conspicuously unrealistic colours, excessively reduce or enlarge the encompassing space, what are they doing if not calling attention to the contrived nature of their work? Painting then appears as what it is: the implementation of certain figurative choices. Classical art minimizes the role of artifice as if to persuade us that its conventions express a figurative order as natural and as indisputable as the order of things it claims to reproduce. With *All's Well* and *Measure for Measure*, Shakespeare still appears clad in Prospero's mantle, but it is worn inside out as if to show off the stitching. These two plays demonstrate *in vivo* the mechanisms of the theatre. In *Hamlet*, the play-within-the-play is the emblem of theatre generating truth *and* deceit. In *Troilus*, isolated elements of parody metonymically refer to the parodic spirit of the entire work. In *All's Well* and *Measure for Measure*, Shakespeare further develops his meditation on the theatre, now focusing specifically on the mechanisms of a certain type of tragicomedy. In these two plays, the fable is dramatized in such a way as to make plainly visible the indissoluble, consubstantial union of art and artifice. Superimposed on the adventures of Bertram, Helena and Parolles, of Angelo, Claudio and Isabella, another adventure unfolds before our eyes: one no less exciting, in its own metadramatic way – that of the artist at work.

Seen from this angle, *All's Well* and *Measure for Measure* are less 'problematic' than is often thought. The denouement of the two plays has long been the subject of questions and demurral (fortunately more from critics than from audiences) because of the strong impression that everything has been sacrificed to the convention that all ends well. How can we explain, let alone justify, the deficiency of Bertram's speech when faced with the 'resurrection' of Helena as she arrives to claim her due (her husband's love) after having overcome the hurdles he himself had laid before her?

> HEL.   There is your ring,
> And, look you, here's your letter. This it says:
> *When from my finger you can get this ring*
> *And is by me with child & c.* This is done;
> Will you be mine now you are doubly won?
> BER.   If she, my liege, can make me know this clearly
> I'll love her dearly, ever, ever, dearly.
>
> v, iii, 304–10

There is no lack of psychological explanations: we can read it as a divine pardon which is so overwhelming that it deprives its beneficiary of speech; but could it not be the simple surrender of the taciturn soldier recognizing defeat? Some critics question the sincerity of Bertram's repentance, because he asks for forgiveness in the most ordinary way possible: 'O pardon!' (v, iii, 302). They doubt the sincerity of his love because of his opportunistic tendency to lie, and they fear that Helena will be the one to pay in their marriage. One thing stands out disconcertingly: this denouement is no apotheosis; it is not the moving, festive reconciliation of romantic comedy, even less the mystical vision of grace descending upon the sinner as in Baroque tragicomedy (*Pericles*, *The Winter's Tale*). Why such a platitude after Helena's spectacular reappearance? Shakespeare's text suggests an answer.

Bertram lays down a surprising condition for the love he owes his wife: that first she explain 'clearly' (no less!) how she managed to deceive him twice – by retrieving the family ring he had given to Diana and by becoming pregnant by him. Our psychologists (who are also moralists) will deem this sheer effrontery. But more than the impertinence of the request, it is its non-pertinence which calls for comment. At the moment when an effusion of great feeling would seem natural and dramatically desirable, Shakespeare disappoints our expectations and uses Bertram's ultimate intervention to bring us back to the manoeuvring skill of Helena. The dramatic impact of this privileged moment, which sanctions the long-awaited reunion of the two spouses and the possible birth of reciprocated love, is omitted to make room for an insistent reminder of Helena's role as an intriguer at a time when the intrigue has been definitely unravelled and Helena has just appeared under the halo of her mysterious 'resurrection', cast in the quasi-allegorical features of Clemency. Thanks to a typically Mannerist displacement, the emotional potential of the present moment is neutralized, as if Shakespeare's primary concern before the close was to remind us how much shrewdness it took Helena, and how much artifice it took him, to take up the impossible challenge. Significantly, a few lines further on, the King himself voices a desire to hear the story of the events 'from point to point'. A request for clarification, a promise of explanation or a plain unfolding of such mysteries often accompany Shakespeare's denouements. In *The Merchant of Venice*, Portia willingly submits to questions on what has happened. In *Much Ado About Nothing*, the Friar promises everyone to recount the fake death of Hero once the marriage rites are performed. In *Twelfth Night*, Fabian dismantles the trap set for Malvolio. In *Hamlet*, Horatio gives his version of the facts for the benefit of Fortinbras. But the explanations requested, promised or obtained do not constitute the whole of the denouement. In no way do they modify the atmosphere of joy or sadness surrounding the conclusion of the play. In *All's Well*, which seems to be lacking in festive spirit, the impatience to discover the solution to the riddle, echoed by Helena's commitment to speak the truth, fills the void created by the absence of celebration and sentimental outpouring. Typically, the only concession to emotion is made in comic form; Lafew says, 'Mine eyes smell onions' (v, iii, 314), as if Shakespeare were making a point of avoiding sentiment and excluding pathos. What counts is not to celebrate the reconciliation of husband and wife, still less to predict the advent of wedded bliss, as the King's fittingly ambiguous last words seem to suggest: 'All yet seems well, and if it end so meet,/The bitter past, more welcome is the sweet' (v, iii, 327–8). What counts is to revitalize in the audience, with the aid of the applause-seeking Epilogue, the impression of a superbly constructed play, a dazzling feat of theatrical art culminating in a finale where Bertram's successive lies cause a stream of twists and turns, until the appearance of Helena alive and well precipitates the unworthy husband's repentance and concludes the story of his humiliations. But this has negative repercussions: W.W. Lawrence rightly maintains that the most direct way (let us say, the least Mannerist) would have been to reintroduce Helena earlier, so that she could beg for justice. Thus we would have been spared those misunderstandings and reversals of situation which 'sacrifice psychological consistency to purely theatrical effect'.[1] But what if the aim of the 'play' were in fact theatrical effect, a display of artifice? One may well ascribe Shakespeare's disregard of psychological 'truth' to the 'inconsistencies' of the Elizabethan era; yet why is it that Shakespeare's denouements are not *always* so glaringly artificial? The Mannerist hypothesis is more plausible: such display of artifice reflects an aesthetic purpose in which all the effects make us marvel at the artist's craft and the excellence of his 'manner'.

Two speeches by Diana, partly written in rhyming couplets, herald Helena's entry. They serve to create an atmosphere of mystery and prepare us for the fulfilment of a 'miracle':

> KING. Wherefore hast thou accus'd him all this while?
> DIA.   Because he's guilty and he is not guilty.
>   He knows I am no maid, and he'll swear to't;
>   I'll swear I am a maid and he knows not.
>   Great king, I am no strumpet; by my life
>   I am either maid or else this man's old wife.
>
>   v, iii, 282–7

> DIA.   He knows himself my bed he hath defil'd;
>   And at that time he got his wife and child.
>   Dead though she be she feels her young one kick.
>   So there's my riddle: one that's dead is quick,
>   And now behold the meaning.
>
>   v, iii, 294–8

When well directed, Helena's 'resurrection' should fill its witnesses (characters and audience) with wonder, as at Hermione's 'resurrection' set up by Paulina, the reunion of Pericles and Thaïsa in the temple of Diana in Ephesus, or the vision of Miranda and Ferdinand playing chess which Prospero 'discovers' for his visitors. But we wonder at different things depending on whether we are faced with a tragicomedy like *All's Well*, or romances like *The Winter's Tale, Pericles* or *The Tempest*. The happy ending of the romances appears to stem more from the beneficial action of Providence and the regenerating effect of Time than from the technical skill of the playwright; it is as if Shakespeare writing his last plays cared as little to show off his virtuosity as did Michelangelo sculpting his last *Pietà*. *The Tempest* is an admirable construction, one in which the action follows a straightforward, effortless course. In *All's Well* and *Measure for Measure* this supreme state of artistic self-effacement has not yet been reached. Art is pushed to the forefront, even if the denouement of *All's Well*, even more than that of *Measure for Measure*, suggests that the author has entrusted a share of his prerogatives to Providence. In this respect, *All's Well* is closer to the romances. Helena's character is a combination of the two traditional figures of the Shrewd Woman and the Providential Agent, and it is therefore predictable that her reappearance, sanctioning the triumph of the ruse, should also be shrouded in an atmosphere of miracle. But the manner in which the event is inserted into the middle of a series of virtuoso *coups de théâtre*, and the emphasis laid on the obstacles Helena has had to overcome, make me wonder whether the most amazing miracle of all is not, in the last analysis, the 'magic' of theatre, which creates such wonders. All things considered, the marvel obtained from Helena's reappearance, so magnificently staged by herself (with the complicity of Diana), merges with the way we marvel at the art of the playwright, supreme master of dramatic art. The denouement of *All's Well* does its utmost to limit its emotional appeal in order to focus the audience's attention more effectively on the artistry with which it is engineered.

But the sense of staging and the systematic exploitation of theatrical conventions culminate in the denouement of *Measure for Measure*. This, exceptionally, takes a whole act, itself consisting of one scene, as if Shakespeare's editors wanted to stress the unity of the final episode. Contrary to his natural preference for surreptitious ploys rather than open displays, the Duke of Vienna instigates a spectacular open-air trial for the people and nobles assembled, with himself topping the bill. Once the order has been given to send Angelo the head of Ragozine in place of that of Claudio (IV, iii), the rest of the fourth act (about 150 lines) is entirely devoted to the preparations for the final confrontation which, as in a classic detective story, will bring the truth to light. Assured of the logistic support of the Provost and Friar Peter, the Duke gives weight to the idea that Isabella's brother really has been executed, so that she can play her role of accuser thoroughly; he persuades her, behind the scenes, to make a false declaration whereby she claims to have given in to Angelo's advances. Meanwhile, the Duke receives from Lucio the unsolicited confession that he had abandoned the woman who bore his child, which confirms the accusation already formulated against him by Mistress Overdone. He informs Mariana, also behind the scenes, of the role she will have to play, and sends Angelo and Escalus news of his imminent return and of his decision to hold a public hearing of his subjects' grievances. He even goes as far as settling material details, like choosing friends to escort him and ordering trumpets to salute his arrival at the town gates. The one episode in which the Duke does not intervene is Angelo's introspective monologue at the end of Act IV, scene iv, the function of which is to acquaint the audience with the state of mind of the accused-to-be prior to his trial and to give a vague foretaste of the two opposing tendencies which will then determine his behaviour: a bad conscience which will prompt Angelo to wish his own death in all sincerity when he sees himself confounded; yet also an unimpaired confidence in the credibility of his word (owing to his function as head of State), which leads him to feign indignation in response to the accusations of Isabella and Mariana. To avoid an effect of laboriousness and to keep the action going at the same brisk pace, Shakespeare has certain preparatory steps taken behind the scenes and thus compresses dramatic time. Except for Angelo and Lucio, who stand accused, and Escalus, who is kept out of the plot so that he can sincerely speak up for the judiciary when the Duke himself (disguised as a monk) derides it , all the participants in the grand trial scene to follow now know what they have to do. In this bustle, there is to me something of the feverish atmosphere that holds the stage before a first night. But then the trumpets sound, as in the Globe before the play starts. Enter the Duke. Make way for the court! Make way for the theatre!

In structure, the single scene of Act v resembles the final scene of *All's Well*; the action progresses by way of carefully measured revelations and craftily wrought reversals of situation. Although the denouement of *Measure for Measure* includes no 'miraculous' appearance, the unmasking of three characters (Mariana, the Duke and Claudio) makes it just as spectacular. Moreover, it offers a brilliant sample of courtroom verbal display, ranging from Isabella's passionate rhetoric to Lucio's burlesque interventions.

No account of this sensational trial can fittingly render the almost diabolical skill in which Shakespeare arranges the entrances and exists, organizes the twists and turns, apportions the high and low points and creates a climate of never-flagging suspense throughout this rigged hearing, the result of which is known in advance. Many denouements in comedies outshine this one in drollness, wit or emotion, but none equals the denouement of *Measure for Measure* in sheer virtuosity. Shakespeare's manipulation of his characters is so amazing that critics are indeed amazed to find that even the proud, rigid Isabella can be so easily manipulated. But the audience is thrilled, giving itself up to the delights of the game and forgetting psychological coherence.

The price to be paid for this breathtaking display of theatrical craftsmanship is language that is uncommonly wooden and a sullen atmosphere. But Mannerist art is seldom warm. Except for Isabella's theatrical vehemence at the beginning of her deposition, emotions are conveyed with maximum restraint. True, when the Duke promises Mariana a better husband than Angelo, her reply is touching: 'O my dear Lord,/I crave no other, nor no better man' (v, i 423–4). And we are moved to think how much love and wisdom such an apparently trivial generalization conceals:

> They say best men are moulded out of faults,
> And, for the most, become much more the better
> For being a little bad.
>
> v, i, 437–9

As in Bertram's 'O pardon!', Shakespeare is bent on avoiding explosion of speech, a call for help, the imploring desire to see Angelo snatched from the hands of the executioner. Isabella speaks not a single line to voice her joy at seeing her brother alive, nor does Angelo to thank the sovereign for the leniency he does not deserve, nor Claudio or Juliet to celebrate the happiness of being reunited. Lucio alone, who does not benefit totally from the Duke's leniency, indulges in a half-comical, half-resigned comment: 'Marrying a punk, my Lord, is pressing to death,/Whipping, and hanging' (v, i, 520–21). E. Schanzer observes that Angelo's conversion is treated 'perfunctorily' and ascribes this negligence to 'the general bustle of the *dénouement*'.[2] But this overlooks the fact that Shakespeare does *not* intend his audience to focus on Angelo's state of mind, any more than on Bertram's, at the moment when, after being cornered, he admits his infamy. Confessing and repenting are not treated here from a psychological standpoint, but as a necessary element of dramaturgy.

Schanzer also remarks that Isabella's appeal in favour of Angelo is disgustingly legalistic, since it seeks to establish his innocence *de facto* and *de jure*, whilst recognizing the guilt of his intentions. Schanzer concludes that Isabella's plea is a speech for the defence with an acquittal in mind but not the surge of charity a Christian should feel for his or her enemy, the very opposite of the pardon Isabella had requested from Angelo for her brother. Schanzer is partially right: Isabella's speech is designed to appeal to the monarch's sense of justice rather than to his duty of charity. The fact remains that the original impetus behind it derives both from a desire for justice as regards Mariana (to return good for good) and from a desire for charity as regards Angelo (to return good for evil). It is clear that Isabella accomplishes that which Angelo could not. More interesting, however, is the reason why Shakespeare has Isabella speak in legalistic terms which seemingly distort the true meaning of her motives. Was it perhaps necessary for the dramatist once again to liken Isabella to Angelo, two puritan figures, apt to value the Letter higher than the Spirit? There is, however, another, more convincing, reason: the rational discourse of the law and of attenuating circumstances is the only one suitable to the atmosphere Shakespeare intends to create surrounding the trial, the only one leaving the Duke the possibility of *rejecting* the request made to him ('Your suit's unprofitable . . .'); for what is important is to prolong the suspense ('I have bethought me of another fault') until the decisive moment when Claudio will be brought to the court to be unmasked. It is the reappearance of Claudio alive (following the non-execution of the death-warrant) which saves Angelo, rather than the Duke's kindness:

> DUKE. By this Lord Angelo perceives he's safe;
> Methinks I see a quickening in his eye.
> Well, Angelo, your evil quits you well.
> v, i, 492–4

Life calls for life; the authorities endorse the fact. Salvation comes less from the Duke's leniency than from the successful outcome of his contrivance, whereby he has warded off the effects of Angelo's cruelty. Thus Shakespeare underlines the prodigious efficiency of his *deus ex machina* and the real motivation of his benevolence, which is humanity and political wisdom rather than true Christian forgiveness inspired by selfless love. In no way is the denouement so contrived as to evoke, however slightly, the sublimity of Baroque apotheosis.

Why does Isabella not answer the marriage proposal the Duke makes on two occasions? Arguably, the young girl's silence conforms to psychology and decorum: a novice can hardly be expected to acquiesce immediately to such an astounding and totally unexpected request. But this silence means neither consent, nor refusal motivated by an irrevocable attachment to the chastity of the cloister. Isabella simply says nothing. The true cause for this abstention should be sought once again in the dramatic mode: nothing should intervene which might distract the audience's attention from the technical prowess of the denouement. As for the reasons behind the Duke's proposal, they have nothing to do with psychology or sentiment. They are symbolic and theatrical. Symbolically, there is the need to incorporate Christian virtues as embodied by Isabella into the art of good government, and the need to associate human love with divine love in the play's spiritual landscape. Only two virtuous characters like the Duke and Isabella can bring these two forms of love to perfect fruition. At this level, the symbolic meaning of the Duke's plan matters more than its possible fulfilment. This explains why the audience is not in the least disturbed by the uncertainty hanging over the two characters' future. The Duke's proposal is so devoid of sentiment that it is made to appear as a purely dramatic motif, a theatrical convention, yet another artifice. This prospective marriage comes as the crowning piece to three actual marriages; it is the finishing touch without which the play would have been theatrically incomplete.

At the risk of disappointing those who expect comedy to end with happy certainties (conjugal bliss, social harmony, the restoration of values etc.) Shakespeare does not anticipate the future. Bertram marries Helena, and we like to think that this already fertile union will rejuvenate the exquisite, yet ageing, society represented by the King of France, Lafew and the Countess. Yet the King's 'seems' ('All yet seems well') hangs heavy, as does Gertrude's 'seems' in *Hamlet*. Claudio marries Juliet and Angelo marries Mariana, but Shakespeare does not commit himself on Isabella's future and on Vienna's return to morality under the Duke's more stringent rule. *All's Well* and *Measure for Measure* end exactly where the threads of the plots unravel. In his Mannerist comedies, Shakespeare cultivates the idea that the theatre is sufficient in itself and should close quite naturally on the contemplation of its own magic. The task of morally concluding this 'regrettable' *nonfinito* falls into the pious hands of the good, only slightly Mannerist Mary Lamb: 'When she became Duchess of Vienna, the excellent example of the virtuous Isabella worked such a complete reformation among the young ladies of that city, that from that time none ever fell into the transgression of Juliet, the repentant wife of the reformed Claudio.'[3] We should be grateful to Shakespeare for never having ended a play on such a depressing note.

Shakespeare foils the hopes of the supporters of justice in much the same way. From Dr Johnson to Elizabeth Pope, including Coleridge,[4] critics have rightly noted that the general amnesty in favour of Angelo, Claudio, Barnardine and Lucio (with a reservation concerning the latter) wrongs our sense of justice and belies all hope raised by the play's title. There are well-known ideological reasons for this: as in *All's Well* where Bertram is given a total pardon, as in *The Merchant of Venice* where Shylock is punished for not having shown pity, in *Measure for Measure* Shakespeare evokes the superior value of clemency, even when its generous use entails some injustice. From the moment that Isabella pleads for Angelo's pardon at a time when she still believes he is guilty of her brother's death, in a play dedicated to denouncing someone unable to forgive, the Duke could do no less than embark on the road of clemency for all. But once again these reasons tie up with others that are specifically theatrical. As W.W. Lawrence puts it: 'The claims of strict justice are secondary to those of stage entertainment.'[5] Meting out punishment at the denouement would have prevented or delayed the repairing of the wrongs done to Mariana and Juliet. Marriage had to be both punishment for the guilty and compensation for the victims, and the beginnings of rejuvenation for all. Between the strict, ethical administration of justice and the respect of the conventions of comedy, Shakespeare chooses the conventions. Moreover, the decision to punish would have obliged the dramatist to mete out fitting sentences and Shakespeare was not interested in this kind of calculation. A package deal for all, as expeditiously served as can be, was indeed the only solution compatible with the requirements of entertainment and the sense of wonder aimed at by the technical prowess of the last act. Pardon for all, with neither discrimination nor deliberation, without outpouring or apotheosis, best fitted the Mannerist spirit of the denouement. What does it matter if we cannot totally adhere to the justice of this Duke of comedy and if we harbour lingering doubts as to his qualities as a statesman? The aesthetic pleasure we derive from this beautifully orchestrated finale makes us forget all the rest.

All's Well and *Measure for Measure* end like a game of chess between grand-masters, when the winner reaps the fruit of a strategy carefully elaborated throughout the game. Ultimately, it is the dramatist who pockets the winnings amassed by the manipulating characters, Helena and Duke Vincentio, who are themselves his creatures. By doing this, he runs the risk of making the characters appear hollow and the situations artificial. This is a very real risk; as characters in the theatre are not like the pieces on a chessboard, their actions cannot be reduced to simple tactical movements, and theatrical situations are not just the preparatory phases for a good move. The dramatist manipulates, but he also imitates. He must give an air of reality to the shows he proposes, including the show of his own skill. Freedom to use the artifice of theatre is hemmed in by the need for a sufficiently credible image of reality allowing the spectator to play the game. I am broaching here a much-debated question and one often raised in relation to *All's Well* and *Measure for Measure*, that of realism and artifice.

Though artifice holds undisputed sway at the denouement, it also appears throughout these two plays. It is there in the King's recovery thanks to Helena's miracle cure, in the exchange of rings which finally confounds Bertram, in the substitution of Helena for Diana in Bertram's bed, of Mariana for Isabella in Angelo's, in the false news of Helena's death and of Claudio's execution, in the sending of Ragozine's head in place of Claudio's, not to mention in the unmaskings, both metaphorical like that of Parolles and literal like those of Mariana, Claudio and the Duke, and the reappearances already mentioned. But the art of the dramatist is not confined to the ravelling and unravelling of those marvellous plots redolent of childhood story-telling. It gives us other, more 'adult' pleasures, such as seeing Helena languishing at the thought of the young, inaccessible aristocrat whom she loves in secret, then confiding in the Countess with such embarrassment and cunning; seeing Helena despairing at being cast away far from her husband, her distress at the thought of Bertram's possible death at war, and her restored confidence when her plan succeeds. In a darker mood, we hold our breath at Isabella's efforts to wrench her brother's pardon from Angelo; our somewhat voyeuristic attention is tensely focused on Angelo's mounting desire, on the purity of Isabella clad in her novice's dress which he finds more arousing than her physical beauty; we lose nothing of the misunderstandings and insinuations – deliberate and accidental – between

Isabella and Angelo during their second meeting, before desire and anger are unleashed; we shudder when, in a moment of almost unbearable violence, Isabella leaves Claudio to die, under the pretext that he is weak enough to prefer his life to his sister's virginity; and we are aghast at the sight of Claudio, so sensually in love with life, gripped by the anguish of death which turns the warm, throbbing body of the living man into 'A kneaded clod' and congeals the fickle spirit into 'thick-ribbed' ice. Alongside such privileged moments, which foster the illusion of an intense psychological existence, there are others which, though less tense, ring just as true and reflect something of the heterogeneous substance of reality: Lucio's scandalmongering and mischievousness, relieved by surges of heartfelt goodness; the Duke's predilection for 'dark corners' and underhand manoeuvres, compounded with a capricious nonchalance in the running of state affairs; Parolles' verbal and sartorial self-conceit concealing a mean soul nevertheless aware of its mediocrity; Lavatch's melancholy bawdiness bound up with a puritan conscience obsessed by sin, and not forgetting the sordid but likeable fauna of Vienna's red-light district: Mistress Overdone, Pompey, Froth, Elbow etc.

Admittedly, every Shakespeare comedy has its own share of romantic situations, brought about by the whims of Fortune, the cunning of man or the intervention of supernatural creatures. But there is not one play, however dependent on the artifices of comedy, which does not claim to hold a mirror up to nature, even through the most unbelievable situations authorized by the conventions of theatre. It is not therefore the unavoidable combination of realism and artifice which differentiates *All's Well* and *Measure for Measure* from the other comedies, but the manner – unprecedented, I think – in which these two components are forced to coexist throughout. It seems that Shakespeare, always on the look-out for experiments, has determined to push realism and artifice to the extreme, thus banking on the yet untapped possibilities afforded by the exacerbation of disparities.

It is enlightening at this point to ponder Shakespeare's use of his sources both fictional and dramatic, but since the question has been thoroughly investigated,[6] I will satisfy myself with the remark that Shakespeare was working in two opposite directions: (1) towards a more complex portrayal of feelings and conduct, a deepening of moral and spiritual issues and the building up around the main characters of a rich, vivid human environment thanks to realistically drawn minor characters; (2) towards a proportional heightening of romance and artifice.

Shakespeare not only retained the romantic situations supplied by his sources – the healing of the King as rite of passage on the way to marriage, the substitution of one woman for another in the bed of a man as a means to save virginity in peril and to consummate a lawful union, and the tyranny of the corrupt magistrate who demands a salary in kind – but he borrowed from folklore the theme of the sovereign in disguise spying incognito on his subjects. Unlike Boccaccio, who had attributed the recovery of the King to the efficacy of Giletta's therapy, Shakespeare presents it as a miracle, thereby stressing the overtly fictional nature of the episode; counting on Providence, he sees to it that Helena chances upon Bertram in the course of her pilgrimage, whereas Boccaccio had his Giletta set out purposely to find Beltramo. Even more significantly, Shakespeare organizes Helena's magic reappearance after the false news of her death. *Measure for Measure* sees the use of the bed-trick already found in *All's Well*, but the major innovation is the role assigned to the ruler. Giraldi Cinthio's Emperor Maximian and George Whetstone's King Corvinus intervened only to judge and pardon; Shakespeare's Duke Vincentio is a fully-fledged, omnipresent and almost omnipotent *deus ex machina* plotting and lying on behalf of Truth and Good. In Mannerist fashion, Shakespeare administers to his audience an overdose of realism and romance, seemingly to impress upon them how much art is needed to cope with such heterogeneous material and how much artifice is necessary to bring the severe trials inflicted upon his characters to a happy conclusion.

Structurally, however, the two plays are very different. *Measure for Measure* is a diptych hinging on the pivotal Act III, scene i. The first half of the play deals with the conflicts arising among Angelo, Isabella and Claudio and within each of them as a result of the arrest of Claudio and the threats hanging over his life. The second half is devoted to the setting up of the stratagem contrived by Duke Vincentio disguised as a friar. This binary mode of composition, called 'split structure' by Bernard Beckerman, its chief proponent,[7] was common practice with Shakespeare, but nowhere else carried to such extremes, with such dazzling, almost provocative clarity. Thus the story falls into two very distinct parts that might be summarized respectively as 'the time of ordeals' and 'how to pull through', a method that most critics from Walter Pater to Philip Edwards have deemed curiously primitive and aesthetically crude.[8] Indeed, it may be frustrating to see the poignant 'drama of choice and decision' (Edwards), as it is played out in the first part, not followed by an equally emotional exploration of the dire consequences of such crucial decisions as Angelo's resolve to seduce Isabella and her refusal to buy her brother's life through the gift of her virginity. From the time the Duke offers to help – 'Vouchsafe a word, young sister, but one word' (III, i, 151) – our hope for more drama of the kind we have enjoyed so far is blighted by the Duke's setting into motion the more prosaic, even at times comic, machinery of 'how to pull through'.

C.K. Stead makes an interesting distinction between 'narrative structure' and 'poetic texture', and argues that, whilst the two are kept in 'rich and dynamic balance' in the first part, in the second we are instead 'led to inspect the convention rather than to experience the play', as if, he goes on, 'Shakespeare was explaining his way towards the comic resolution instead of writing his way there'.[9] Stead is right; Shakespeare's demonstration of the theatrical conventions necessary to achieve the comic resolution he is aiming at is so systematic in the last act that these read almost like a pedagogical treatise in action (or a practical meta-discourse) on the art of fashioning potentially tragic material into a comic form.

That such dichotomy exists is beyond question, but is it so detrimental to the unity of the play that we must resort to an allegorical interpretation to rescue it? The fact is that on stage the split structure of *Measure for Measure* is not necessarily perceived as an artistic disaster. Director John Barton agrees that the play, 'which has in the first half been poetically intense and psychologically subtle, is then worked out on a lower, almost fairy-tale level', but, as he observes from firsthand experience, this change, 'obvious enough in the study', disappears in the theatre 'because the actors, if they have brought their characters to life in exploring the first half, can carry through that life into the play's more superficial resolution'.[10] Shakespeare, as an actor himself and possibly a director of his own plays, though not with the regal prerogatives attached to the directing profession today, must have known that efficient acting can produce lasting impressions that outlive the stimuli that cause them. Pursuing Barton's line of thought, I feel that it is precisely because the dramatist starts by portraying emotions with maximum intensity that he can later afford to shift ground to focus on other aspects of his 'art' such as the manipulation of situations and characters in compliance with the artificial conventions of tragicomedy.

It is worth noting, however, that the near effacement of Isabella, Claudio and Angelo during the second part of the play is counteracted by the dramatization of minor characters that had hitherto been sketchily drawn. The Provost, for example, acquires substance as a character through his anguished compassion for Claudio as the fateful hour approaches together with the dilemma he faces, a little later, when the Duke in disguise asks him to have Barnardine executed instead of Claudio. Similarly, Escalus' celebrated insight into the Duke's elusive personality ('One that, above all other strifes, contended especially to know himself,' III, ii, 226) provides the stereotyped figure of the faithful counsellor and even-handed magistrate with a new, interesting dimension. Shakespeare also rounds off his portrayal of Lucio: not only does he further enrich the image of Lucio as a waggish peddler of gossip – a lesser evil when Angelo is concerned – but he develops him into a vile slanderer of the Duke and a loving, sympathetic friend of Claudio and Isabella. At the same time, Shakespeare enhances the picturesque realism of the prison world thanks to memorable figures like Abhorson, who is as finicky as can be regarding the honour of his corporation, Barnardine, a drunken miscreant 'insensible of mortality' who has been rotting for nine years in a dungeon but who, none the less, refuses to be executed until he decides he is ready for the journey, and Pompey, promoted assistant executioner, who thus links Vienna's world of brothels to its world of prisons.

As for the Duke, who is all too often denied human credibility because his role is mainly to activate the action and instigate the denouement, he too benefits from dramatic attention at least equal to that afforded less prominent characters. His disguise forces him to hear Lucio rant on about him, without being able to stop his mouth: this is the comic ransom for going around incognito, the ephemeral revenge of licence over authority, of play over gravity, the intrusion of carnival-like misrule in the heart of austere and depraved Vienna, until one of the two partners breaks the game of involuntary connivance by restoring the other to his true identity, thus ending the time for unrestrained speech. It matters little that Lucio's gossip is unfounded; what counts, setting aside the comic effect, is that the Duke is caught under the fire of commentary, however false, so that his character is not confined to the impersonal role of a *deus ex machina*. The Duke is not only a busy director handing out roles, settling difficult situations (like Barnardine's refusal to be executed) and giving instructions for the forthcoming trial; at times, he takes on the posture of a pensive character drawing lessons from experience couched in well-pondered Euphuistic maxims:

> ESC.   What news abroad i'th'world?
> DUKE. None, but that there is so great a fever on goodness
>   that the dissolution of it must cure it. Novelty is

only in request, and it is as dangerous to be aged in
any kind of course as it is virtuous to be constant in
any undertaking. There is scarce truth enough alive
to make societies secure; but security enough to
make fellowships accurst. Much upon this riddle
runs the wisdom of the world.

III, ii, 215–23

The Duke is also a most fallible demiurge. On at least two occasions
events turn against him; when Angelo's letter arrives, he rashly believes
that Claudio has been pardoned and seizes upon this opportunity to
deliver another moralizing aside, this time in rhyming couplets as if to
make this new demonstration of political wisdom weightier; it is one of
Shakespeare's master-strokes of irony:

This is his pardon, purchas'd by such sin
For which the pardoner himself is in.
Hence hath offence his quick celerity,
When it is borne in high authority.
When vice makes mercy, mercy's so extended
That for the fault's love is th'offender friended.

IV, ii, 106–11

As soon as he hears from the Provost that the letter means death for
Claudio, he still confidently launches his emergency plan of action: why
not execute Barnardine? But there comes a second disappointment
when this new plan fails, demonstrating once again the Duke's miscalcu-
lation. Thereupon the arch-manipulator finds himself short of ideas,
until the Provost comes to his rescue by proposing the Ragozine solution.
It is dramatically and psychologically important that the Duke should
come to feel the resistance or the relative intractability of the human
environment. Such hitches contribute to feed the suspense and human-
ize the character. He thought he knew Angelo? That was without counting on the latter's duplicity. He thought that Barnardine's execution
would be a mere formality? That was without counting on the Provost's
loyalty towards the lawful authorities and on the possibility that even the
most brutish of men may feel concerned by the salvation of their souls.
The Duke is not even spared the discomfort of having to contradict
himself within a few minutes. He confidently asserts that Angelo is just:

were he meal'd with that
Which he corrects, then were he tyrannous;
But this being so, he's just.

IV, ii, 81–3

Yet this must give way to his recognition that Angelo is no less guilty than Claudio:

> Claudio, whom here you have warrant to execute,
> is no greater forfeit to the law than Angelo who
> hath sentenced him.
>
> IV, ii, 156–8

Finally, the pseudo-friar is forced to play his master card earlier than planned and 'go further' than he wished: he produces a letter signed by the Duke announcing his imminent return. So the implementation of the stratagem, however ingeniously contrived, carries within itself a lesson of humility. The providential man is neither an abstraction nor a simple cog (the main one) in a complicated machine, but a human character exposed to Shakespeare's irony. All through the play, even if only unobtrusively, Shakespeare confronts his audience with the usual theme of the moral, and political, improvement of the individual through experience. Applied to the Duke, this is in keeping with the traditional motif of the disguised sovereign who, by righting wrongs, pursues his learning of human nature and good government.

Even with these reservations, it remains true that these secondary characters never acquire such emotionally intense presence on stage as do Isabella, Claudio and Angelo in the first half of the play. The prime motivation behind their actions and their speech is, for the most part, subservient to the practical necessities of the plot. But a similar conclusion applies to these three characters. Take, for example, Angelo's monologue in Act II, scene iv, and that in Act IV, scene v. The first is full of passionate rhetoric loaded with metaphors:

> Heaven hath my empty words,
> Whilst my invention, hearing not my tongue,
> Anchors on Isabel: Heaven in my mouth,
> As if I did but only chew his name,
> And in my heart the strong and swelling evil
> Of my conception.
>
> II, iv, 2–7

The second monologue, on the contrary, though still metaphorical, tones down the spontaneous and violent expression of discomfort:

> This deed unshapes me quite; makes me unpregnant
> And dull to all proceedings. A deflower'd maid;
> And by an eminent body that enforc'd
> The law against it!
>
> IV, iv, 18–21

What now prevails is a reflection on the credibility of Isabella's and Angelo's testimonies, as well as on the legitimacy of Claudio's execution. Angelo's remorse is expressed in a voluntarily flat way, with simple words set in a laboriously and overtly discursive structure:

> But that her tender shame
> Will not proclaim against her maiden loss,
> How might she tongue me! Yet reason dares her no,
> For my authority bears so credent bulk
> That no particular scandal once can touch,
> But it confounds the breather. He should have liv'd;
> Save that his riotous youth, with dangerous sense,
> Might in the times to come have ta'en revenge
> By so receiving a dishonour'd life
> With ransom of such shame. Would yet he had lived.
>
> IV, iv, 21–30

We are struck once again by the restraint put on the expression of feeling, as if the point at this stage were to prevent the characters from giving free rein to their emotions, but to position them on the chessboard of the imminent resolution. This exemplifies the depreciation of the 'poetic' in favour of the 'narrative'.

It is tempting to view *All's Well* as a first draft for the bipartite division found in *Measure for Measure*. The turning-point in the former play comes a little earlier, in Act II, scene ii, when Helena, in obedience to her husband's order to return to Rossillion, arrives in the Countess' home with a letter from Bertram informing her of his decision to bar her from his bed unless she satisfies the two conditions we know to be impossible. This is a very gloomy episode, further darkened by the announcement that Bertram has fled the country to wage war in Italy. In the final monologue – the most poignant of the play – Helena feels anguished at the thought that Bertram is risking his life and she is remorseful for having pushed him to this extreme:

> O you leaden messengers,
> That ride upon the violent speed of fire,
> Fly with false aim; move the still-piecing air
> That sings with piercing; do not touch my Lord.
> Whoever shoots at him, I set him there;
> Whoever charges on his forward breast;
> I am the caitiff that do hold him to't;
> And though I kill him not, I am the cause
> His death was so effected.
>
> III, ii, 108–16

She herself decides to leave so as to allow the son and the beloved spouse to return home:

> I will be gone,
> That pitiful rumour may report my flight
> To consolate thine ear. Come, night; end, day;
> For with the dark, poor thief, I'll steal away.
>
> III, ii, 126–9

The invocation to the night sounds like the end of a tragedy and ironically contrasts with the image of light which radiated through Helena's first monologue:

> 'twere all one
> That I should love a bright particular star
> And think to wed it, he is so above me.
> In his bright radiance and collateral light
> Must I be comforted, not in his sphere.
>
> I, i, 83–7

As long as Bertram was out of reach, Helena could hope to collect some of the 'collateral light' from this bright star. Now that she 'possesses' him and that he is fleeing from her, she is plunged into the dark despair of an unconsummated marriage. At this moment, Helena does not yet know of the restoring power of night. Darkness, which ordinarily lends its black cloak to infamy, can also shroud beneficent enterprises with its protective veil: it is the night which will allow the substitution of Helena for Diana in Bertram's bed and the unmasking of Parolles. Having won the husband she wanted, Helena has lost the man she loves: the second half of the play relates that obstinate conquest of love, just as the first half relates the obstinate conquest of the spouse. Located as it is, at the turning-point in the play, where success and failure intersect, marriage appears like a Mannerist oxymoron for the paradigm of union and disunion.

As G.K. Hunter has noted, in the second half Helena no longer holds the privileged position that was hers in the first.[11] She has less time on stage, and the psychological description of her is briefer, as if Shakespeare had tried out in *All's Well* the methods he was to use shortly afterwards in *Measure for Measure*. This feeling is also borne out by the case of certain minor characters like the Countess, Lafew, the King of France and Lavatch. Shakespeare is careful to describe them realistically in their social and human surroundings, as if to establish them solidly once and for all. But the analogy with *Measure for Measure* stops there. Two important characters acquire substance and stature in the second half: Parolles and Bertram. A significant dimension is added to the former when the bragging and dressing ritual of the 'gallant militarist' are shown to end in real cowardice. The three-stage machination (III, iv; IV, i; IV, iii), which brings this out, counts for a great deal in the action of the second half and serves as the main source of comedy for the whole play. As for Bertram's presence on stage, it increases as Helena's decreases. As his character develops, Bertram becomes more of a paradox: as a man of honour, he fights courageously and, for this reason alone, is the worthy son of his father; but he slights the honour of his lineage when he presents his mistress with an ancestral ring in return for a night of love. The unmasking of Parolles, the Countess' reprimands and the false news of Helena's death all seem to open his eyes and lead him to repent; yet when his reputation is questioned in public, he turns into a brazen liar before his pride finally succumbs under the shock caused by the reappearance of Helena alive. It appears that Shakespeare could not make do with the initial, brief outline of Bertram. He had to give enough credibility to his recalcitrant, yet well-loved, man, if only to justify Helena's untiring fervour to conquer the love of her husband. However urgent her desire to 'lose her virginity to her liking' may have been, this could not suffice. Bertram had to be allowed to exhaust his ability to behave badly, and to suggest in passing some positive qualities so that, at the end of a Jonsonian therapy of purging humours, he is ripe for repentance.

The two French Lords, who initiate the plot against Parolles, abound with wisdom. They voice deep thoughts with a distinctly Shakespearian ring about them:

> FIRST LORD.   As we are
> ourselves, what things are we!
> SECOND LORD. Merely our own traitors. And as in the common
> course of all treasons we still see them reveal
> themselves till they attain to their abhorr'd ends;
> so he that in this action contrives against his own
> nobility, in his proper stream o'erflows himself.
> IV, iii, 18–24

And later in the same scene:

> FIRST LORD.   The web of our life is of a mingled yarn, good and
> ill together; our virtues would be proud if our
> faults whipp'd them not, and our crimes would
> despair if they were not cherish'd by our virtues.
> IV, iii, 68–71

Restored to their dramatic context, these moral considerations have a specific purpose: to make Bertram, to whom these words allude, into the prototype of Man, capable of the best and the worst. The attraction he holds over Helena and over the spectator (why pretend otherwise?) is not a simple matter of physical beauty and youthful freshness; he, more than anyone else, exemplifies the paradox of human nature marred with imperfections, but rich with promise.

I would therefore tone down G.K. Hunter's opinion, that 'this [second] half is too full of "contrivance" and too little irradiated by personality'. We should be wary of looking at *All's Well* through the prism of *Measure for Measure*. No doubt the recourse to artifice is more insistent in the second half: Helena has to obtain through cunning that which she has not obtained otherwise; but artifice was already very present in the first half. What is the healing of the King, if not the artifice by which Helena manages to become Bertram's equal socially in order to be worthy of him? The honour of healing one's king is worth all the degrees of noble lineage. As for the idea that 'the second half of the play is less concerned with human will and more with a sense of "All's Well that End's Well" – things working out under the pressure of forces other than the personal',[12] this is only partly true. The relative effacement of Helena does not mean she has become a passive character committed to impersonal forces. Her energy and ingenuity are intact: it is she who buys the services of Diana, after negotiations with the Widow of Florence, settles the practical details of the stratagem, finalizes the exchange of rings, propagates the false news of her death and plans out her return to France, accompanied by the Widow and her daughter who will serve as witnesses for the prosecution in Bertram's 'trial'. Helena's reiterated certainty that all is well (IV, iv, 35 and V, i, 25) is no different from the conviction she felt about the miraculous effectiveness of the cure her father had bequeathed her: 'There's something in't/More than my father's skill' (I, iii, 237–8). Strengthened by the very same faith, she will eventually overcome the resistance of the King, despite his philosophical distrust of 'empirics'. Against all 'common sense', he surrenders to Helena's 'senseless help' and divinely inspired speech: 'Methinks in thee some blessed spirit doth speak' (II, i, 174). In *Measure for Measure*, the Duke is an agent of Providence only in so far as he is the sovereign, invested with the temporal powers attached to his status as vicar of God on earth. In *All's Well*, Helena is a commoner who compensates for the baseness of her rank with the royal and divine protection she enjoys. In *Measure for Measure*, artifice is a matter of manipulation and skill. In *All's*

Well, artifice implies cunning, but also the effective intervention of Providence. This is why *All's Well*, more than *Measure for Measure*, prefigures the romances. At one moment, Shakespeare stresses the miraculous aspect, but, as noted before, Helena's determination to heal the King is also part of her strategy for social advancement. At the next moment, Shakespeare stresses the element of cunning and manipulation, as in the second half, but here again nothing is possible without Providence: the simultaneous presence of Helena and Bertram in Florence is clearly one of Fortune's good turns, and Helena regards her meeting and coming to terms with Diana as a heaven-sent opportunity for both parties:

> HEL.   Doubt not but heaven
> Hath brought me up to be your daughter's dower,
> As it hath fated for her to be my motive
> And helper to a husband.
>
> IV, iv, 18–21

At the end, what the spectators know to be the acme of cunning is in fact experienced by the witnesses to the event as a second miracle: after the healing of the King, there comes (perhaps) the healing of Bertram.

It appears then that the notion of artifice does not have exactly the same content in both plays. The structure of *Measure for Measure* is discrete and stamped with excess. An overtly paroxysmal portrayal of feelings abruptly gives way to an equally overt and paroxysmal display of artifice. In *All's Well*, the close-knit structure of which is marked with ambiguity, Shakespeare spared his audience this shock treatment and accustomed the spectator to the sustained, if no less bizarre, alliance of psychological realism and theatrical manipulation, a form of artifice in which the tricks engineered by the manipulatory character are always inspired and endorsed by Providence, whose supernatural, beneficent power is always felt at work behind the scenes. These are two different strategies with a single Mannerist purpose: to show the theatre at its most dramatic and at its most theatrical.

Like the great tragedies they lead up to, *All's Well* and *Measure for Measure* credit the forces of evil with fearsome power but in a manner congruent with the comic genre. The basic assumption underlying these sister plays is that human predicaments have little or no chance to sort themselves out alone and that human beings accordingly can hardly pull through unhelped. This is why, more patently than elsewhere, the dramatist must rely on those conventions of comedy that ensure a happy ending; and he does so notably by entrusting some of his demiurgic powers to surrogate characters like Helena, Diana and Duke Vincentio.

Though we know, of course – and from the start – that the worst will not come to pass and that all must and will end well, we still have to discover as the play unfolds how much artifice is needed to reach the foregone conclusion of comedy. Despite our abstract certainty, we feel relieved, if somehow disappointed, to catch the first signs that at last, if perhaps too soon, there is something brewing that will unmistakably overcome so many complications and bring us to a satisfactory outcome.

Swinburne was the first to express disappointment at having the 'machinery', as he called it, of *Measure for Measure* thus laid bare to the public eye.[13] He thought the device was inelegant aesthetically and morally unworthy of Shakespeare, and he would have liked to prove the dramatist innocent of the undignified manipulations of the trickster-Duke. I have the feeling that, in true Mannerist fashion, Shakespeare would have been more likely to regard this outstanding piece of theatrical virtuosity as a legitimate achievement by no means inferior to the building up of passionate, pathetic or burlesque episodes. During four decisive events in these two plays we find pure Shakespearian inventions that owe nothing to the source material: the rigged trials of Parolles, Bertram and Angelo that Shakespeare delights in protracting beyond measure, and Helena's equally rigged reappearance at the close of *All's Well*. These notorious pieces of trickery are also superb pieces of stagecraft, real productions within the theatre, metadramatic moments of artistic truth during which the dramatist ironically casts himself as the artist at work.

In 'Pyramus and Thisby' (the play-within-the-play in *A Midsummer Night's Dream*), where some Athenian artisans play in front of Duke Theseus and his court as their special contribution to his nuptials, the exposure of theatrical conventions is held up to ridicule as part of the entertainment that concludes the play. In *Hamlet*, 'The Murder of Gonzago' gives the audience serious cause to reflect on the ambiguous nature of Claudius' Elsinore and on the truthful deceptiveness of theatre. In *All's Well* and *Measure for Measure*, those highly theatrical scenes shed ironic light on the dramatist as conjuror. Classical art excels at persuading us that Art and Nature are one. Mannerist art maintains the dichotomy between the two and increases their disparity. To achieve a sense of 'dramatic coquetry' that may sometimes verge on discomfort, Mannerist art brings to the fore the implicit paradox that all theatregoers experience consciously or not: to believe, and not to believe.

CHAPTER 8

The end of the Mannerist moment

Was it because Shakespeare had stifled tragic emotion long enough, or because he realized the impasse into which his Mannerist plays had led him, that he wrote *Othello* in 1604, the same year as *Measure for Measure?*

Othello marks the second wind of Shakespeare's drama at that period, a deep breath of fresh air regenerating the somewhat rarefied atmosphere of Mannerism. After the deconstruction of the tragic hero in *Julius Caesar* and *Hamlet* and the ironic negation of the genre itself in *Troilus and Cressida*, after the laying bare of certain mechanisms of dramaturgy anatomized in *All's Well* and *Measure for Measure*, now was the time for a recomposition of tragedy in a powerful movement which carried the intensity of tragic feeling and the destructiveness of passion to unprecedented heights. *Othello*, *King Lear* and *Macbeth* come to mind, but also, to a lesser degree, *Timon of Athens*, *Coriolanus* and *Antony and Cleopatra*. It is *Othello* that signals the end of the Mannerist moment together with the advent of what R.A. Foakes has aptly called 'heroic tragedy'.[1] But why should *Hamlet* come under this heading? It seems to me that to describe *Hamlet* as a heroic tragedy which depends for its effect on our full engagement with the hero, or as a play in which 'the clash of fell and mighty opposites represents a conflict of absolute values', tends to ignore the strategy of Mannerist distancing used as a means of closing up the Kydian vein of revenge tragedy.[2]

What I find of outstanding novelty in *Hamlet* is not that the Prince and the usurper should find themselves at loggerheads on ethical grounds, a fact that no one would deny, but it is rather that both belong to the new Elsinore born of the fratricide. Although this Elsinore is not committed to absolute evil any more than the former was committed to good, yet they are now part of a place contaminated by obliquity and manoeuvring and deprived of its original simplicity. This is why Claudius' villainy and Hamlet's goodness are somehow impure or vitiated. At the risk of contradicting Hamlet himself, whose words in any case are seldom meant to be taken at their face value, one entertains the belief that the play-world in no way admits of the aforesaid clash of 'fell and mighty opposites' evoked by Foakes. The fierce and grandiose struggle of extremes can only truly be played out in the untainted, univocal space of the Baroque theatre, but it is incompatible with Mannerism. If we are to speak of commitments to Hamlet's side, it is therefore not so much the man of good that wins our sympathies as the man of thought, the representative of modern conscience in crisis. Our sense of kinship with Hamlet is more intellectual than emotional or ethical. It assumes the form of an intimate and problematic complicity unassailed by the formidable storms which rock heroic tragedies and in which good and evil confront each other unvizarded in fearsome cosmic battle.

OTHELLO, OR THE BREAK

In *Othello*, the 'conflict of absolute values' is present to a degree of exceptional clarity. The love between the Moor and the young Venetian makes no mystery of what it is: an irreversible transgression which is assumed as such by the protagonists. They transgress the code in the name of a superior positivity which suffers neither question nor compromise. The play epitomizes the absoluteness of love between a man and a woman whose union is an outrage to Venetian society. Shakespeare endows this guilty love with an aura of Platonic spirituality in which body and soul reflect upon each other in perfect symmetry:

> OTH. She lov'd me for the dangers I had pass'd,
> And I lov'd her that she did pity them.
> 1, iii, 167–8

> DES. I saw Othello's visage in his mind,
> And to his honours, and his valiant parts
> Did I my soul and fortunes consecrate.
> 1, iii, 252–4

While the couple's departure for Cyprus answers the need for strategic defence against Turkish menace, it also symbolizes the banishment of the absolute from the sphere of the relative. The love between Othello and Desdemona cannot live out its fatal and grandiose destiny on the banks of the *laguna*. Venice is too much concerned with preserving that honourable mediocrity which guarantees the viability of the State and society to give shelter to a relationship alternately described as the radiant union of two exceptional beings and the monstrous coupling of two bestial creatures. The story of Othello and Desdemona demands a more appropriate setting than the cramped space of respectable and legalistic Venice; it needs a faraway land opening onto, and enclosed by, boundless sea and sky. Cyprus is a real, yet mythical, isle where extremes clash and meet when 'chidden billows seem to pelt the clouds', thus conjoining heaven and hell, until the waves becalmed by the beauty of 'divine Desdemona' deliver the noble lady and Iago, her devilish escort, in safety to the port. Like a Christian Venus rising from the waves, Desdemona appears shrouded in celestial grace. She is the ambassadress of love and renewal, and the inhabitants of Cyprus kneel to her. A little later, but in an equally exalted mode, she is reunited with Othello who has just landed. It is a moment of sheer bliss (the only one in the play), of ineffable pleasure so replete with harmony and tenderness that Othello is overjoyed to a degree seemingly disproportionate to the circumstances, as if he cannot or will not come to terms with the stunning miracle of his own marriage. But the blessed reunion of these two fair warriors, taking place after their dearly won victory against Venice and the storm, and in the presence of Iago, ironically foreshadows another confrontation of 'mighty opposites', this time between the almost deathlike pleasuring in the present moment and the throes of real death which the future holds in store for them, between the perfect harmony of this ephemeral duo and the awesome discordance of the same two instruments once Iago has unstrung them:

> OTH. O my fair warrior!
> DES.   My dear Othello!
> OTH. It gives me wonder great as my content
>   To see you here before me: O my soul's joy,
>   If after every tempest come such calm,
>   May the winds blow, till they have waken'd death,
>   And let the labouring bark climb hills of seas,
>   Olympus-high, and duck again as low
>   As hell's from heaven. If it were now to die
>   'Twere now to be most happy, for I fear
>   My soul hath her content so absolute,
>   That not another comfort, like to this
>   Succeeds in unknown fate.
> DES.   The heavens forbid
>   But that our loves and comforts should increase,
>   Even as our days do grow.
> OTH.   Amen to that, sweet powers!
>   I cannot speak enough of this content,

It stops me here, it is too much of joy:
And this, and this, the greatest discord be   [they kiss]
That e'er our hearts shall make!
IAGO. [Aside] O, you are well tun'd now,
But I'll set down the pegs that make this music,
As honest as I am.

                                      II, i, 182–201

Prior to Othello's landing, the audience is treated to a recreational scene between Iago, acting the role of the witty, insolent jester, and Desdemona, his 'mistress' who gives him his cues. This is a traditional piece of comedy, an apparently harmless interlude between two moments of lyrical exaltation. Yet amid this innocent banter, one finds lying as if in ambush the most casual and powerful definition of absolute evil in the whole play. Iago says of himself: 'I am nothing, if not critical' (II, i, 119).[3] Opposite Desdemona, who is Purity incarnate, looms the antithetical figure of Iago, whose being is reduced to his function, namely to blight and destroy every manifestation of nobility, inclination to goodness and longing for happiness in the soul of man. But Iago is powerless before Desdemona because he knows that she pits the infallibility of good against his infallibility of evil. The role of the destroying angel is not to attack the good angel but to vie with it for the soul of man. Iago and Desdemona have just enough psychological depth to become alive theatrically, but no more. Iago is sheer strategy, and to say that he 'embodies' evil is almost to credit him with more reality than he actually has; he is rather the active principle of evil, its quintessence, almost divested of human detail. As Coleridge suggested, his 'motiveless malignity' is of theological essence, despite the personal grudges with which it is clothed – his suspicion of having been cuckolded by Othello and his resentment at Cassio's promotion. His villainy resembles only superficially that of the ordinary 'malcontent', and his tireless energy as 'demon ex machina' is matched only by his human flimsiness. The creation of Iago, in a play written the same year as *Measure for Measure*, suggests that Shakespeare was at that time particularly interested in the figure of the manipulator; but unlike Duke Vincentio, whose 'nature' cannot be reduced to his dramatic function, Iago operates essentially as a symbol. At the denouement of the play, he appears walled in silence, walling out death. 'If that thou be'st a devil, I cannot kill thee', Othello realizes. It is indeed difficult to imagine Iago dying or even suffering, either repentant or triumphant. The only means, dramatically and ethically, to dispose of him is to bundle him off stage and consign him to the ubiquitous place of torment to which he belongs and which we conveniently dub hell on earth. Once he ceases to be active because he is no longer needed, he virtually continues his existence on an abstract mode, resuming his former status as 'ancient' or ensign, and signalling the ineradicable presence of evil.

Diametrically opposed to absolute negativity, Desdemona stands for absolute positivity. Her existence posits that virtue is no vain word and that happiness is attainable, if only temporarily, even in a world beset with precariousness. But in the loaded context of unfair competition between good and evil that Shakespeare chose for his play, Desdemona embodies a total absence of strategy. Against the machinations of the other side, she has nothing to offer but her radiant presence, a mode of being rather than acting, in accordance with the necessities of tragedy where it is the onslaught of evil against good that invariably triggers the action, as well as Christian theology in which evil derives its existence only from its negation of good, ontologically the primary and sole reality.

Subjected to the conflicting attraction of two magnetic poles, Othello migrates from one to the other. As a black man among whites and a stranger in Venice, since he has been uprooted from his native soil, Othello becomes estranged from his own identity and from that inner refuge that the two spouses had fashioned for themselves. It is precisely Iago's strategy to establish between them a sense of estrangement analogous to that which exists between Othello and Venice. Iago sees to it that the Moor internalizes the cultural prejudices linked to their differences so that the marriage appears to Othello not only as a challenge to culture (which it is), but also as a challenge to nature, which until then only the Venetians had believed. Iago therefore has no need to dramatize Desdemona's fault in order to lend it credibility; quite the reverse, he needs to trivialize it, so that her supposed adultery with Cassio, a man of her race, will appear as the all-too-possible outcome of an unnatural marriage, the revenge of the natural order infringed by her initial disobedience. This suffices to restore Othello to a sense of his own blackness and make him espouse the image of the barbarian propagated by Venice. Henceforth, this is how he wants Desdemona and the audience to see him, since he himself sees her as one specimen among others of the fickleness of Venetian womanhood. Beyond the unspeakable horror of Desdemona's strangling, the play reaches a pitch of moral distress when we see the forces of evil thus playing havoc with the hero's mind and soul. A cataclysm of such magnitude is unprecedented in Shakespeare and totally incompatible with the aesthetics of Mannerism.

From the moment Othello is contaminated by doubt, he is lost. If there is one thing that lies beyond his reach, it is precisely an ability to cope with doubt, until he can obtain the proof he needs. However harrowing doubt may be for a Mannerist character, at best it provides free space for thought in a world where everything is uncertain, ephemeral and contingent. To Othello, doubt spells suspicion, a deadly poison gnawing at his mind, and this is more than he can bear. This is why he is doomed to move into the vicious circle of certainties, true or false. By doubting Desdemona's faith, he is already convinced of her guilt:

> to be once in doubt,
> Is once to be resolv'd.
> III, iii, 183–4

By becoming convinced of her guilt, he already loves her no longer:

> Now do I see 'tis true; look here Iago,
> All my fond love thus do I blow to heaven, . . .
> 'Tis gone.
> III, iii, 451–3

By showing himself dishonoured, he has already sentenced a faithless wife to death and promoted Iago to Cassio's position:

> Damn her, lewd minx: O, damn her!
> Come, go with me apart, I will withdraw
> To furnish me with some swift means of death,
> For the fair devil: now art thou my lieutenant.
> III, iii, 482–5

By awakening to his error, he has already resolved on his own death, while undergoing the hellish torments of damnation:

> Whip me, you devils,
> From the possession of this heavenly sight,
> Blow me about in winds, roast me in sulphur,
> Wash me in steep-down gulfs of liquid fire!
> V, ii, 278–81

Othello can only conceive of the relationship between thought and action, and more generally between cause and effect, in terms of some terrifying instantaneousness, leaving the executioner and the victim no chance for second thoughts. Such an imperative sense of the here and now negating time and becoming is nowhere better expressed than in the suppression of the future tense:

and when I love thee not,
Chaos is come again.
III, iii, 92–3

In *Hamlet*, on the contrary, between the desire to act and action itself, time stretches out as a rich purveyor of experience, allowing the main character to pursue his meandering course and give himself over to the rumination of thought, with its unpredictable advances and its stand-stills, until Hamlet eventually seizes his revenge as if catching Fortune by the hair, like an unpremeditated, last-minute affair.

When Troilus has before him the irrefutable proof of Cressida's betrayal, he still tries to delude himself and, as Thersites puts it, 'Swagger himself out on's own eyes'. By dint of intellectual and verbal extrava-gance on the theme of 'This is, and is not Cressid', Troilus ends up losing sight of the actual fact, and indulges in complacent scrutiny of his own divided consciousness: 'With my soul there does conduce a fight'.[4] Self-delusion keeps Troilus' mind alert and thought forges excuses in order to impugn the evidence of the senses. Othello instead hankers after ocular proof.

Like Othello, for whom the end of love means the return of chaos; like Lear, for whom the storm is an emblem of the monstrous complicity of nature and evil as well as of nature's rebellion against his unnatural daughters, so Troilus associates his misfortune with the collapse of cosmic order: 'The bonds of heaven are slipp'd, dissolv'd, and loos'd', and his flights of vengeful eloquence sound like an anticipation of Lear or Timon's imprecations:

Not the dreadful spout
Which shipmen do the hurricano call,
Constring'd in mass by the almighty sun,
Shall dizzy with more clamour Neptune's ear
In his descent than shall my prompted sword
Falling on Diomed.
Troilus and Cressida, v, ii, 170–5

But it is difficult to avoid the realization that the heavily prosaic and definition-like interpolated clause 'which shipmen do . . .' pinions the whole tirade, causing Troilus to sound somehow wrong, as did his former protestations of love which invariably capsize under their top-heavy load of frenzied narcissism. Despite thematic resemblances, the above is a far cry from Lear's sublimity of speech, which supposes spontaneous aban-donment to the power of the word and certainly not this sort of meta-linguistic self-consciousness.

Had the tragicomic story of Troilus and Cressida been treated in the Fletcherian mode, it would have given rise to a duel bringing the two rivals close to death. In Shakespeare's Mannerist play, the combat between sworn enemies is reduced to two inconclusive and briefly glimpsed bouts of fighting. Instead of a grand show-down between Troilus and Diomedes, the audience fare rather poorly with a story about some stolen horse, as if the offended Troilus had almost forgotten his more serious cause for harbouring a grudge against the thief:

> O traitor Diomed! Turn thy false face, thou traitor,
> And pay the life thou ow'st me for my horse.
>
> v, vi, 6–7

It is bad taste to suggest that 'my horse' might stand for Cressida too, but a well-directed actor could still raise a laugh there if he is able to stress the ironic discrepancy between the alliterative pompousness of the first line and the anticlimactic derision of the second. Whilst paralleling the motif of the stolen armour, this anecdote is one more indication of Shakespeare's concern to avoid all semblance of pathos at the denouement. Ethically speaking, Troilus' attitude can only be interpreted with reference to a world of perverted values, given over to triviality and abandoned to the passing solicitations of the present moment. In the tragic vision of *Othello* and the subsequent tragedies, the transgression-retribution pattern vouches for the solidity of values and the validity of a time-scheme which safeguards the continuity between past, present and future.

LATER TRAGEDIES AND ROMANCES

Shakespeare's later tragedies, *Timon of Athens*, *Coriolanus* and *Antony and Cleopatra*, all written about 1607–8, may seem a promising field for someone prospecting for Mannerism, in that they eschew the grandiose clash of good and evil characterizing the earlier tragedies. Here dichotomies are blurred again and ambivalence holds sway as if Shakespeare were applying to characters and themes the paradox expressed by the witches in *Macbeth* – the last of his so-called 'great' tragedies – that 'Fair is foul, and foul is fair'. In these later plays, evil is shown to be the other side of good or excess of good. Timon's generosity is overwhelmingly tyrannical in that it deprives its beneficiaries of the right to refuse it or to find moral gratification in their acceptance of it. Timon's selfish altruism is a bane to his entourage, holding them under an irredeemable obligation, with ingratitude as the sole way out.

Coriolanus' outstanding valour is a civic disaster since it discountenances the legitimate aspirations of lesser people to some form of dignity. By wanting to live out desire to the full and die for it, Antony and Cleopatra achieve epic grandeur, and Shakespeare clothes in splendid poetry the erotic fusion of East and West. But the protagonists' glorious yielding to love and to nothing else, while the fate of the world is being played out on the political scene, stands against a background of lust and cunning, self-ishness and fickleness, treason and caprice, as if to signify that exclusive devotion to Eros feasts upon the sublime and the sordid alike.

In these plays, the centre of interest shifts from the plane of ethics to that of psychology, which explains why the heroes of the later tragedies are more akin to the Mannerist figures of Julius Caesar, Brutus, Hamlet, Troilus, Bertram and Angelo, than to their more recent predecessors like Othello, Lear or Macbeth, who are more clearly positioned in the scale of moral values. If they suffer and succumb in their struggle against a hostile environment, it is not essentially because they are part of the uni-versal conflict between 'mighty opposites', but because of their psycho-logical make-up which renders them tragically unsuited to the world around them. Each of these heroes is a fascinating case of aberrant conduct: Timon, or the pathology of goodness felt as a compulsion; Coriolanus, or the pathology of patriotic pride in an immature man; Antony, or the pathology of self-destructive desire. In the earlier tragedies, the prevailing feeling at the denouement is one of irreparable loss. Here this feeling is toned down by a sense of relief. Alcibiades' Athens without Timon, Menenius Agrippa's Rome without Coriolanus and Octavius' Roman Empire without Antony are not exactly elating prospects, but they are less cruelly penalized, less tragically bereaved than Fortinbras' Denmark without Hamlet, Lodovico's Venice without Othello and Desdemona, and Albany's Britain without Lear and Cordelia. Between ourselves and the heroes of the later tragedies, a more distant relationship is fostered and our emotional involvement diminished accordingly. Foakes suggests, rightly I think, that this is due to 'the discordances of a variety of persectives upon them'. Whilst this method of character-drawing may evoke Mannerism, yet there is one essential feature absent from Mannerist characters which these later heroes possess to a high degree: I mean a heightened sense of their own identity. Exploring the concept of self-consciousness in Montaigne and Shakespeare, Robert Ellrodt remarks that of the three plays (*Hamlet, Troilus and Cressida* and *Measure for Measure*), that are judged to be most in accordance with the spirit of Montaigne, two are tragicomedies while

Hamlet is akin to the 'Problem Plays' because of its intellectuality. Hence the bold yet plausible hypothesis of a certain incompatibility between the tragic mode and that particular form of self-consciousness *à la Montaigne* which tends to destroy the sense of identity rather than to consolidate it: 'The full tragic response calls for a heightened consciousness of identity – evident in Lear, Othello or Macbeth – not for the kind of self-consciousness that may dissolve identity. Shakespeare the tragedian had to part company with Montaigne.'[5] To me, this observation is also applicable to Timon, Coriolanus and Antony. Not only do these characters experience a 'heightened consciousness of identity', but they are imbued with a sense of uniqueness. In their pursuit of dreams impossible to fulfil in a world tainted with mediocrity, they yearn for the absolute and prefer suicide to compromise as the only way to perpetuate the strong image they have fashioned for themselves and others, one which they have identified with once for all and against all and sundry. Their sense of their own identity is by no means problematic to them; it is of the order of the given, not something they feverishly hanker after, in contrast to Julius Caesar, Brutus, Hamlet or Troilus. This is why these characters have no need to posture experimentally or to assume successive viewpoints in the hope of perceiving themselves as coherent, viable entities. From the start, they are in symbiosis with themselves, filling as it were the entire space of their inner selves. On the other hand, they are tragically vulnerable, all the more so as they believe in the indissociable wholeness of personality, experiencing each of their thoughts and actions as an investment and a commitment of the entire being. When Timon's steward visits his master who has retreated to the woods, Timon is forced to acknowledge that fallen mankind still includes at least one good man and Shakespeare emphasizes his dawning awareness. First, Timon lies shamelessly:

> Then I know thee not;
> I never had honest man about me.
> IV, iii, 479–80

Then comes recognition, but phrased in the interrogative mode:

> Had I a steward
> So true, so just, and now so comfortable?
> IV, iii, 494–5

And finally a sense of regret for the apparently more comfortable and as yet unchanged position of universal reviler that he has been assuming since his voluntary exile:

> How fain would I have hated all mankind,
> And thou redeem'st thyself.
>
> IV, iii, 503–4

Despite this flash of lucidity, Timon resolves to withdraw once again into a species of misanthropy, quite as inveterate and irrational as his former philanthropy. He dismisses his servant violently, orders him to hate mankind and showers him with gold, in the hope that the evil power of money will corrupt his innate goodness. It is not so much Timon's wilful persistence in error that Shakespeare dramatizes at this point as his compulsive surrender to absolute hatred as the only alternative to absolute love. The tragedy of Timon, Coriolanus and Antony perhaps lies in this regressive suicidal obstinacy in being themselves in a changing world. When a pragmatic ability to adapt and political realism become the dominant values, there seems to be no room any more for this particular brand of heroism.

Unlike the more traditional hero of tragedy, the Mannerist hero knows himself to be essentially double-natured, unstable and contradictory. Inherent in his own particular brand of self-consciousness is perhaps the sense of an inner void, a feeling of incompleteness within himself and before the world, as if his inner ear and eye were destined to hear him speak and watch him act and think even in situations requiring the utmost abandon through effacement of the self-regarding ego. This inner distance from self to self mediates speech and mode of action, as seen notably in Julius Caesar, Hamlet, Troilus and Angelo. Montaigne, I mean the narrator-figure that the author of the *Essays* puts on stage, and Hamlet, most conspicuously, discover and uncover themselves, in constant astonishment at what they find. They are onlookers, never forgetting that they are being observed even by their own unsparing gaze. It is not surprising therefore that the very special kind of emotion that one feels when contemplating a Mannerist work, be it drama, literature, music or the visual arts, should always stop short of true, deep-felt tragic or comic experience. So when Shakespeare turned to tragedy, not only did he part company with Montaigne, but he veered away from the aesthetics of Mannerism as well.

A few months before the plague broke out in London, causing the theatres to close between the summer of 1608 and the autumn of the following year, a new play entitled *Pericles* was put on at the Globe, initiating a change of orientation that was to occupy Shakespeare for the next three years; *Pericles* was followed by *Cymbeline* (1609?), *The Winter's Tale* (1611?) and *The Tempest* (1611). Like Mannerist comedy, Shakespearian romance makes a point of cultivating artifice to ensure the happy ending required by the genre. But unlike Mannerist comedy, which flaunts its claim to realism as ostentatiously as it does its right to artifice, the romance presents itself from the beginning as the transposition to the theatre of a purely fictitious tale. *Pericles* begins with a long monologue in rhyming tetrameters in which Gower, the medieval poet, momentarily resurrected to act as narrator, recounts the incest of King Antiochus with his daughter and the beheading of her suitors, following their failure to solve a certain riddle. The twofold purpose of this 'song that old was sung' is of course to provide the facts prior to Pericles' adventures, but more importantly to introduce the audience to the fabulous atmosphere of the play-world. Similarly, Leontes' sudden and carefully unmotivated fit of jealousy in the second scene of *The Winter's Tale* is an intimation that it is inexplicable by the ordinary criteria of psychology. Thus warned, the audience will bear the death of young Mamillius with relative serenity and learn with ever more equanimity the absurd fate of Antigonus, who is eaten by a bear, after the safe delivery of the new-born Perdita to the improbable shore of Bohemia. Thus warned again, no one would invoke psychological verisimilitude in order to wince at Polixenes' murderous frenzy when he learns that his son Florizel has fallen in love with a shepherdess, or to complain about Leontes' credulousness when he sees Hermione's statue come to life before his very eyes. Likewise, *Cymbeline*'s audience feels immersed in a world of folklore and fairy-tale when hearing that the King of Britain has had his two infant sons stolen from him, that his second wicked queen is an expert in poison and that Imogen, his daughter, has disregarded the wishes of her father and stepmother and married a young man without fortune, named Posthumus, himself an orphan brought up at court. Henceforth the audience is prepared to accept the most extraordinary happenings, including the grotesquely macabre scene of Cloten's decapitated body which Imogen wrongly identifies, almost limb by limb, as her beloved husband's, not forgetting the apparition of Jupiter riding an eagle and depositing on the chest of Posthumus (asleep in gaol) a tablet informing him in cryptic terms that his misfortunes are soon to end. In *The Tempest*, Miranda's first words are to beg her father to calm the tempest he has himself magically provoked, whereupon Prospero assures her and the audience that nobody has perished. On Prospero's island where he exerts his 'art' with the complicity of Providence, we know from then on that Ariel's ethereal invisibility or Caliban's earthy bestiality are no less 'real' than the motley humanity of the shipwrecked voyagers.

In *The Dramaturgy of Shakespeare's Romances*, Barbara B. Mowat takes up the classical distinction made long ago by Alexander Bakshy between two forms of drama, the 'representational' mode seeking to produce a mimetic image of life and the 'presentational' mode conveying a sense of theatricality.[6] Her argument is that in the romances the two modes are found side by side, so that at certain moments the audience are led to believe and participate in the events shown on stage, whereas at other times the artifice and the conventions of the presentational mode preclude all identification. Whilst this observation certainly holds true of Shakespeare's Mannerist comedies, it is less relevant to the romances. In *All's Well* and *Measure for Measure*, Shakespeare goes to great lengths to counteract through artifice the sense of reality achieved through realistic portrayal of characters and situations. But to me, the theatrical experience afforded by the romances can by no means be reduced to another version of 'dramatic coquetry'. Contrary to what Mowat maintains, Shakespeare has no need to 'remind' us that we are confronted with a fictitious world because we are never allowed to forget it. From the very beginning, we are, as it were, conditioned to welcome and endorse artificiality and improbability, often at their most blatant, and it is our whole view of the play, including its most lifelike or illusionistic sequences, that is thereby modified. Like those Mannerist paintings which draw their effect from the 'discord of parts', Shakespeare's Problem comedies aim at destabilizing our vision, forcing us to strive to embrace their uneasy compound of realism and artificiality. In the romances, the disparate elements are blended into a homogeneous texture instead of being kept in a state of tension, and so the effects that were experienced and sometimes resented as dissonant in *All's Well* and *Measure for Measure* betoken in the romances a higher level of coherence. Here the world is looked at from further away and higher up in a perspective that renders it barely distinguishable from 'such stuff/As dreams are made on'. This is where the usual dichotomy between emotion and detachment proves irrelevant. The romances elicit from their audiences a unified response. In *All's Well*, the healing of the King, the cunning of Helena, the unmasking of Bertram and the final reappearance of the heroine spell theatrical artifice as well as providential benevolence. In *Measure for Measure*, it is the Duke's manipulative skills and the playwright's technical prowess rather than the saving action of Providence which bring about the sparing of Claudio's life, the preservation of Isabella's chastity and the confounding of Angelo. But in the romances, it is no longer a priority to exhibit art. Art is now seen joining hands with Nature to shape the destinies of men;

and artifice, which is in Shakespeare's Mannerist comedies a metaphor of theatrical art whereby an intractable raw material seemingly drawn from life is successfully forced into the conventions of the comic genre, becomes a metonymy of life itself, part of its very substance. Lysimachus' conversion to virtue in the Mytilene brothel where chaste Marina is confined, Pericles' reunion with his daughter and wife, Hermione's 'resurrection' and Prospero's magic tempest as a prelude to the initiatory progress through a magic island imposed on those who have been shipwrecked allegorize life as convincingly as do the moral and physical sufferings inflicted on them by the magician, the unjust deaths of Mamillius and Antigonus, as well as the preventive death of Cloten, a potential rapist, and the just deserts of wicked Antiochus and Dioniza. Never before had the human condition been portrayed on stage from such an all-inclusive viewpoint, taking in both the ordinary vicissitudes and contingencies of life and the unaccountable ways of Providence. However artificial and incredible these stories may be, we view them as a recognizable, if stylized, representation of human experience at its most meaningful.

Though it is unfashionable today to interpret Prospero's abjuration of magic as Shakespeare's valediction to the stage, this powerful gesture following the recapitulation of the magician's achievements cannot be dismissed so lightly. In his famous Ovidian invocation to 'Ye elves of hills, brooks, standing lakes, and groves' and 'you demi-puppets whose pastime is to make midnight mushrooms', Prospero claims to have

> bedimm'd
> The noontide sun, call'd forth the mutinous winds
> And 'twixt the green sea and the azur'd vault
> Set roaring war: to the dread rattling thunder
> Have I given fire, and rifted Jove's stout oak
> With his own bolt; the strong-bas'd promontory
> Have I made shake, and by the spurs pluck'd up
> The pine and cedar: graves at my command
> Have wak'd their sleepers, op'd, and let 'em forth
> By my so potent Art.
>
> v, i, 41–50

But how is it that among the feasts he has or could have performed Prospero includes an act of such sacrilegious impiety as waking the dead from their graves, one which so obviously lies beyond the reach of his 'rough magic'? Who else could have achieved this if not Shakespeare the dramatist, who recurrently had used his 'potent art' to that effect in the ghost scenes of *Richard III, Julius Caesar, Hamlet* and *Macbeth*? And where else have we come across or heard mentioned such 'mutinous winds' and rattling thunder if not in *Othello, Macbeth* and *King Lear*? As for the pastoral image of those spirits that 'By moonshine do the green sour ringlets make,/Whereof the ewe not bites', are they not more congenial to the atmosphere of *A Midsummer Night's Dream* than to Prospero's island?

In my view, it is no coincidence that Prospero should promise to bury his staff in the earth, drown his book in the sea and release Ariel to the air. In handing over his instruments of magic to Nature, Prospero is re-enacting symbolically Shakespeare's inaugural gesture as a writer of romances. The demiurge-artist who was so ostensibly, if not obtrusively, an active presence in the Mannerist comedies has now withdrawn from the front-stage as if to place his own powers in Nature's keeping. But, one may argue, this act of apparent self-effacement is but once more an expression of consummate artistry. Well and good, but it is the very insolence of art itself that had to be curbed in order to produce this last-born illusion. When an artist is capable of achieving such a degree of seeming humility, he will perhaps first allow himself, if only for a brief spell, to indulge in a burst of Mannerist pride.

Notes

INTRODUCTION

1 A. Hauser, *The Social History of Art*, 2 vols., London, 1951; repr. in 4 vols., 1962.
   E.R. Curtius, *Europaische Literatur und lateinisches Mittelalter*, Bonn, 1948; transl.
   as *European Literature and the Latin Middle Ages*, London, 1953.
   M. Raymond, *Baroque et Renaissance poétique*, Paris, 1955.
   W. Sypher, *Four Stages of Renaissance Style*, New York, 1955.
   G.R. Hocke, *Manierismus in der Literatur*, Hamburg, 1959.
2 D.B. Rowland, *Mannerism – Style and Mood*, New Haven, 1964.
   C. Hoy, 'Jacobean Tragedy and the Mannerist Style', *SS*, 23, 1973.
   C.G. Dubois, *Le maniérisme*, Paris, 1979.
3 J. Shearman, *Mannerism*, Harmondsworth, 1967.
4 F.S. Boas, *Shakespeare and his Predecessors*, New York, 1896.
5 W.W. Lawrence, *Shakespeare's Problem Comedies*, New York, 1931.
   E.M.W. Tillyard, *Shakespeare's Problem Plays*, London, 1951.
   E. Schanzer, *The Problem Plays of Shakespeare*, London, 1963.
6 E. Souriau, *La correspondance des arts*, Paris, 1969.

1. THE PROBLEM OF MANNERISM

1 G. Weise, 'La doppia origine del concetto di Manierismo', in *Studi vasariani*
   (Atti del Convegno Internazionale per il IV Centenario della prima
   Edizione delle *Vite* del Vasari), Florence, 1952, pp. 181–5.
   E. Battisti, 'Sfortune del Manierismo', in *Rinascimento e Barocco*, Turin, 1960,
   pp. 216–37.
   C.H. Smyth, 'Mannerism and Maniera', in *The Renaissance and Mannerism*,
   Princeton, 1963, vol. II, pp. 174–99.
   J. Shearman, 'Maniera as an Aesthetic Ideal', in ibid., pp. 200–21.
2 Alois Riegl was the real pioneer in this field with *Die Entstehung der Barockkunst
   in Rom*, Vienna, 1908.
3 These two studies were published in English under the title *Mannerism and
   Anti-Mannerism in Italian Painting*, New York, 1957.
4 'The Anti-Mannerist Style', in ibid., 1965 edn, p. 48.
5 See Anthony Blunt, *Artistic Theory in Italy 1450–1600*, Oxford, 1940.

6 Notably Raffaello Borghini, *Il riposo*, Florence, 1594; Giovanni Paolo Lomazzo, *Trattato dell'arte della pittura, scultura ed architettura*, Milan, 1584; Giovanni Battista Armenini, *De' veri precetti della pittura*, Ravenna, 1587.

7 Smyth, 'Mannerism and Maniera', p. 192.

8 Ibid., p. 198.

9 Shearman, 'Maniera as an Aesthetic Ideal', p. 202.

10 Quoted by J. Shearman, ibid., p. 202.

11 Ibid., p. 213.

12 P. Francastel, 'Y a-t-il une esthétique de la Renaissance?', in *Actes du colloque sur la Renaissance organisé par la Société d'Histoire Moderne*, Paris, 1958.

13 P. Francastel, *Peinture et société*, Paris, 1951; 1965 edn, p. 69.

2. FROM ART TO THEATRE: TOWARDS A DEFINITION OF MANNERISM

1 Though the following pages owe nothing to George R. Kernodle's iconographic approach, the title of chapter 2 is a homage to his masterful study of the influence of ancient and medieval staging on Quattrocento painting. (See Kernodle, *From Art to Theatre*, Chicago, 1944; repr. 1964.)

2 W. Sypher, *Four Stages of Renaissance Style*, New York, 1955, p. 10.

3 Ibid., p. 11.

4 Ibid., pp. 116–17.

5 E. Souriau, *La correspondance des arts*, Paris, 1969, p. 36.

6 J. Rousset, 'Saint-Yves et les poètes', in *L'intérieur et l'extérieur*, Paris, 1968, pp. 259, 265.

7 G. Wilson Knight, *The Wheel of Fire*, London, 1930; 1965 edn, p. 3.

8 A. Ubersfeld, *Lire le théâtre*, Paris, 1977, p. 172.

9 D.B. Rowland, *Mannerism – Style and Mood*, New Haven, 1964, p. 15.

3. MANNERISM IN REACTION TO FORMALISM

1 C.G. Dubois, *Le maniérisme*, Paris, 1979, p. 156.

2 F.P. Wilson, *Elizabethan and Jacobean*, London, 1945; 1965 edn, p. 26.

3 M.C. Bradbrook, *The Growth and Structure of Elizabethan Comedy*, London, 1953; 1963 edn, p. 14.

4 A. Hauser, *The Social History of Art*, London, 1951, vol. II, p. 8.

5 Jonas A. Barish, '*The Spanish Tragedy* or The Pleasures and Perils of Rhetoric', in *Elizabethan Theatre*, Stratford-Upon-Avon Studies, 9, London, 1966, p. 72.

6 Leo Salingar, *Shakespeare and the Traditions of Comedy*, Cambridge, 1974, p. 79.

7 E.M.W. Tillyard, *Shakespeare's History Plays*, London, 1944; 1962 edn, p. 159.

8 B. Gibbons in *Romeo and Juliet* (Arden edn), London, 1980.

9 W. Sypher, *Four Stages of Renaissance Style*, New York, 1955, p. 141.

10 Quoted by Patrick Cruttwell in *The Shakespearean Moment*, New York, 1960, p. 40.

11 See Robert Ellrodt's great book, *Les poètes métaphysiques anglais*, 3 vols., Paris, 1960. Whilst comparing Spenser with Donne, Ellrodt insists on the latter's

avoidance of reiterative and symmetrical patterns, a feature 'discernable in the complex structure of the verse and even in the irregular construction of the sentence itself. His lyrical poetry eschews the refrain. When it happens that Donne repeats a line, it is to play with the idea as if he were turning a diamond between his fingers to inspect its facets' (my translation, 1973 edn, p. 73). Donne's rejection of rhetorical formalism together with his playful curiosity in intellectual exploration and verbal manipulation are strong inducements to consider him as a Mannerist, though this requires further investigation.

12 See T.S. Eliot's essay on Ben Jonson (1919), reproduced in *Elizabethan Dramatists*, London, 1963; 1968 edn, pp. 76–7.

13 In his letter to George and Thomas Keats, his brothers, dated 21 December 1817

4. *JULIUS CAESAR* AND 'DRAMATIC COQUETRY'

1 Paul Bacquet, *Les pièces historiques de Shakespeare*, 2 vols., Paris, 1979, vol. II, p. 156.

2 I do not find anything in the text to substantiate the view held by Bacquet and some other critics that the Epilogue spoken by the Chorus invites the audience to look back upon the King as an ultimately ineffectual warmonger, because France came to be lost under the next king. It seems to me that Henry remains 'this star of England' to the very end of the play, though Shakespeare's portrayal of him throughout the play is often touched with irony. The Chorus insists that Henry's valour is not to be ascribed to his personal merits only, but also to Fortune ('Fortune made his sword'), and as expected Fortune turns her wheel against Henry VI, his successor. In fact, the Chorus' last speech serves to put the glorious reign of Henry V in a double perspective: the unfolding of history, which is pre-eminently the site of Fortune's whimsical doings, and the sequence of the Histories 'which oft our stage hath shown'. It is part of the Chorus' pedagogical function to conclude the play on such a relativistic note.

3 See the Prologue to Act v in *Henry V*, in which the Chorus likens Henry's return to London from his wars in France to Caesar's return to Rome from his wars in Gaul. In Act v, scene vii, Fluellen and Gower compare Henry with Alexander the Great.

4 C.G. Dubois, *Le maniérisme*, Paris, 1979, p. 38.

5 E. Schanzer, *The Problem Plays of Shakespeare*, London, 1951, p. 70.

6 R. Willems, 'Ambiguïté et identité dans *Julius Caesar*', in *Aspects du théâtre anglo-saxon*, Publication de l'Université de Rouen, 1981, p. 79.

7 This is the opinion notably of Brents Sterling in *Unity in Shakespearean Tragedy*, New York, 1956.

8 Willems, 'Ambiguïté et identité dans *Julius Caesar*', p. 82.

9 Mildred E. Hartsock, 'The Complexity of *Julius Caesar*', *PMLA*, 81, March 1966, p. 61.

10 T.S. Dorsch (ed.), *Julius Caesar* (Arden edn), London, 1955; 1977 edn, pp. xix–xx.
11 R. Marienstras, *Le proche et le lointain*, Paris, 1981, p. 92 (my translation). The book has been published in English under the title *New Perspectives on the Shakespearean World*, Cambridge, 1985; the passage quoted is p. 60.

5. *HAMLET*: OPTICAL EFFECTS

1 This unoriginal scenario rests on the supposed existence of a pre-Shakespearian *Hamlet* now lost. The information concerning the dates and places of performance of this hypothetical *Ur-Hamlet* is based on three documents: Nashe's Preface to Greene's *Menaphon* (1589), one entry in Henslowe's Diary for June 1594 and Lodge's *Wit Misery* (1596).
2 M.C. Bradbook, in *Shakespeare, the Craftsman*, London, 1969, p. 122, thinks that *Antonio's Revenge*, acted in 1600 by the Children of St Paul, was written before *Hamlet*, but the question is still unsettled.
3 W. Sypher, *Four Stages of Renaissance Style*, New York, 1955, p. 26.
4 See G.R. Hocke, *Die Welt als Labyrinth: Manier und Manie in der europaische Kunst*, Hamburg, 1957, p. 32 (my translation).
5 H. Jenkins, Introduction to *Hamlet* (Arden edn), London, 1982, p. 135.
6 S. Snyder, *The Comic Matrix of Shakespeare's Tragedy*, Princeton, 1979, pp. 91–136.
7 This classic definition of the metaphysical sensibility is taken from Basil Willey, *The Seventeenth Century Background*, London, 1954; 1967 edn, p. 42.
8 Quoted from Burton's *The Anatomy of Melancholy* by Harry Levin in *The Question of Hamlet*, Oxford, 1959; 1966 edn, p. 126.
9 G.K. Hunter, 'The Heroism of Hamlet', in John Russell Brown and Bernard Harris (eds.), *Hamlet*, Stratford-Upon-Avon Studies, 5, 1963; repr. 1965, p. 94.
10 P. Ure, 'Character and Role from *Richard III* to *Hamlet*', in ibid., pp. 9–28.

6. WHEN PLAYING IS FOILING: *TROILUS AND CRESSIDA*

1 The Pyrrhus speech serves different purposes: it is (1) an emblematic representation of a legendary avenger both heroic and barbaric (two qualities Hamlet can hardly claim to possess); (2) a projection of Hamlet's desire and reluctance to take revenge (Pyrrhus has a moment's hesitation before he slays Priam); (3) a demonstration of an actor's ability to feign passion (whereas Hamlet has not yet found the means to translate heartfelt passion into efficient action); (4) an exemplary picture of a truly sorrowful queen (as opposed to what he fancies his mother's attitude had been following the death of her own kingly husband).
2 See Peter Alexander, '*Troilus and Cressida*, 1609', *Library*, 9, 1928–9, pp. 267–86. The author remarks that 'stage' may stand for 'common stage', which does not exclude a private performance, possibly in one of the Inns of Court.

3 M.C. Bradbrook, 'What Shakespeare did to Chaucer's *Troilus and Criseyde*', *SQ*, 9, 1958, p. 311.
4 Concerning the debunking of the chivalrous stance in love and war, see the characters of Hotspur and Falstaff and the derogatory allusions to Troilus and Cressida in the comedies, listed in Kenneth Palmer's Introduction to *Troilus and Cressida*, (Arden edn), London, 1982, p. 28. In *Henry V*, Shakespeare kills two birds with one stone: the play includes a burlesque anticipation of Hector's challenge delivered by Pistol and a reference to Cressid's venereal diseases (II, i, 67–74).
5 John Bayley, 'Time and the Trojans', *EC*, 25, 1975, pp. 55–73; repr. in Priscilla Martin (ed.), *Troilus and Cressida. A Casebook*, London, 1976, pp. 218–38.
6 Brian Morris, 'The Tragic Structure of *Troilus and Cressida*', *SQ*, 10, 1959, p. 484.
7 Kenneth Muir, '*Troilus and Cressida*', *SS*, 1957, p. 37; repr. in Kenneth Muir and Stanley Wells (ed.), *Aspects of Shakespeare's Problem Plays*, Cambridge, 1982, pp. 96–107.
8 Philip Edwards, *Shakespeare and the Confines of Art*, London, 1968, p. 102.
9 Erwin Panofsky, *Studies in Iconology*, Oxford, 1938; 1972 edn, pp. 175–6.
10 Una Ellis-Fermor, *The Frontiers of Drama*, London, 1945; part of it repr. in Martin (ed.), *A Casebook*, pp. 71–81.
11 Troilus twice uses the word 'purity' (III, ii, 165, IV, iv, 23). There are many other references to this lofty moral ideal, all of them touched with dramatic irony.
12 Bayley, 'Time and Trojans', p. 223.
13 R.A. Foakes, *Shakespeare, The Dark Comedies to the Last Plays: From Satire to Celebration*, London, 1971, p. 53.
14 This figure is not a Mannerist invention since it is found in many Quattrocento paintings (see, for example, Domenico Veneziano's *Madonna and Child with Saints* or Filippo Lippi's *Madonna and Child with Two Angels*, both in the Uffizi). The Renaissance commentator is often a major participant in the scene whereas the Mannerist one is more of an outsider, less integrated to the composition and often over-insistent – not to say downright obtrusive – in calling attention to his or her presence or to some detail of apparently doubtful relevance.
15 Palmer, *Troilus and Cressida*, note 106–7, p. 275.
16 Another impersonation scene is when Thersites apes Ajax while Patroclus plays Hector (III, iii, 279–97). For an excellent discussion of this parodic mode through mimicry, see Lawrence Danson, *Tragic Alphabet*, New Haven and London, 1974, pp. 77–80.
17 Arnold Stein, '*Troilus and Cressida*: The Disjunctive Imagination', *ELH*, 36, 1969, pp. 147–67.
18 T. McAlindon, 'Language, Style and Meaning in *Troilus and Cressida*', *PMLA*, 84, 1969, pp. 29–41; part of it repr. in Martin (ed.), *A Casebook*, pp. 191–218.
19 F.S. Boas, *Shakespeare and his Predecessors*, New York, 1896, 1912 edn, pp. 383–4.

7. *MOSTRAR L'ARTE: ALL'S WELL THAT ENDS WELL* **AND** *MEASURE FOR MEASURE*

1 W.W. Lawrence, *Shakespeare's Problem Comedies*, New York, 1931, p. 74.
2 E. Schanzer, *The Problem Plays of Shakespeare*, London, 1963, p. 93.
3 Quoted by P. Edwards in *Shakespeare and the Confines of Art*, London, 1968, p. 116.
4 See Walter Raleigh (ed.), *Johnson on Shakespeare*, London, 1908; Elizabeth M. Pope, 'The Renaissance Background of *Measure for Measure*', SS, 2, 1949, pp. 62–82; S.T. Coleridge, *Shakespearean Criticism*, ed. T. Middleton Raysor, 2 vols., London, 1930.
5 Lawrence, *Shakespeare's Problem Comedies*, p. 117.
6 Notably in G.K. Hunter's Introduction to *All's Well That Ends Well* (Arden edn), London, 1959, pp. xxv–xxix; and J.W. Lever's Introduction to *Measure for Measure* (Arden edn), London, 1965, pp. xxxv–lv.
7 Bernard Beckerman, 'A Shakespearean Experiment: The Dramaturgy of *Measure for Measure*', in David Galloway (ed.), *Elizabethan Theatre II*, Waterloo (Ontario), 1970, pp. 108–23.
8 Walter Pater, 'Measure for Measure', in *Appreciations*, London, 1889; 1904 edn, pp. 178–79.
9 C.K. Stead (ed.), *Measure for Measure. A Casebook*, London, 1971, p. 28.
10 John Barton, 'Directing Problem Plays', in K. Muir and S. Wells (eds.), *Aspects of Shakespeare's Problem Plays*, Cambridge, 1982, p. 3.
11 G.K. Hunter, *All's Well That Ends Well* (Arden edn), p. xxxii.
12 Ibid., p. xxxii.
13 A.C. Swinburne, *A Study of Shakespeare*, London, 1879; part of it repr. in Stead (ed.), *A Casebook*, pp. 62–3.

8. THE END OF THE MANNERIST MOMENT

1 See R.A. Foakes, *Shakespeare, The Dark Comedies to the Last Plays: From Satire to Celebration*, London, 1971, p. 85.
2 Though my approach to *Hamlet* is very different from Stanley Cavell's, I agree with him that in writing this revenge play, Shakespeare wished 'to end revenge plays'. See Stanley Cavell, *Disowning Knowledge*, Cambridge, 1987, p. 181.
3 See R. Marienstras, 'Quelques aspects de la négation dans *Othello*', in *Autour d'Othello*, Presses de l'Université de Picardie, 1987, pp. 96–105.
4 Othello too affirms, and then denies:

> I think my wife be honest, and think she is not,
> I think that thou art just, and think thou are not;
> I'll have some proof.
>
> III, iii, 390–2

But this statement comes *before* he obtains the 'proof'. Othello is not express-ing here the Mannerist view that a thing is both itself and its opposite, but his uncertainty about the true nature of Desdemona and Iago. He is swaying between two contradictory interpretations, but as soon as he obtains the proof of his wife's 'infidelity', this uncertainty disappears.

5   Robert Ellrodt, 'Self-consciousness in Montaigne and Shakespeare', *SS*, 28, 1975, p. 49.

6   Barbara B. Mowat, *The Dramaturgy of Shakespeare's Romances*, Athens (USA), 1976, pp. 63–5. Concerning the distinction between 'representational' and 'presentational' modes, see Alexander Bakshy, *The Theatre Unbound*, London, 1923.

Index of names and titles

Guarini, Giovanni Battista, *Il Pastor Fido*, 18

Hartsock, Mildred E., 83, 85, 86
  'The complexity of *Julius Caesar*', 187n
Hauser, Arnold, 1, 5, 54
  The Social History of Art, 185n, 186n
Heemskerck, Maerten van, 15
Hilliard, Nicholas, 15
  Man and Flames, 21
Hocke, Gustav-René, 1, 88
  Manierismus in der Literatur, 185n
  Die Welt als Labyrinth . . ., 188n
Homer, 119, 121
Hooker, Richard, 49
Horace, 71, 120, 123
  Poetic Art, 119
Hoy, Cyrus, 1
  'Jacobean Tragedy and the Mannerist Style', 185n
Hunter, G.K., 113, 114, 165, 167
  Introduction to *All's Well*, 190n
  'The Heroism of Hamlet', 188n

Jenkins, Harold, 88, 93
  Introduction to *Hamlet*, 188n
Johnson, Samuel, 156, 190n
Jonson, Benjamin, 50, 68–71, 105, 131, 133, 166, 187n
  The Alchemist, 70
  Bartholomew Fair, 70
  The Case is Altered, 59–61
  Cynthia's Revels, 69
  Epicoene, 70
  Every Man In His Humour, 59, 68
  Every Man Out of His Humour, 69, 70
  Poetaster, 69
  The Staple of News, 70
  Volpone, 61, 70
Julius II, 33

Keats, John, 71
  Letter to George and Thomas Keats, 187n

Kernodle, George R., *From Art to Theatre*, 186n
Kyd, Thomas, 4, 5, 50, 51, 58, 87, 88, 93, 170
  The Spanish Tragedy, 54–5, 66, 88, 89, 90, 103

Lamb, Mary, 156
Lanzi, Luigi, *La storia pittorica . . .*, 1
Lassus, Roland de, 1
Laureti, Tomaso, 9
Lavaudant, Georges, 1
Lawrence, W.W., 4, 150, 156
  Shakespeare's Problem Comedies, 185n, 190n
Leo X, 4
Leonardo da Vinci, 25, 51
  The Last Supper, 25
Lever, J.W., Introduction to *Measure for Measure*, 190n
Levin, Harry, *The Question of Hamlet*, 188n
Lippi, Filippino, *Deposition from the Cross* (with Perugino), 39
Lippi, Filippo, *Madonna and Child with Two Angels*, 189n
Lipsius, Justus, 5
Lodge, Thomas, *Wit Misery*, 188n
Lomazzo, Giovanni Paolo, 9, 10
  Trattato dell'arte della pittura . . ., 186n
Lyly, John, 5, 51, 55, 57, 60, 71
  Mother Bombie, 56

McAlindon, T., 142
  'Language, Style and Meaning in *Troilus and Cressida*', 189n
Malvasia, Carlo Cesare, 8, 9, 10
  Felsina pittrice, 8
Mantegna, Andrea, *The Dead Christ*, 39
Marienstras, Richard, 84
  Le proche et le lointain, 188n
  'Quelques aspects de la négation dans *Othello*', 190n